13

Foundation Erratics Bedrock

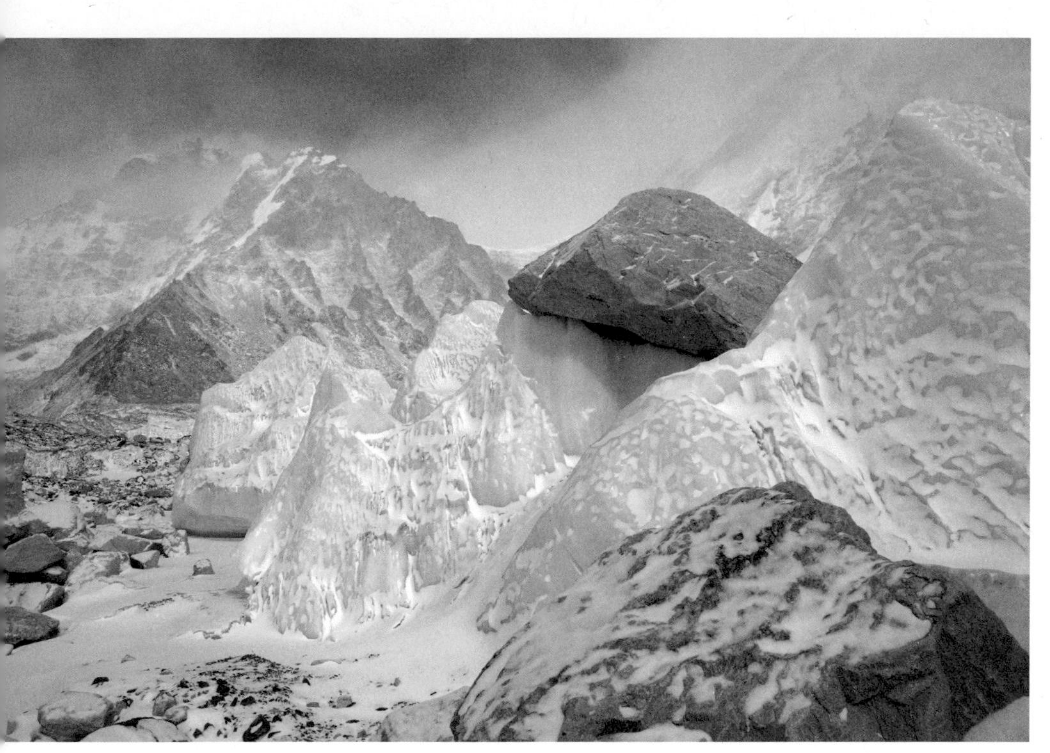

12

Realignment

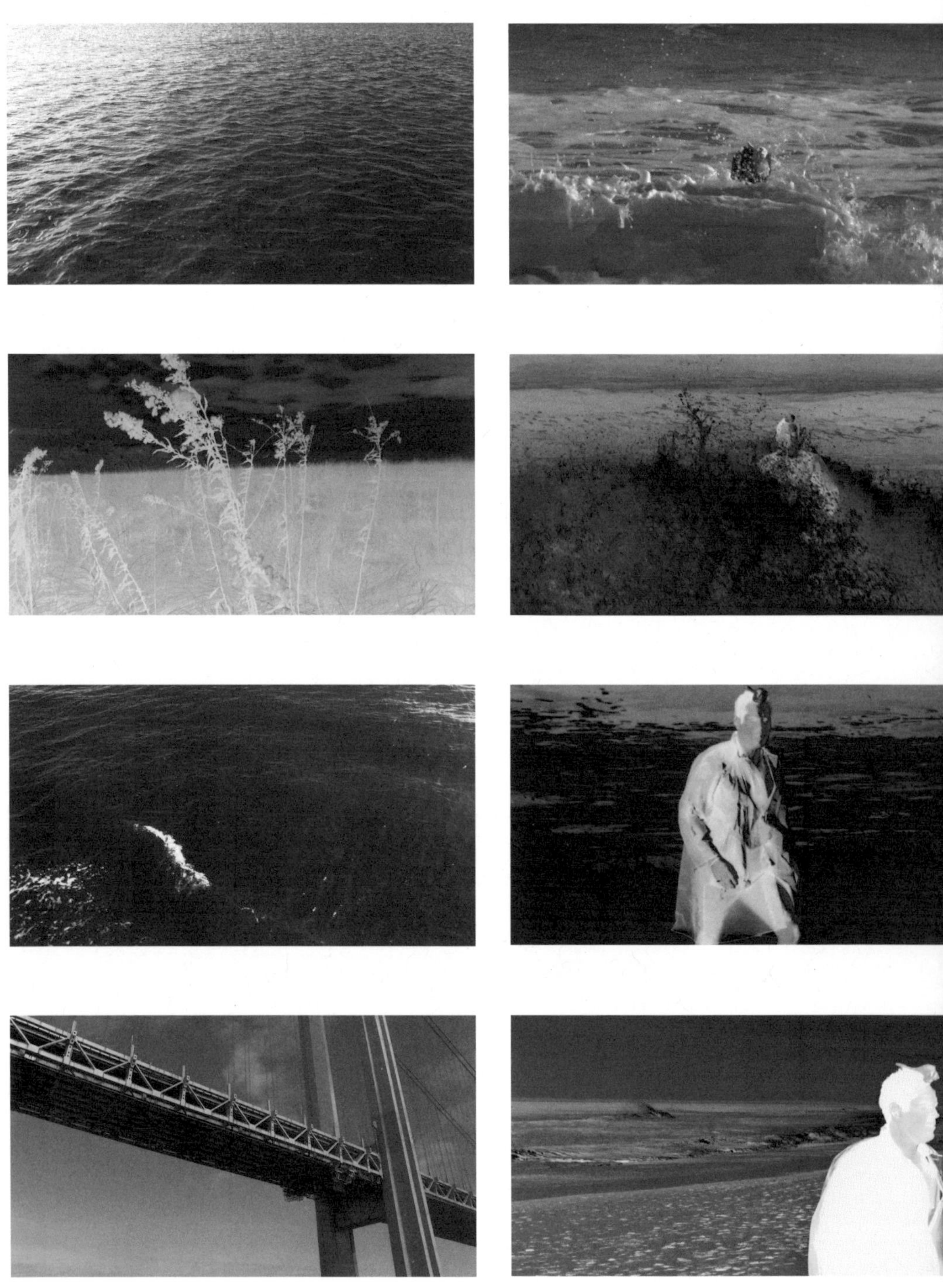

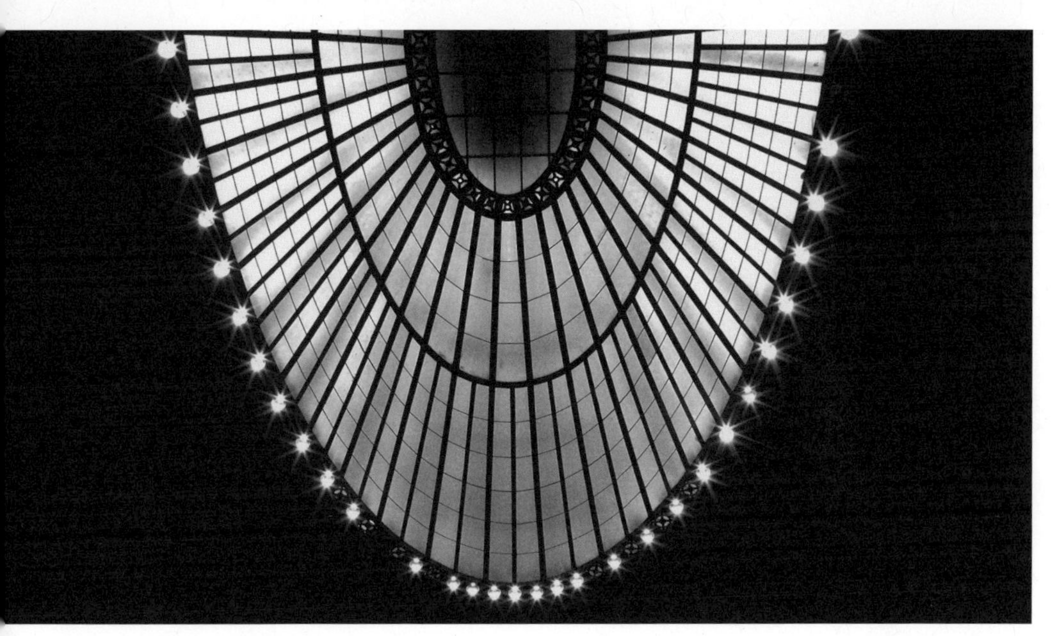

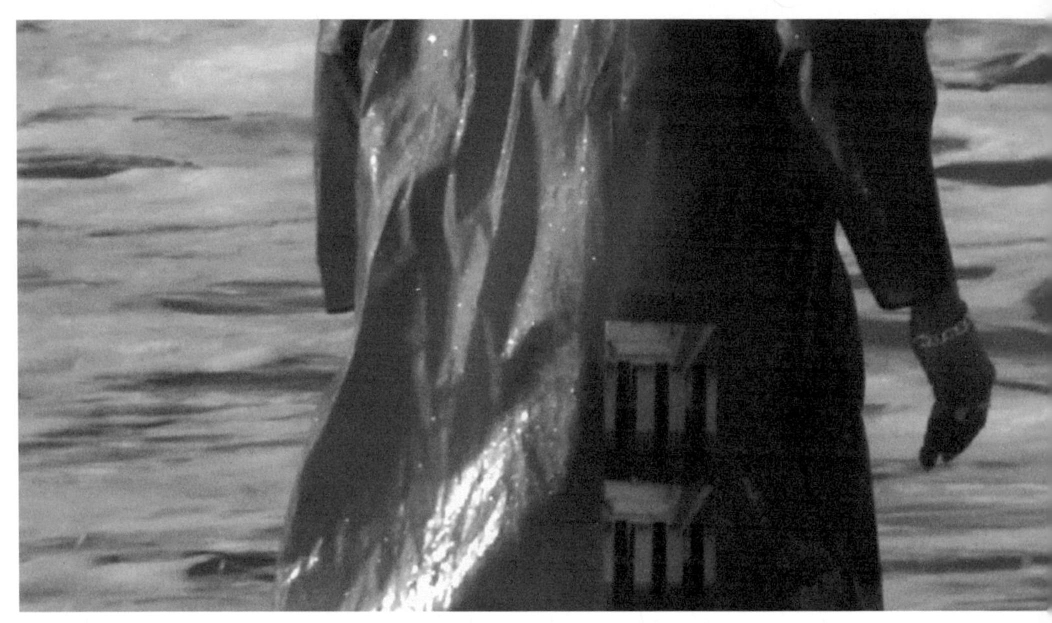

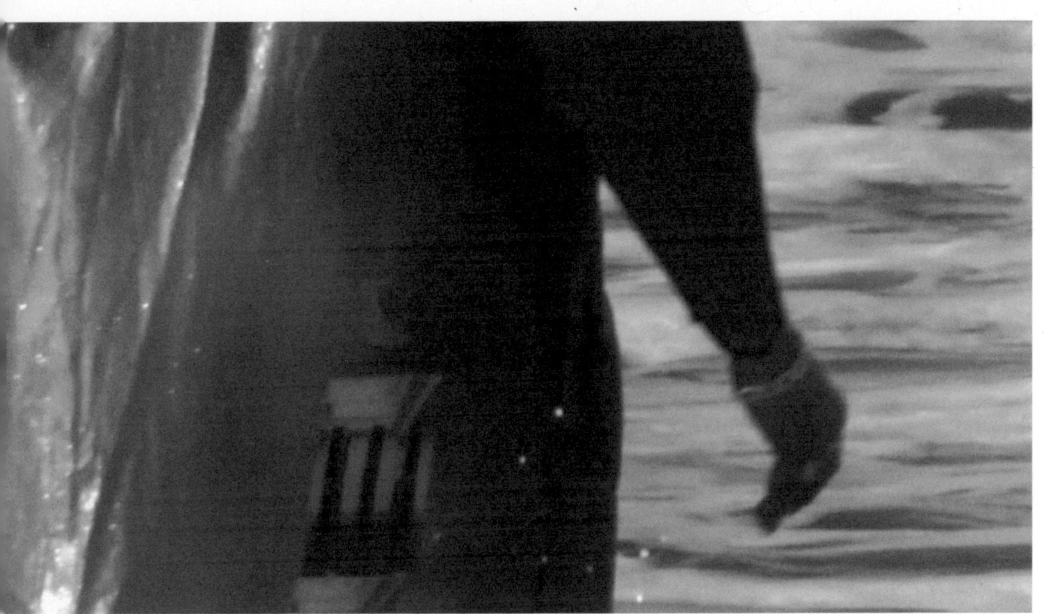

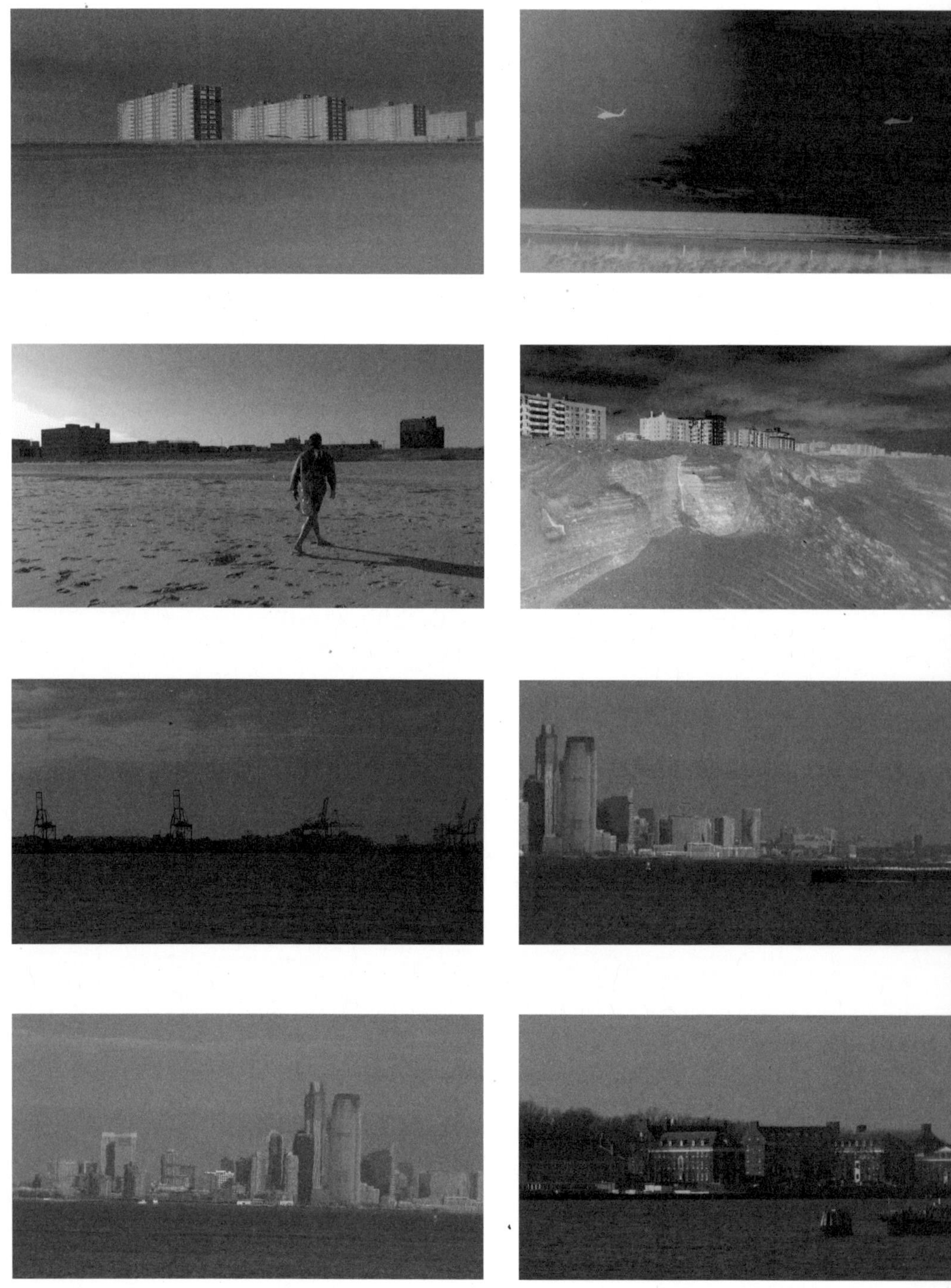

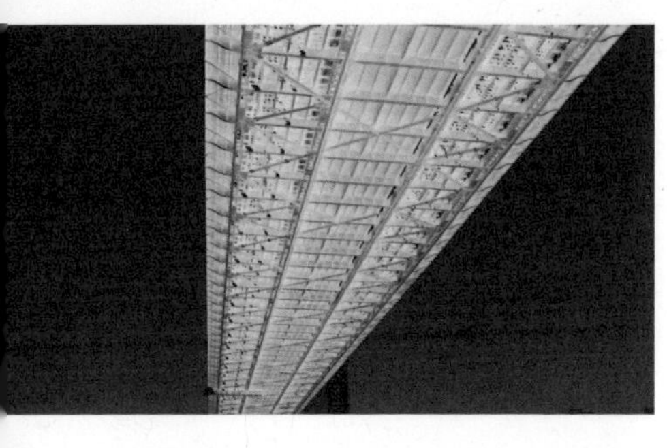

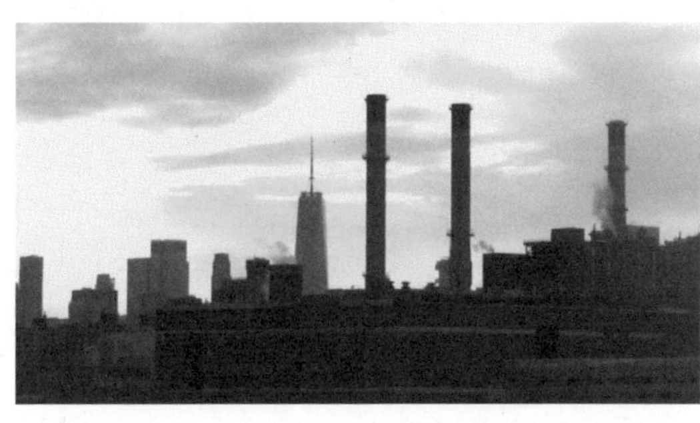

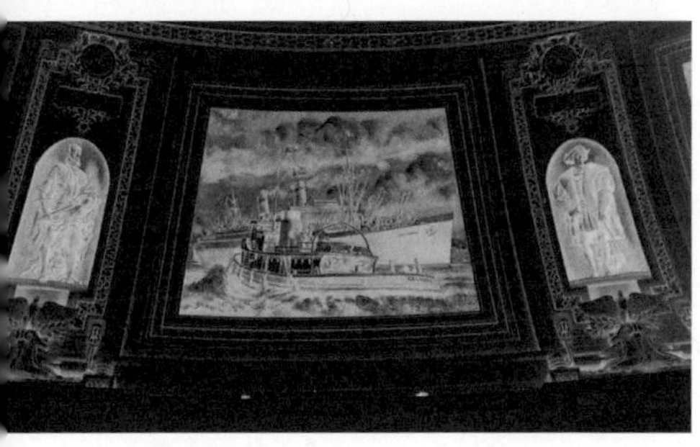

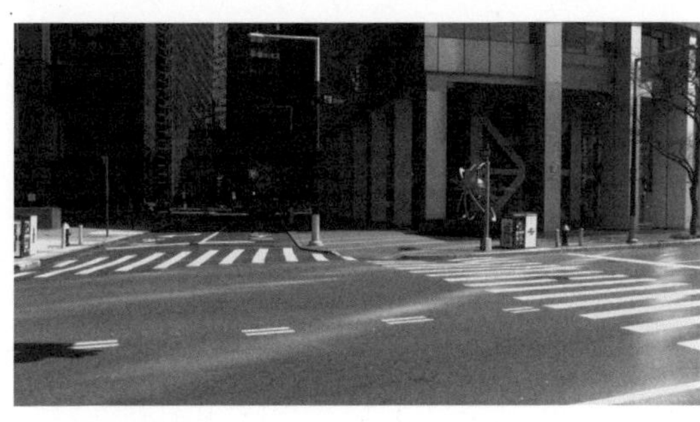

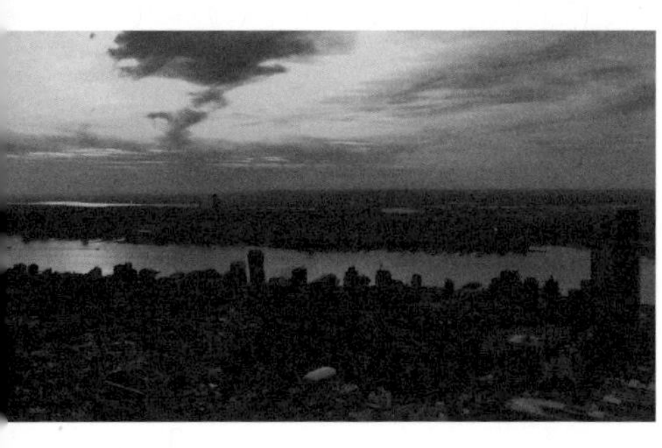

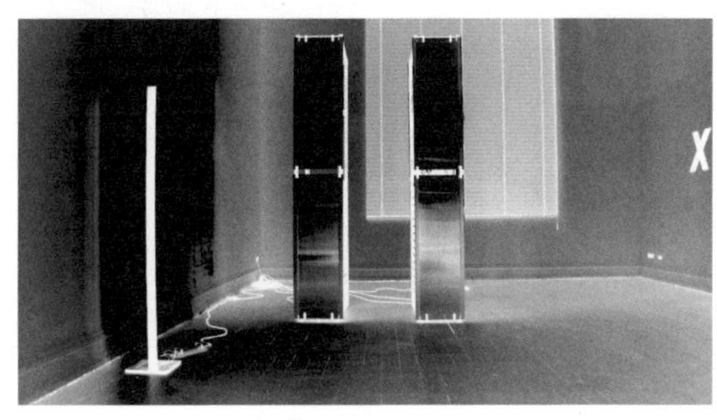
X

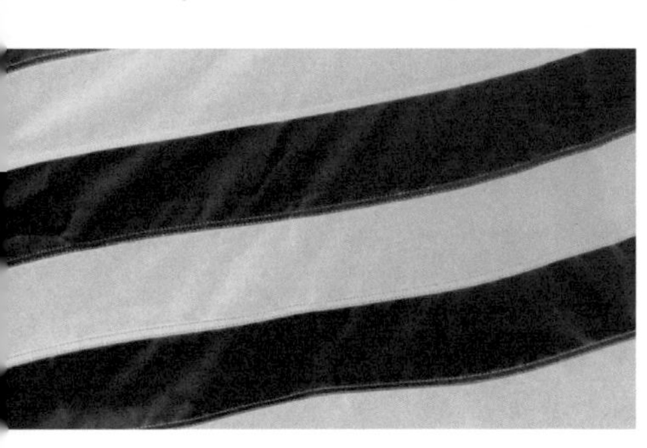

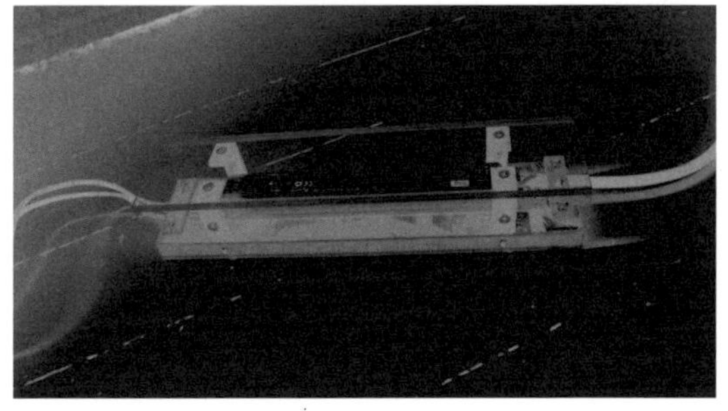

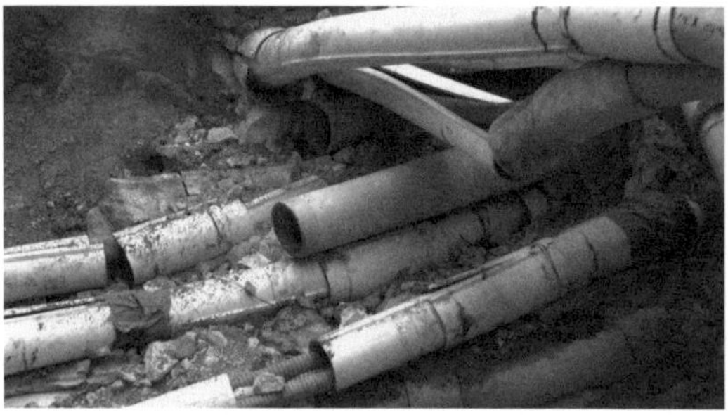

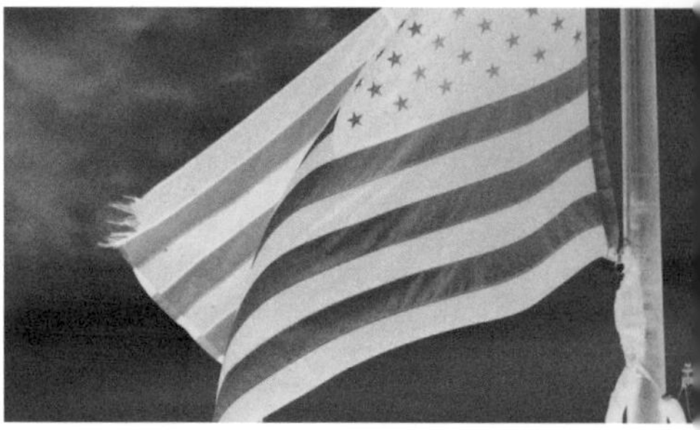

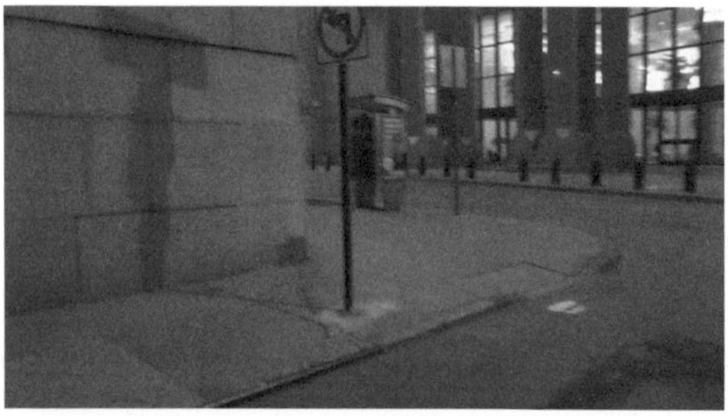

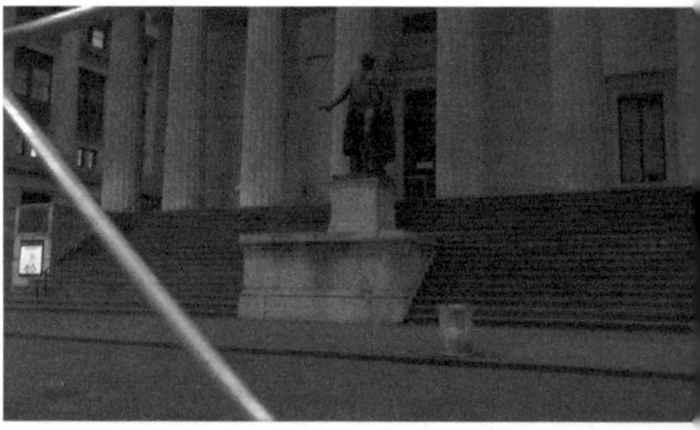

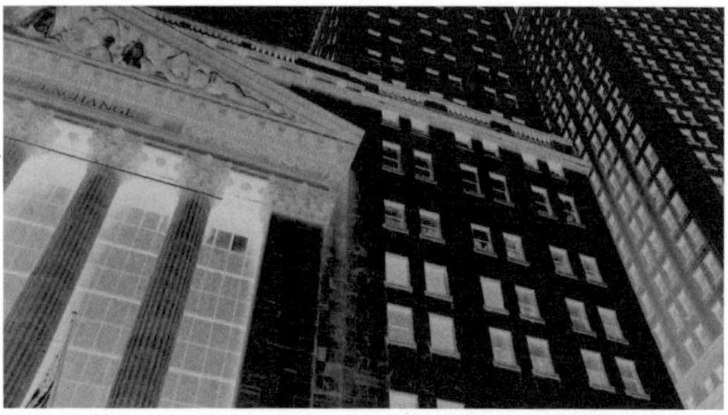

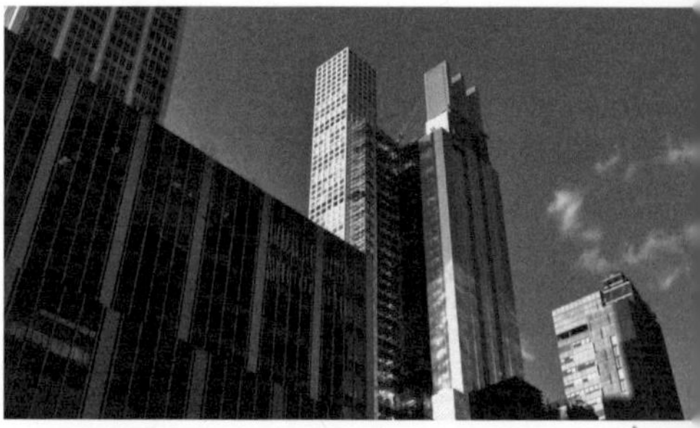

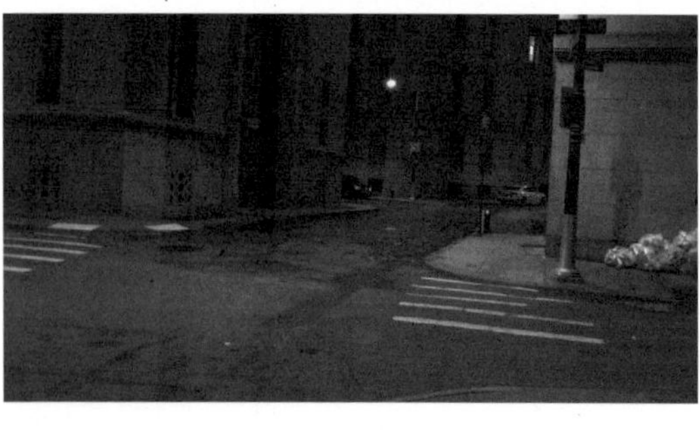

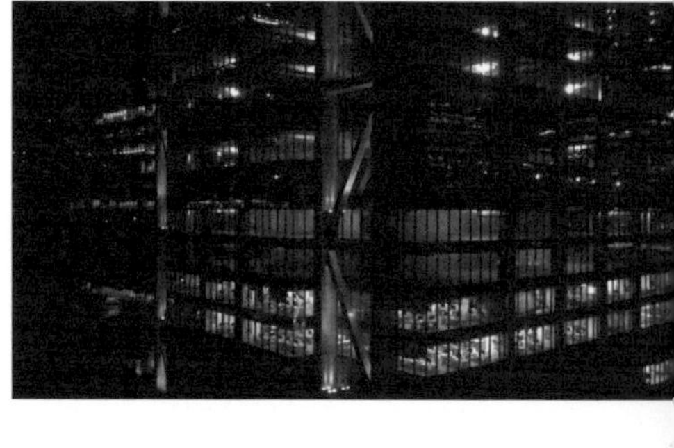

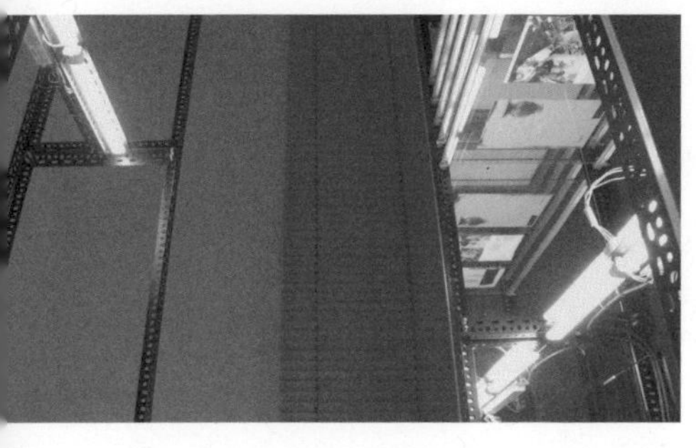

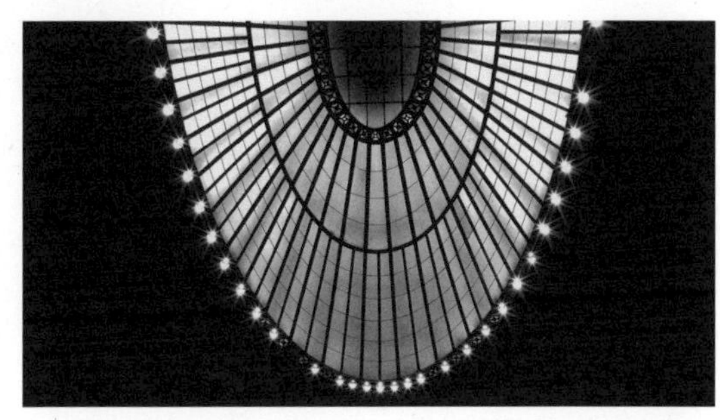

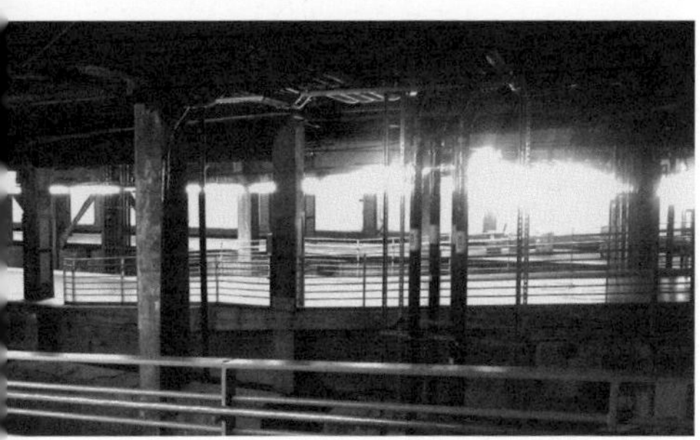

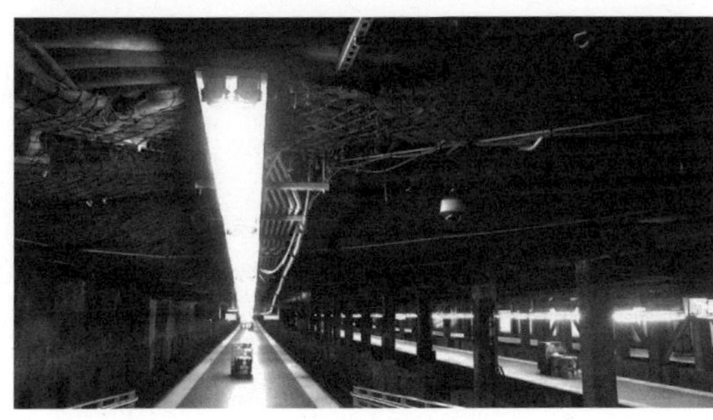

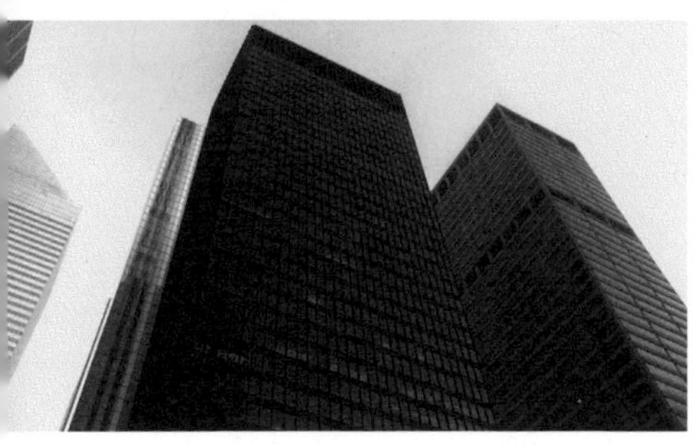

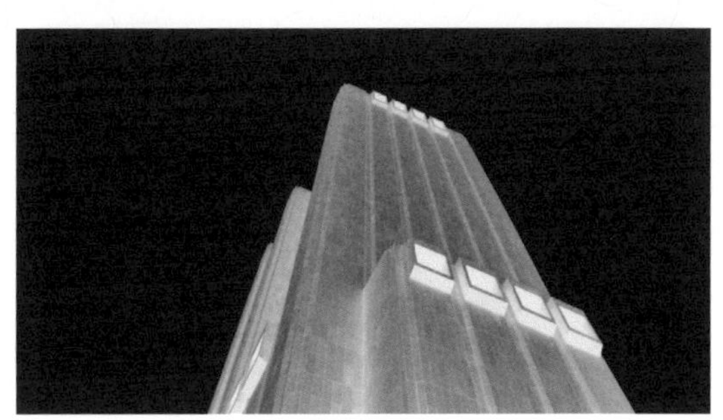

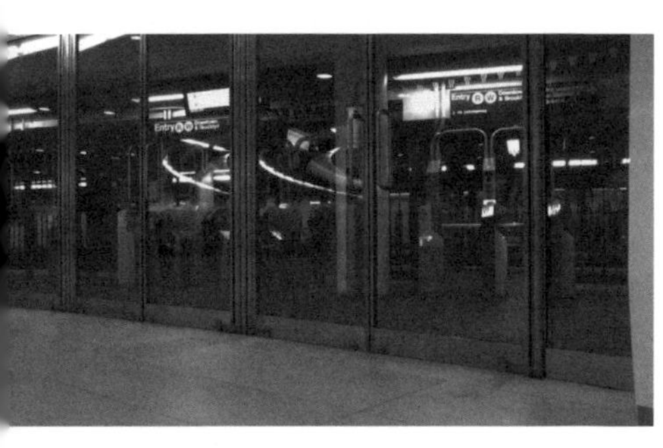
Entry R W
Entry R W

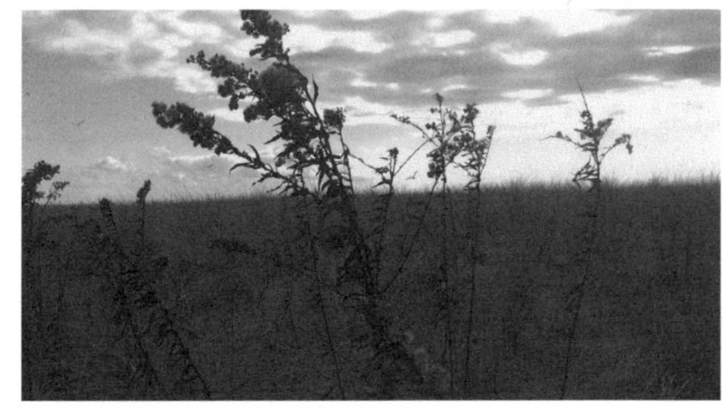

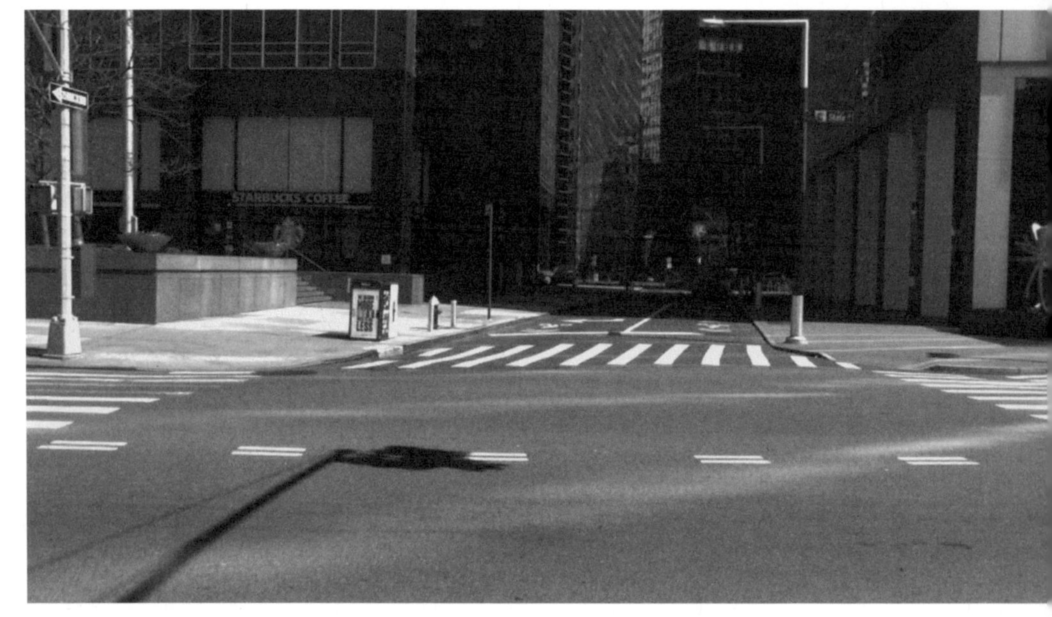
STARBUCKS COFFEE

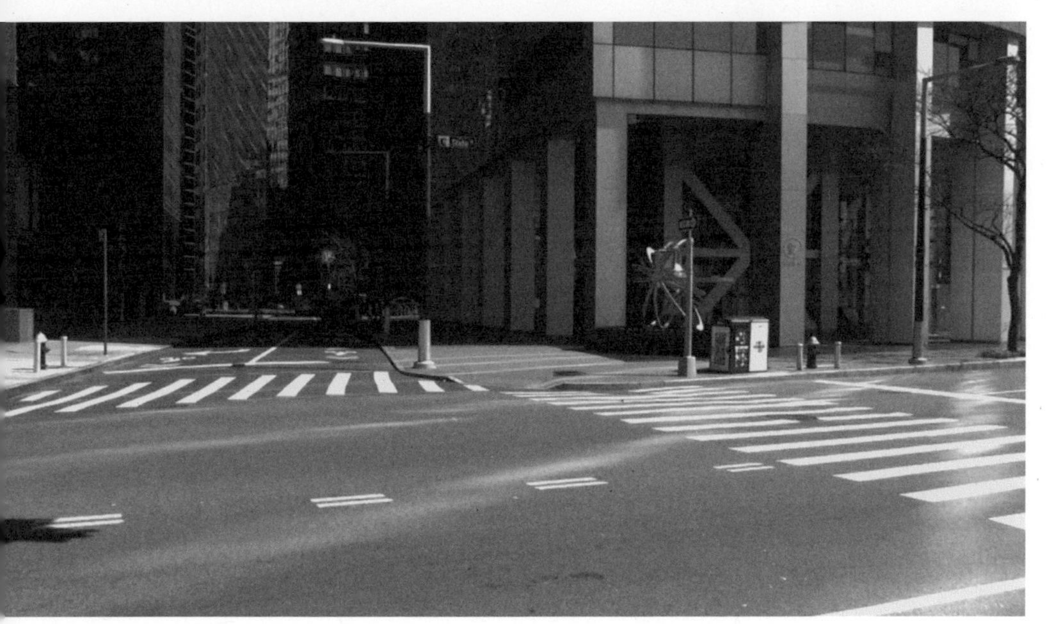

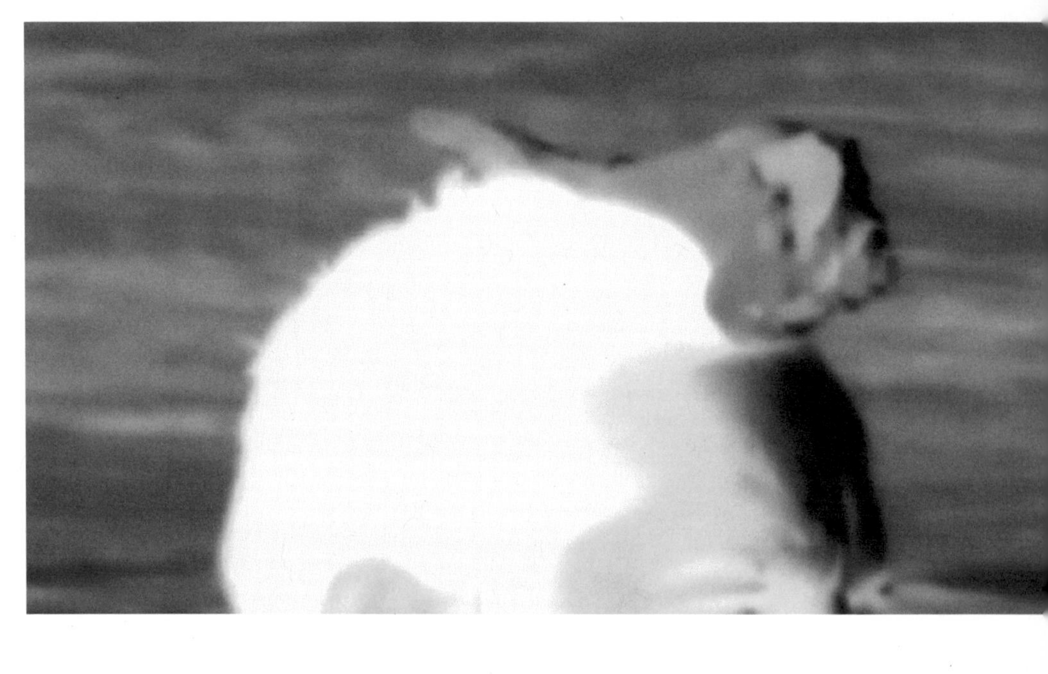

11

Prologue

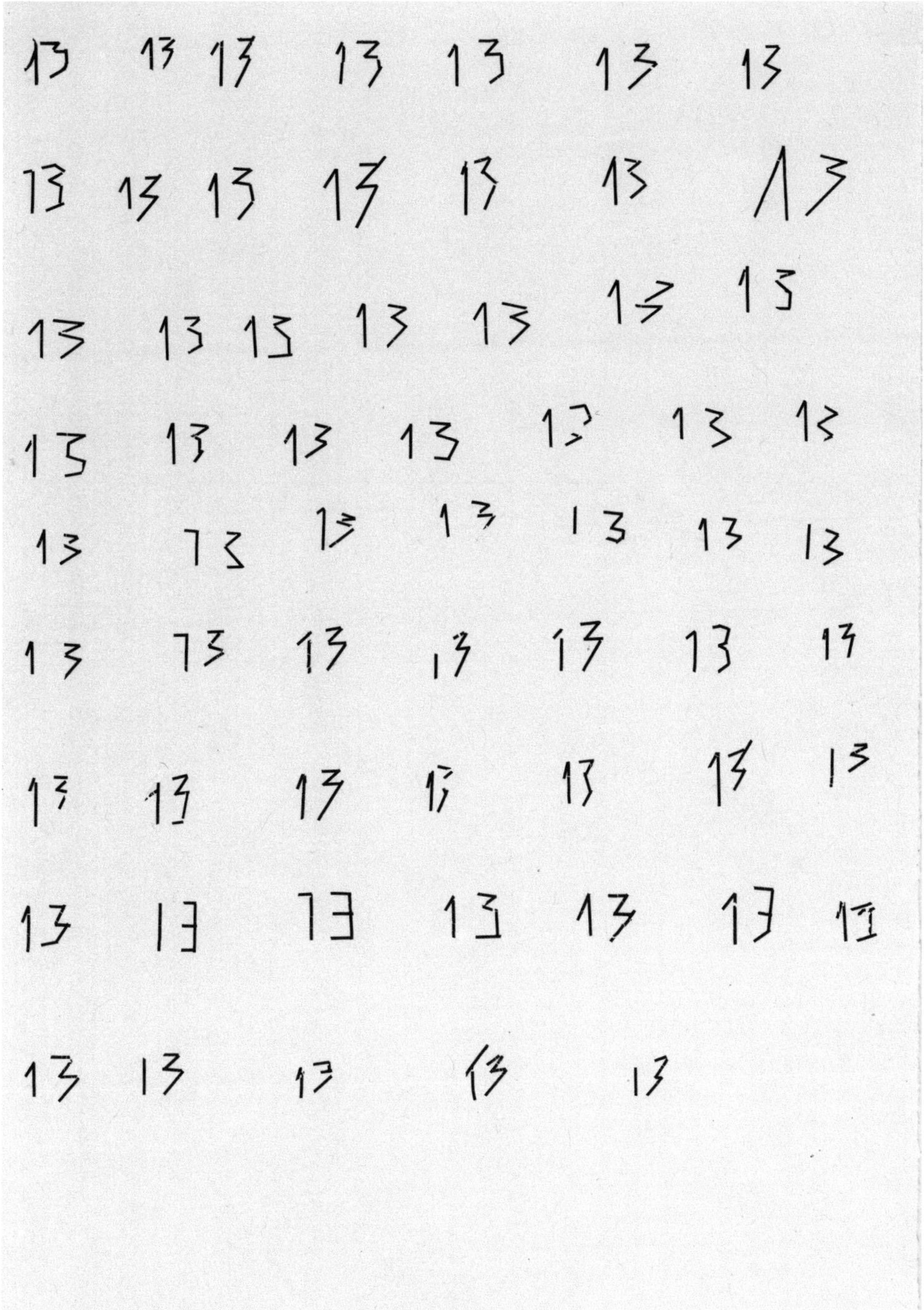
13 13 13 13 13 13 13
13 13 13 13 13 13 13
13 13 13 13 13 13 13
13 13 13 13 13 13 13
13 13 13 13 13 13 13
13 13 13 13 13 13 13
13 13 13 13 13 13 13
13 13 13 13 13 13 13
13 13 13 13 13

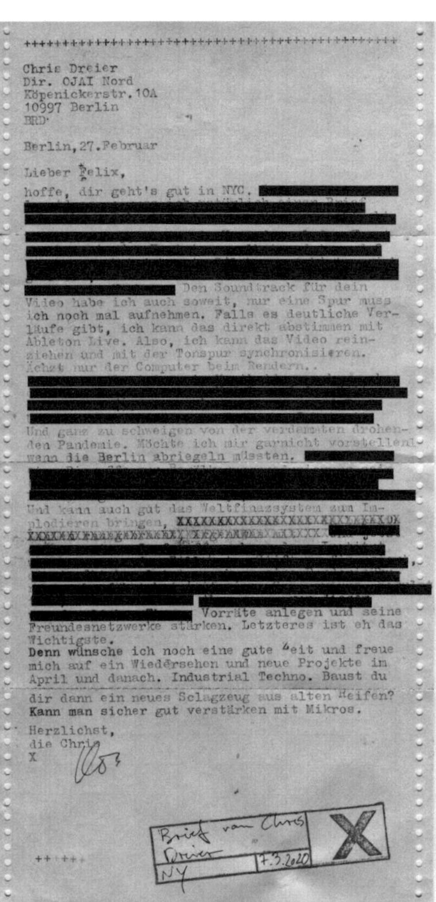

Chris Dreier
Dir. OJAI Nord
Köpenickerstr.10A
10997 Berlin
BRD

Berlin,27.Februar

Lieber Felix,

hoffe, dir geht's gut in NYC.

Den Soundtrack für dein Video habe ich auch soweit, nur eine Spur muss ich noch mal aufnehmen. Falls es deutliche Verläufe gibt, ich kann das direkt abstimmen mit Ableton Live. Also, ich kann das Video reinziehen und mit der Tonspur synchronisieren. Ächzt nur der Computer beim Rendern..

Und ganz zu schweigen von der verdammten drohenden Pandemie. Möchte ich mir garnicht vorstellen, wenn die Berlin abriegeln müssten.

Und kann auch gut das Weltfinazsystem zum Implodieren bringen, XXXXXXXXXXXXXXXXXXXXXXXXXX

Vorräte anlegen und seine Freundesnetzwerke stärken. Letzteres ist eh das Wichtigste.
Denn wünsche ich noch eine gute Zeit und freue mich auf ein Wiedersehen und neue Projekte im April und danach. Industrial Techno. Baust du dir dann ein neues Sclagzeug aus alten Reifen? Kann man sicher gut verstärken mit Mikros.

Herzlichst,
die Chris
X

Brief von Chris Dreier
NY
7.3.2020

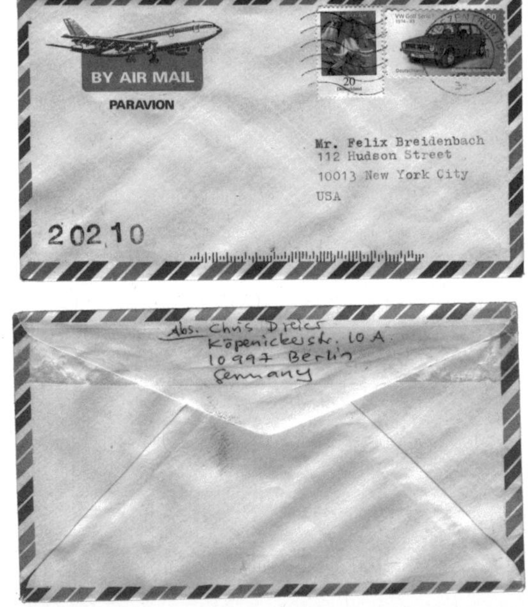

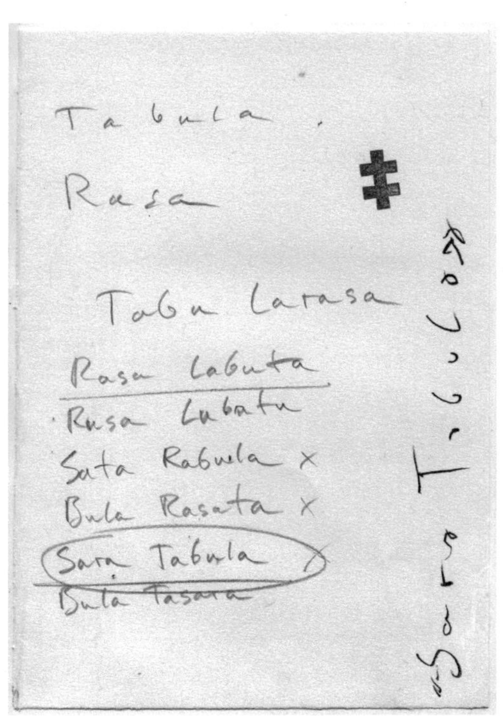
Tabula.
Rasa
Tabu larasa
Rasa Labuta
Rusa Lubatu
Sata Rabula x
Bula Rasata x
Sara Tabula
Bula Tasara

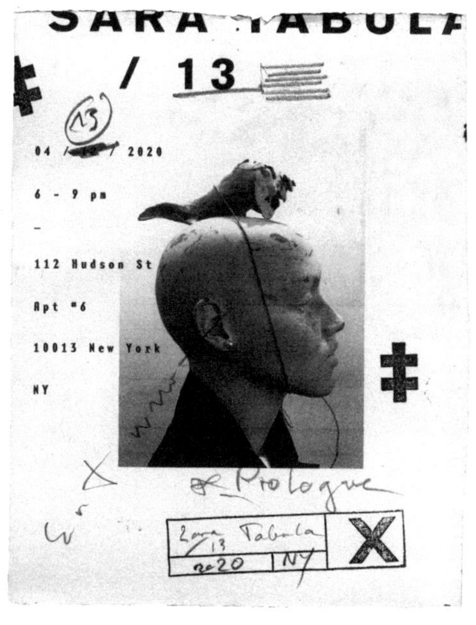
SARA TABULA
/ 13
04 / 2020
6 - 9 pm
112 Hudson St
Apt #6
10013 New York
NY
Prologue
X

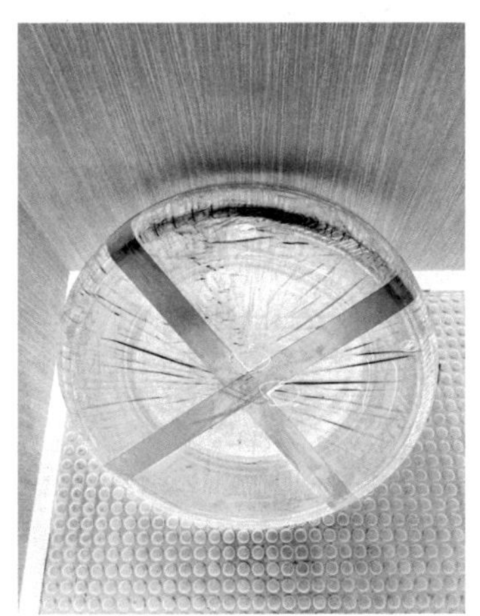

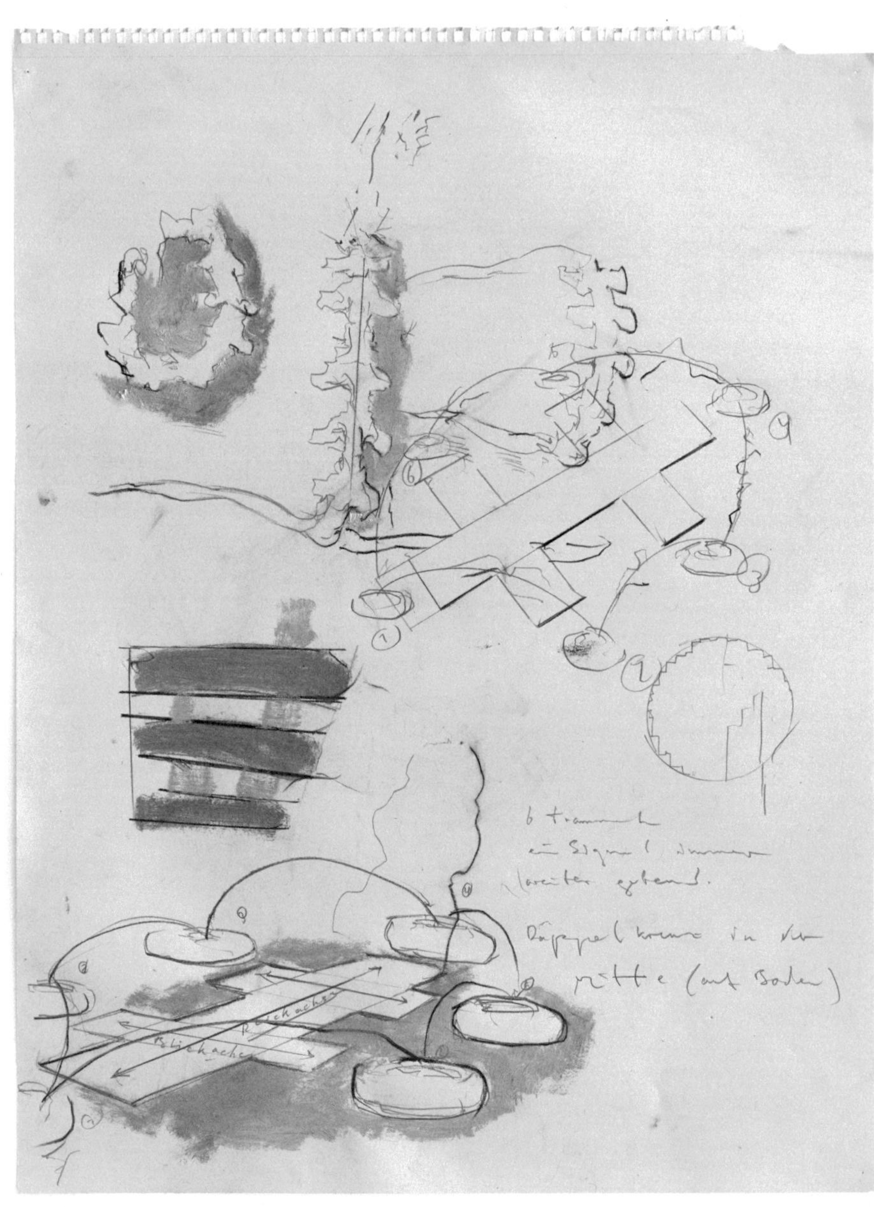

Blickachse
6 trommeln
ein Signal
(weiter gebend).
Doppelkreuz in der
Mitte (auf Boden)

10

Configuration

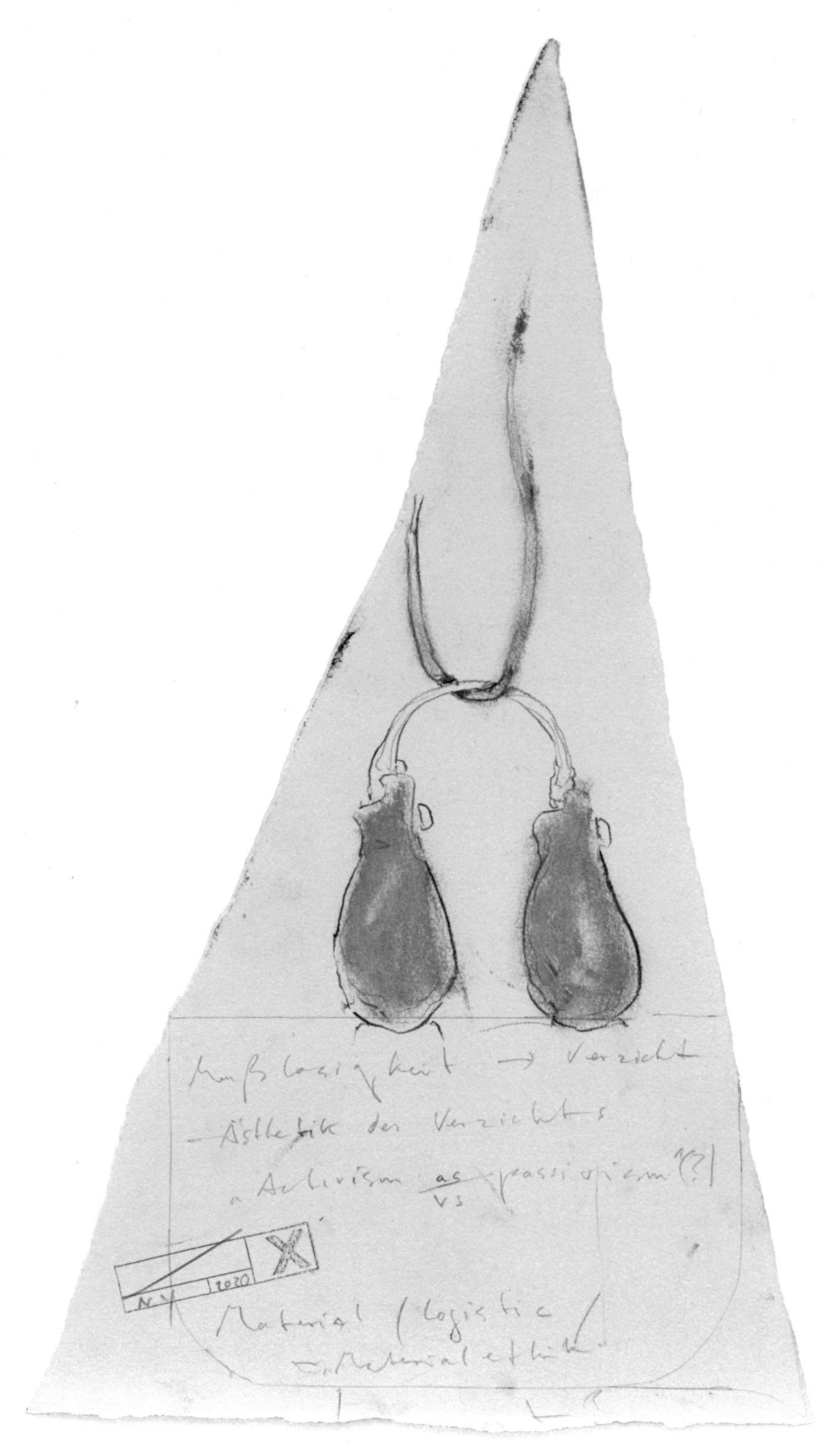
Maßlosigkeit → Verzicht
Ästhetik des Verzichts
Activism as vs
NY
2020
Material / logistic /
Materialethik

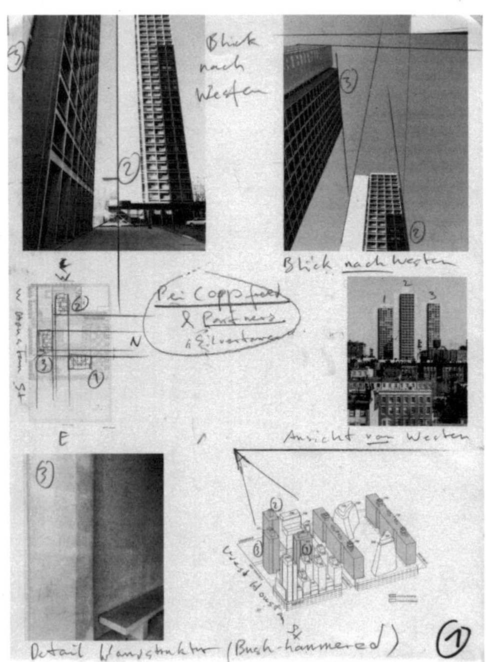
Blick nach Westen
Blick nach Westen
& Partners
„Silvertowers“
N
E
Ansicht von Westen
Detail Wandstruktur (Bush-hammered)
1

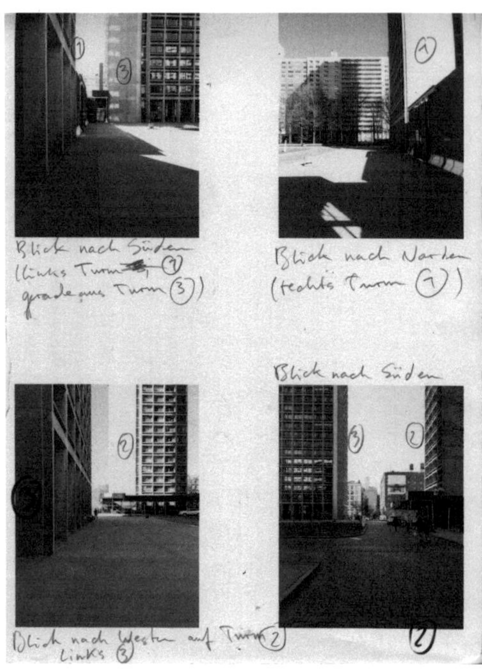
Blick nach Süden
(links Turm 1,
geradeaus Turm 3)
Blick nach Norden
(rechts Turm 1)
Blick nach Süden
Blick nach Westen auf Turm 2
links 3
2

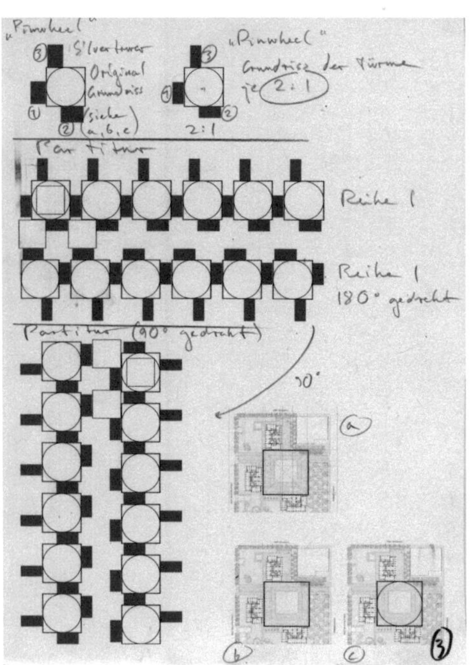
„Pinwheel“
Silvertower
Original
Grundriss
(siehe a, b, c)
„Pinwheel“
Grundriss der Türme
je 2:1
2:1
Partitur
Reihe 1
Reihe 1
180° gedreht
Partitur (90° gedreht)
90°
a
b
c
3

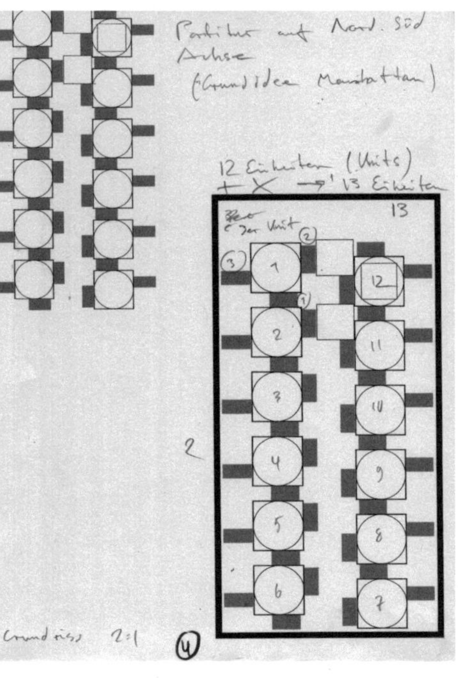
Partitur auf Nord Süd
Achse
(Grundidee Manhattan)
12 Einheiten (Units)
+ X → 13 Einheiten
13
Grundriss 2:1
4

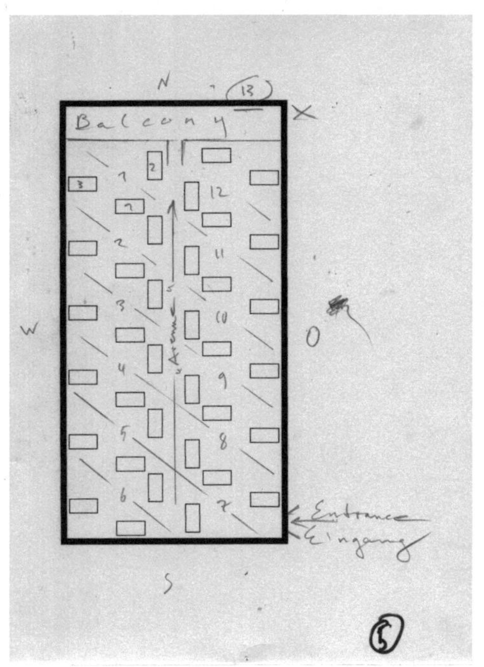
N
13
Balcony
X
W
O
S
Entrance
Eingang

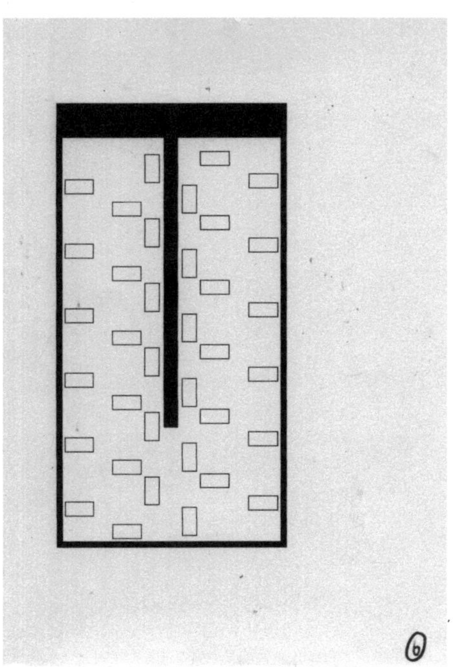

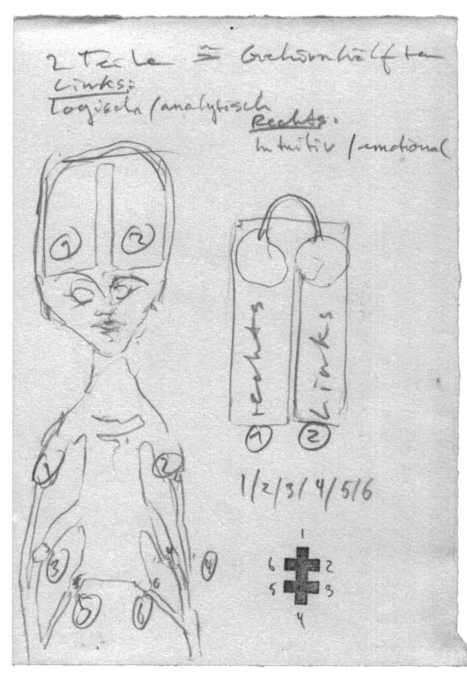
2 Teile ≙ Gehirnhälften
Links:
Logisch/analytisch
Rechts:
Intuitiv/emotional
Rechts
Links
1/2/3/4/5/6

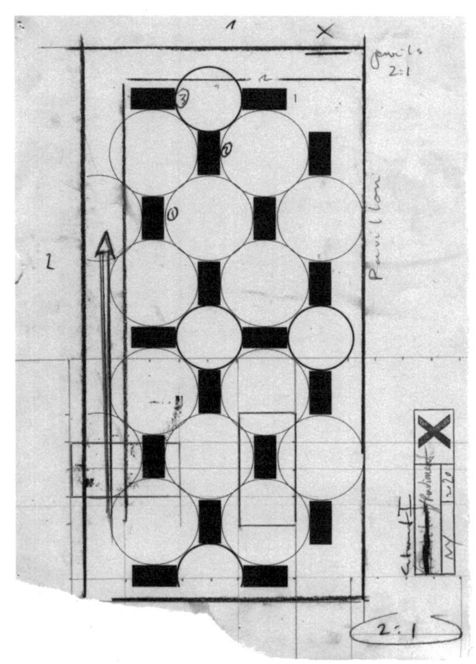
jeweils
2:1
Pavillon
NY
2020
2:1

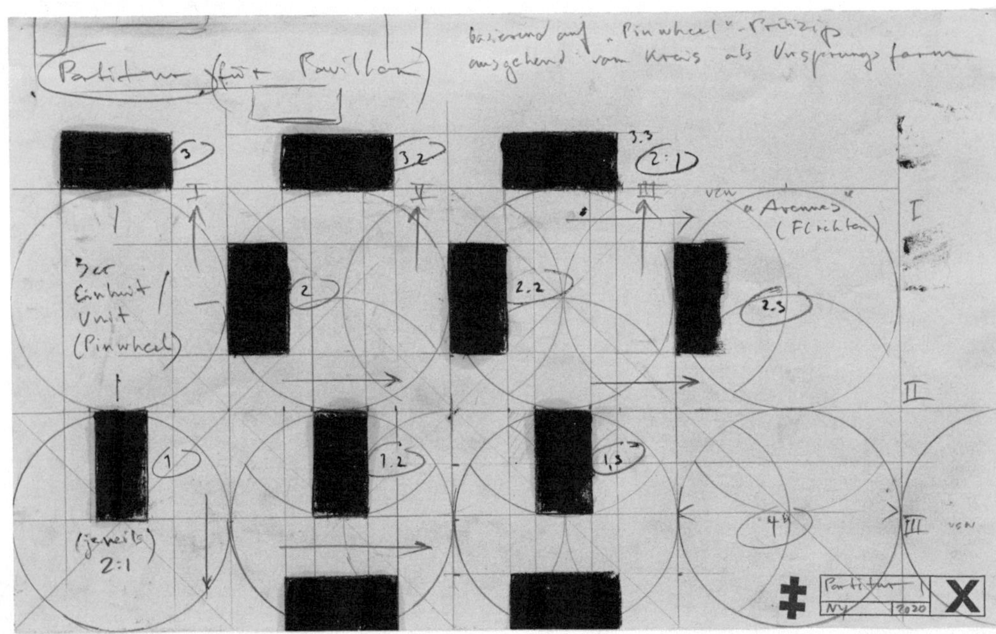
Partitur für Pavillon
basierend auf „Pinwheel"-Prinzip
ausgehend vom Kreis als Ursprungsform
3er
Einheit /
Unit
(Pinwheel)
(jeweils)
2:1
2:1
Partitur
NY
2020

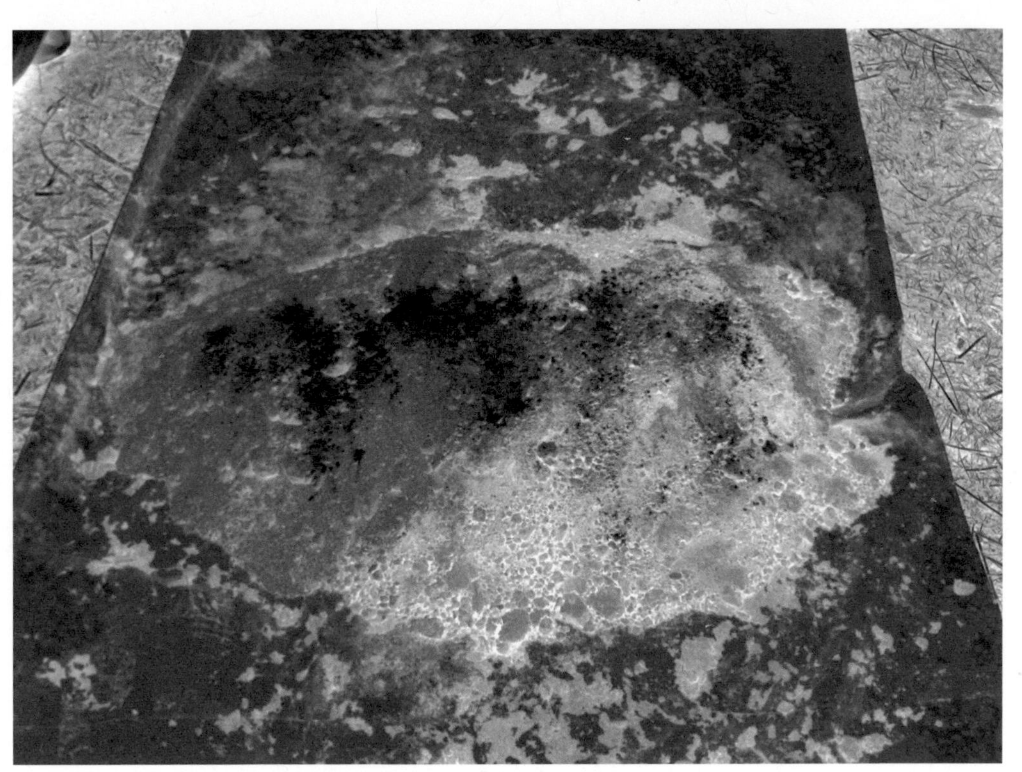

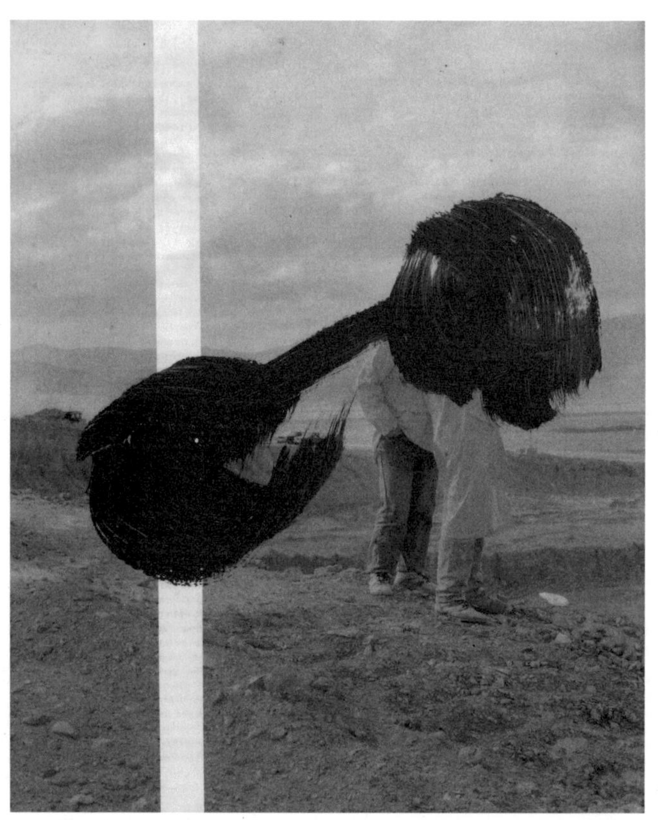

9

Cope
Shell

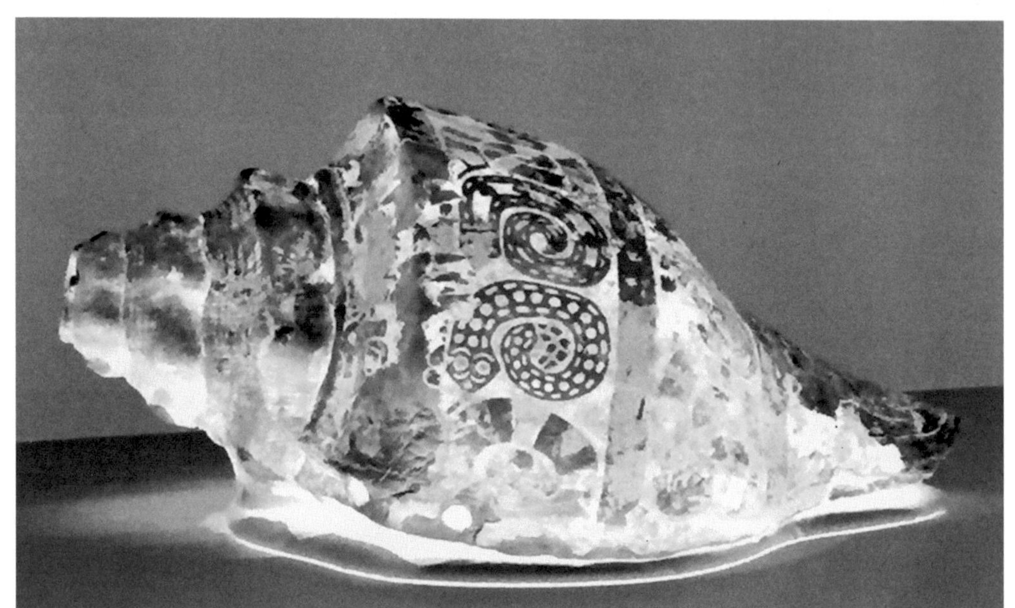

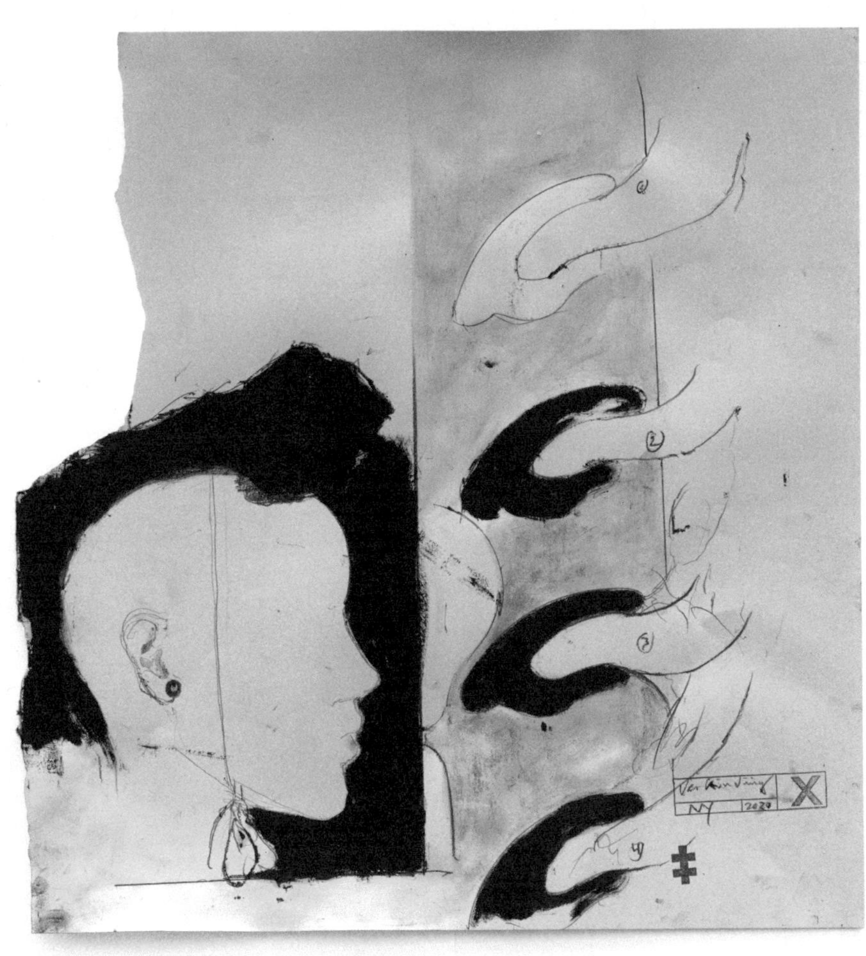
NY
X

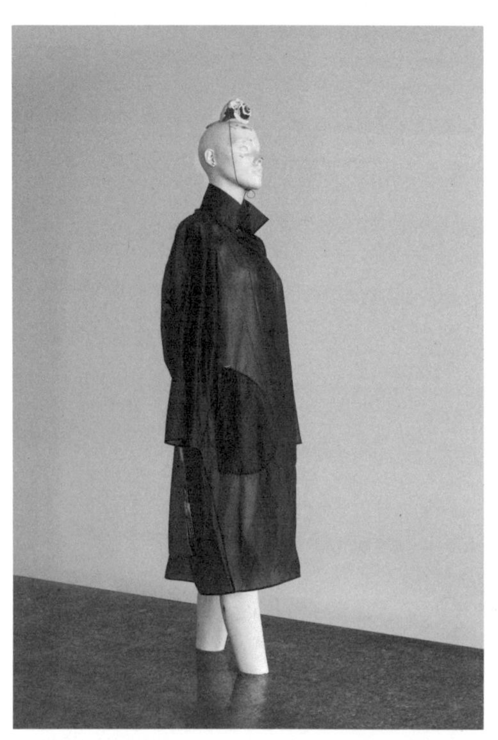

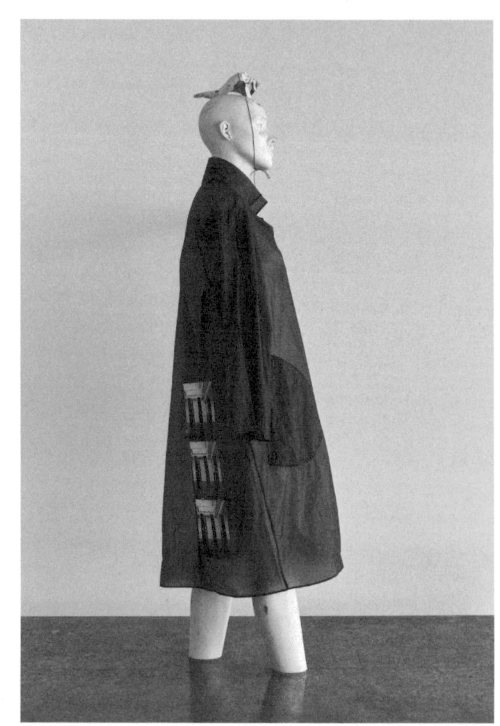

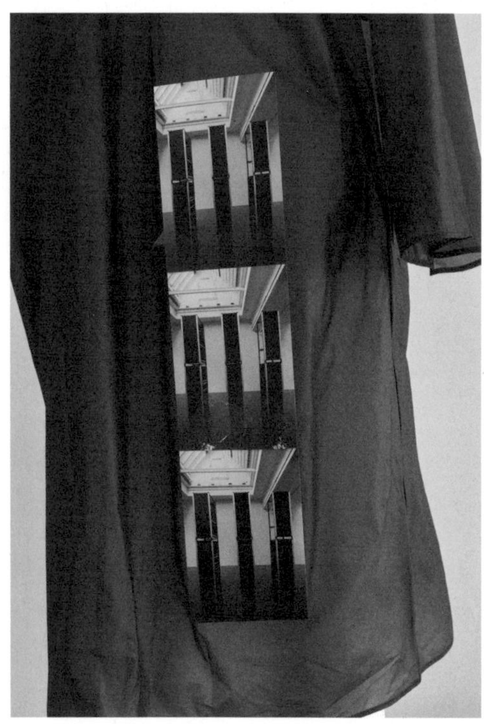

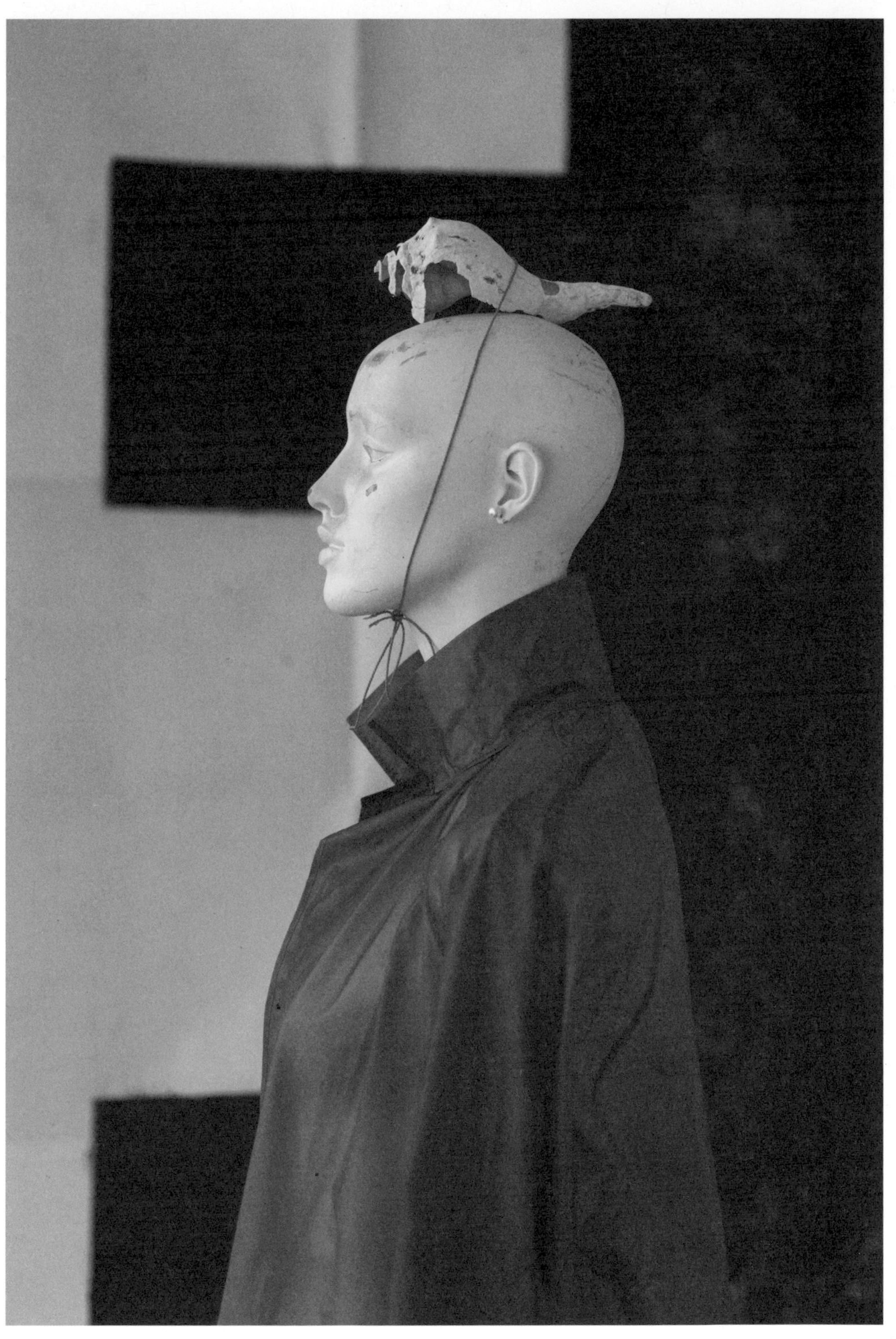

8

Meditation

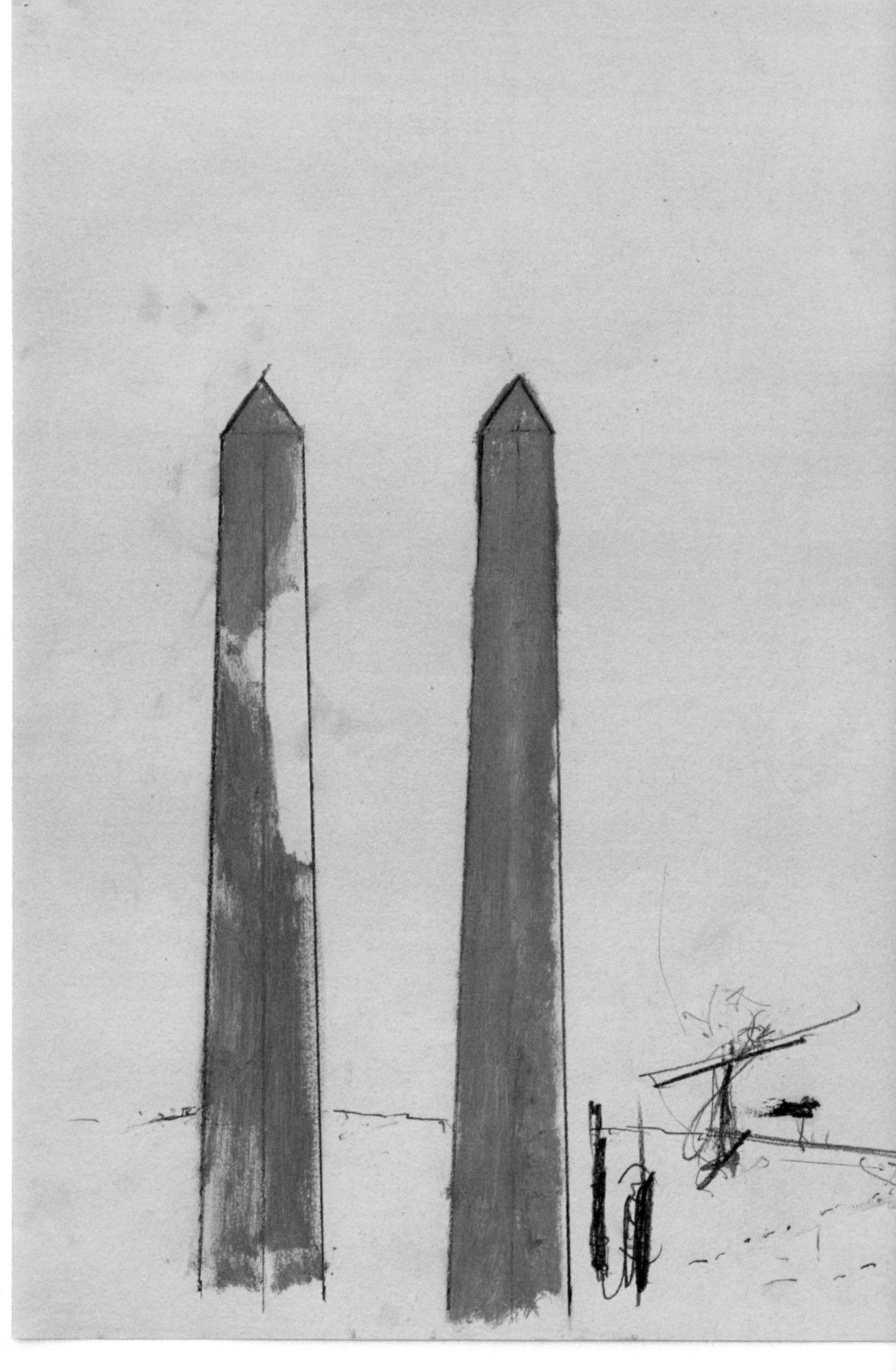

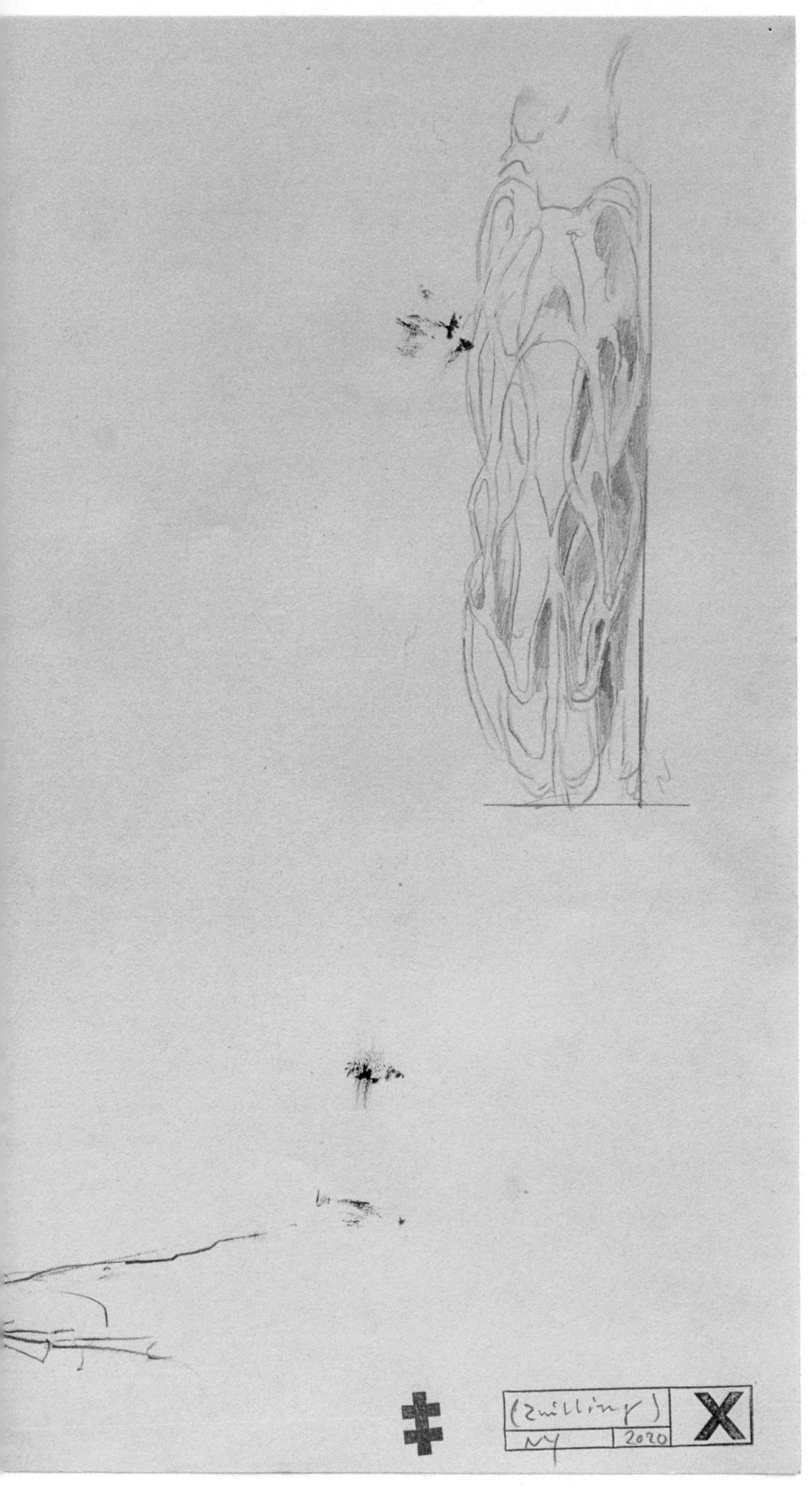
(Zwilling)
NY
2020
X

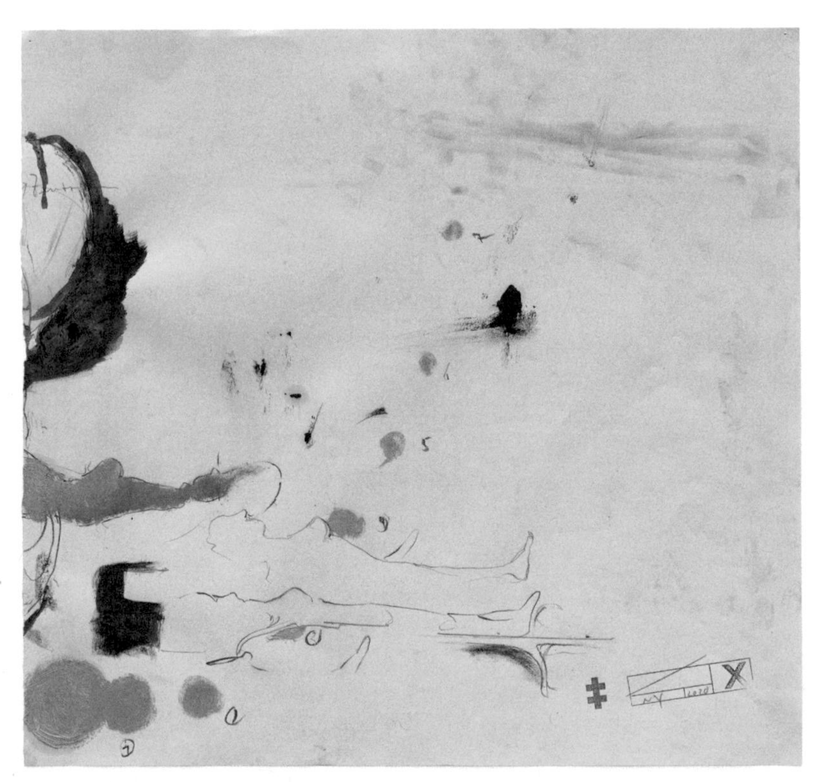

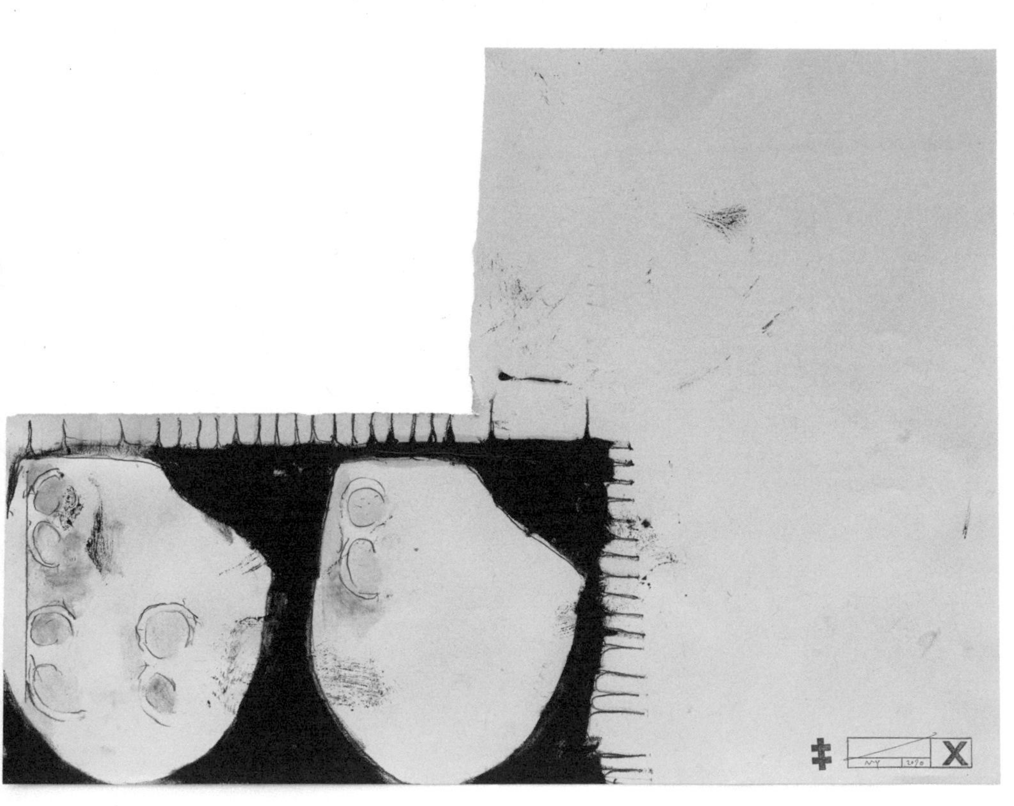

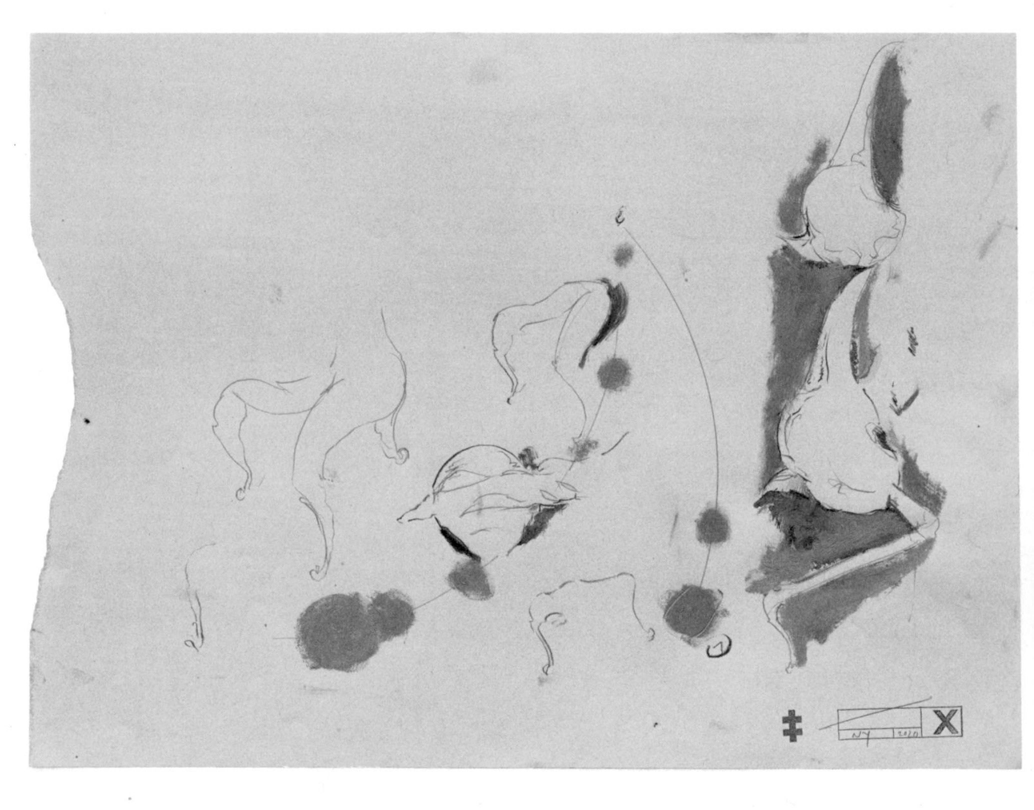

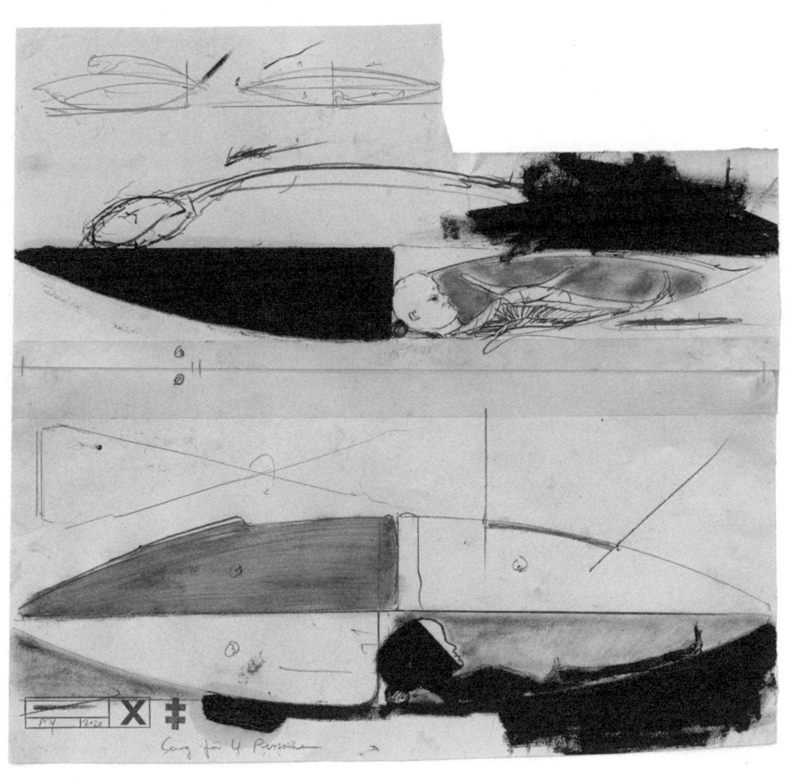

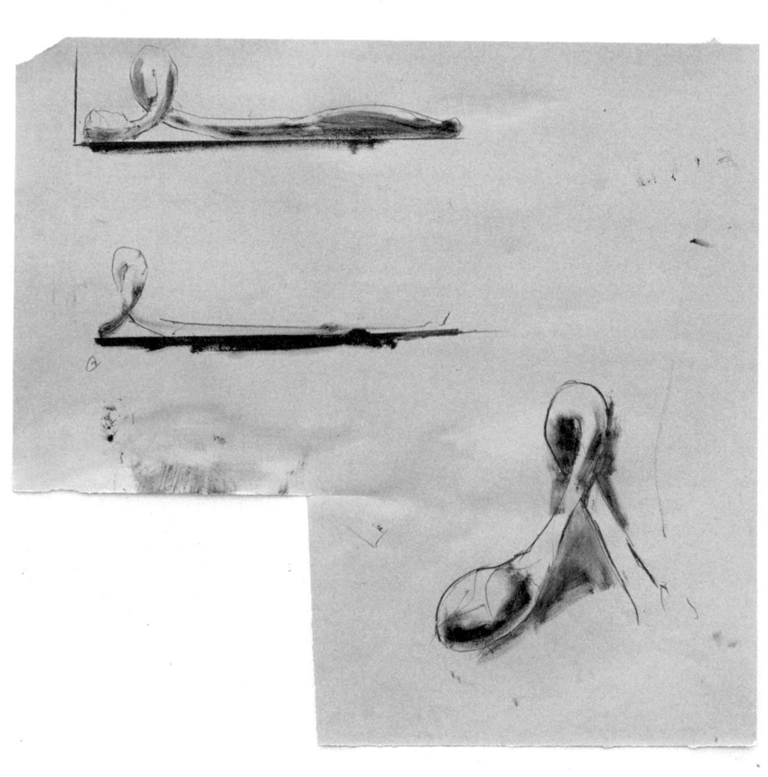

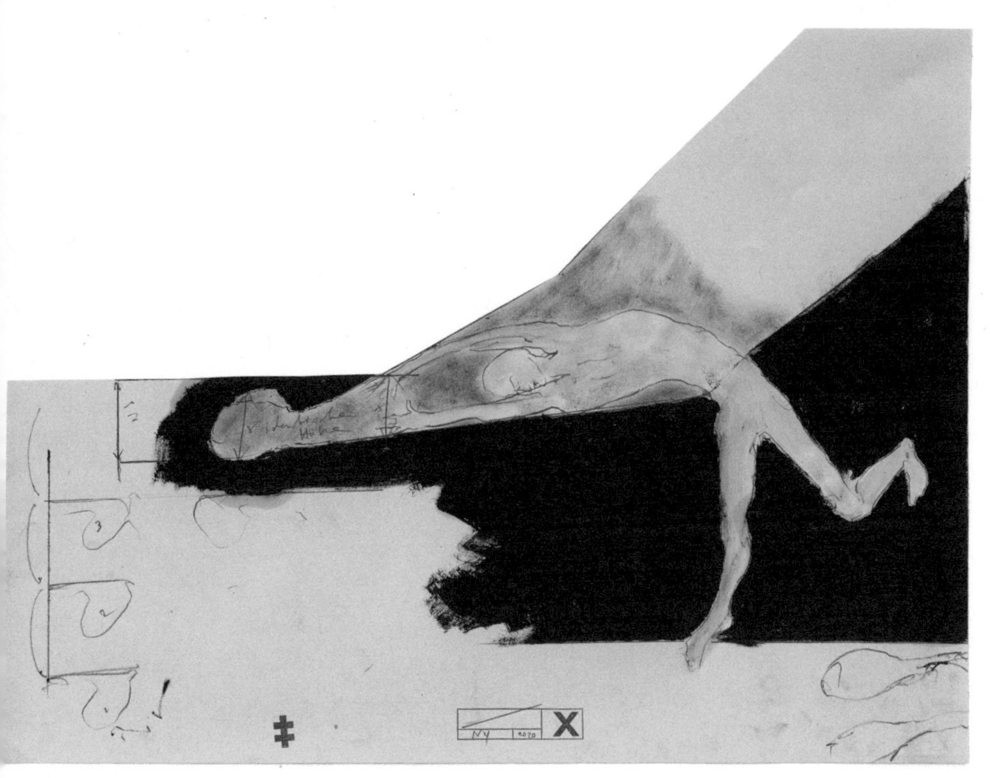

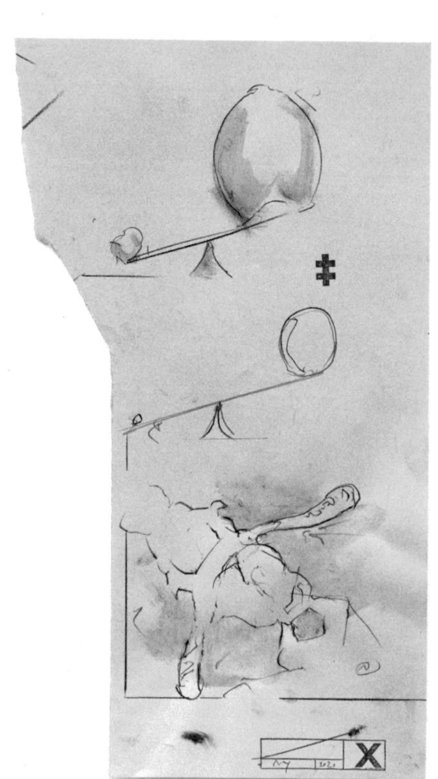

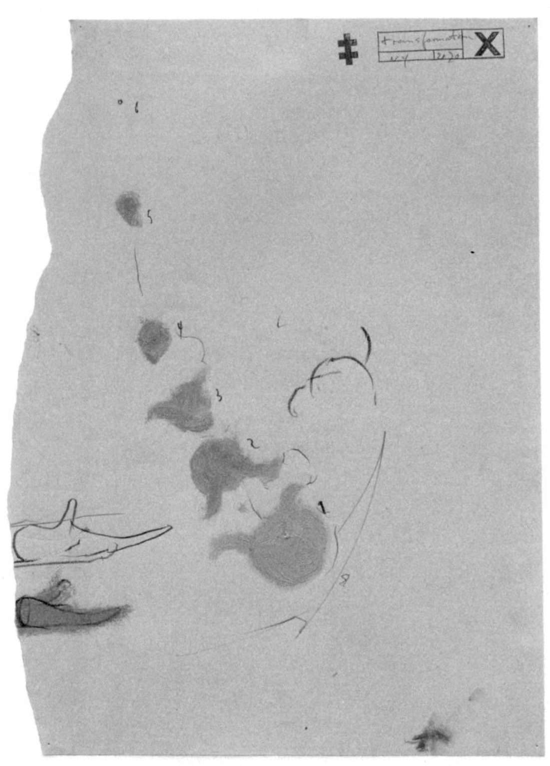

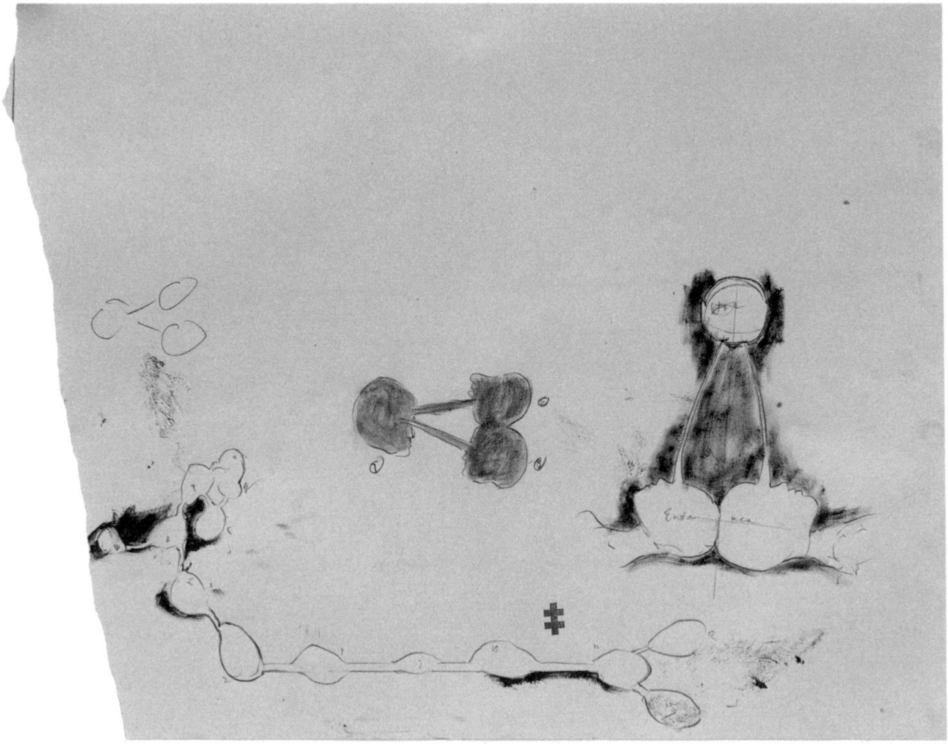

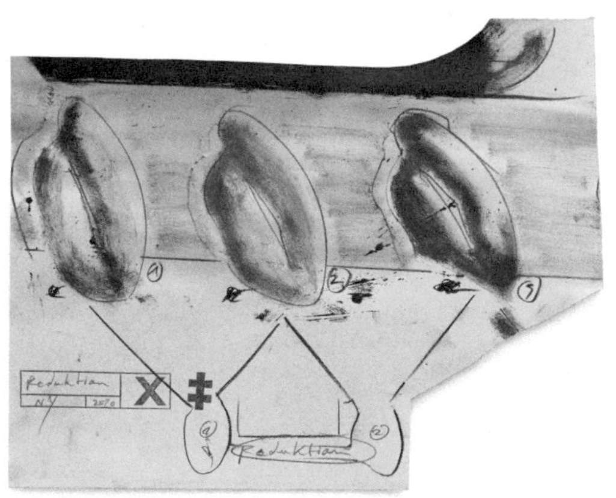

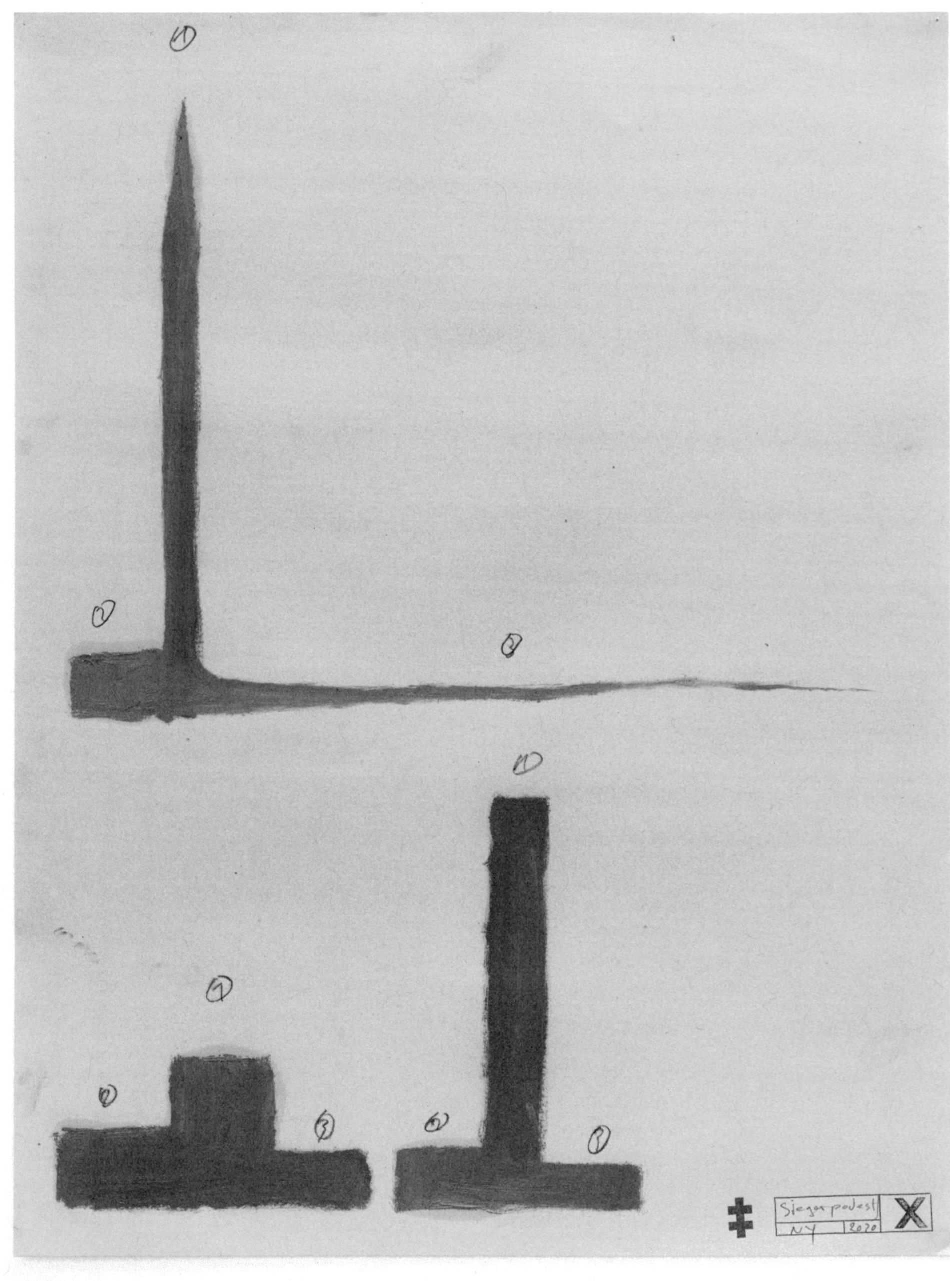
Siegerpodest
NY
2020
X

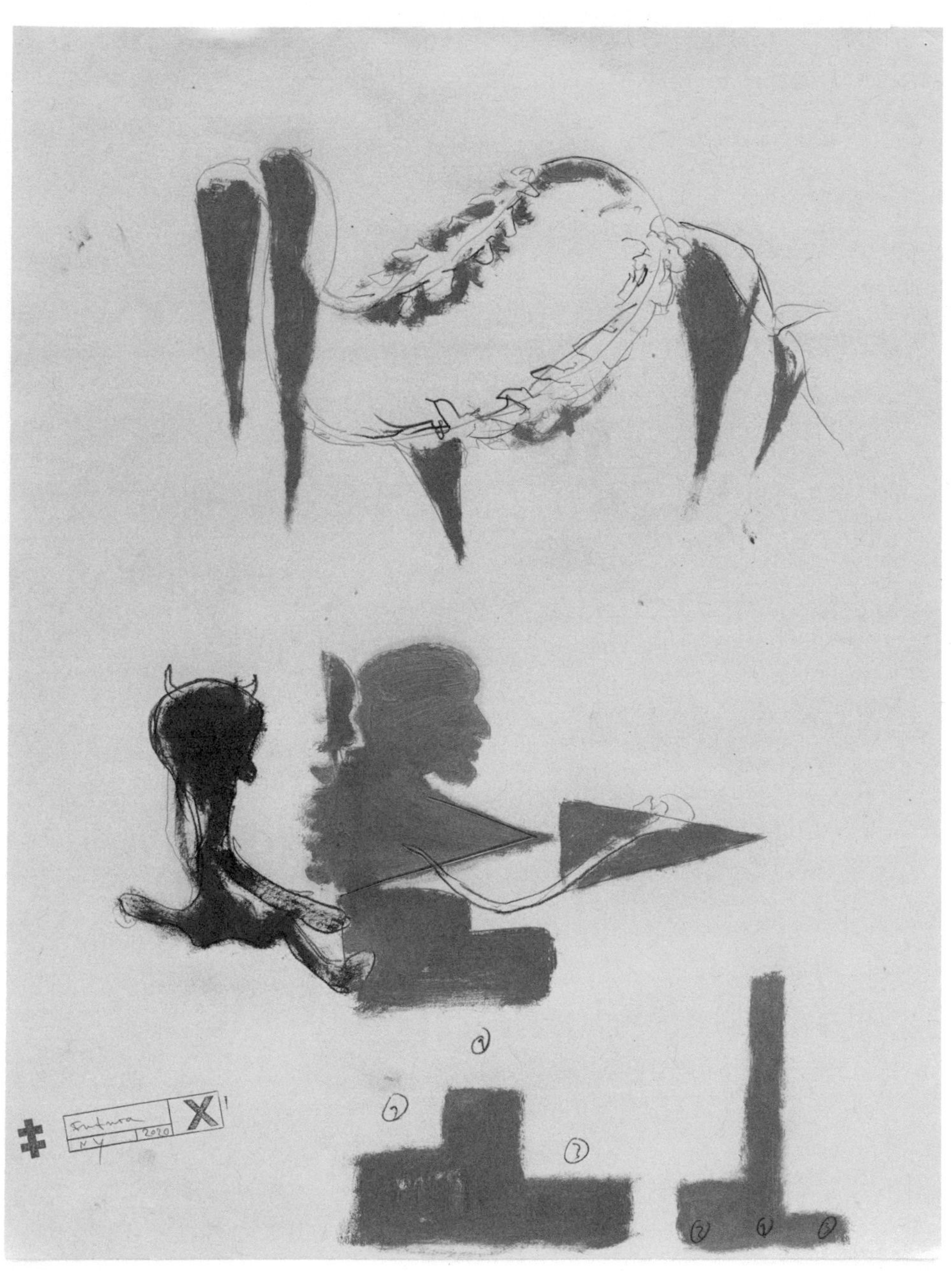

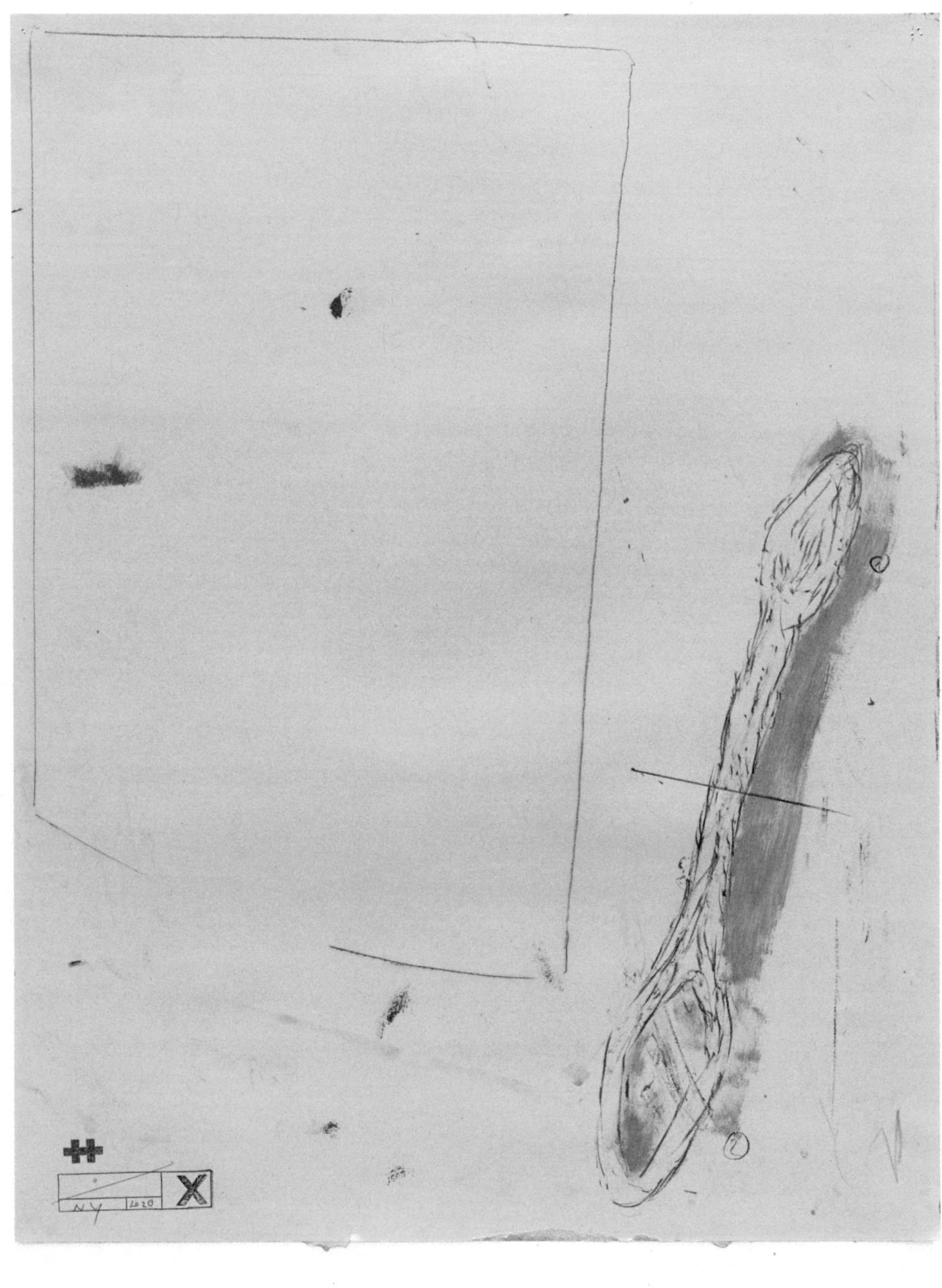

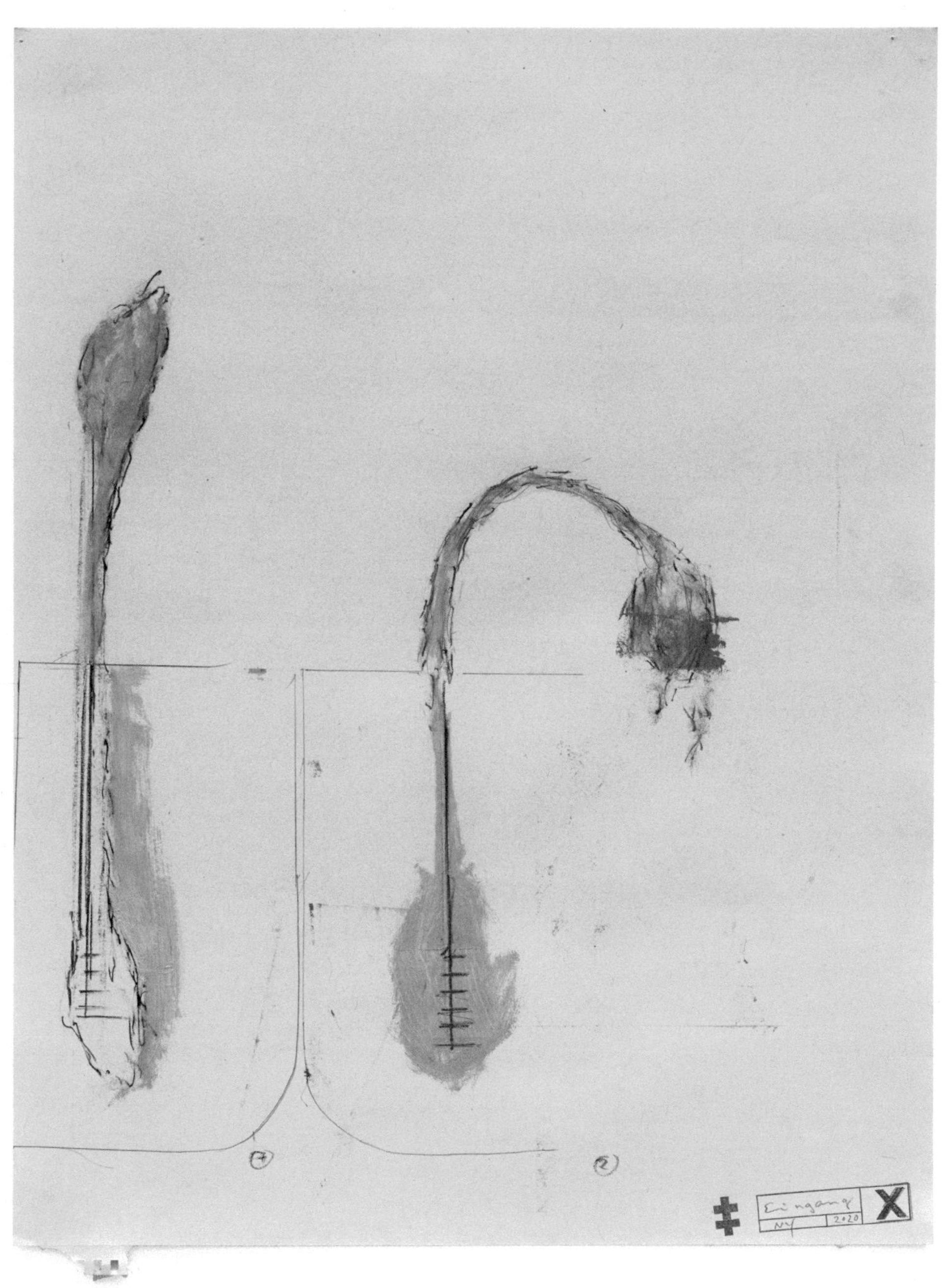
Eingang
NY
2020
X

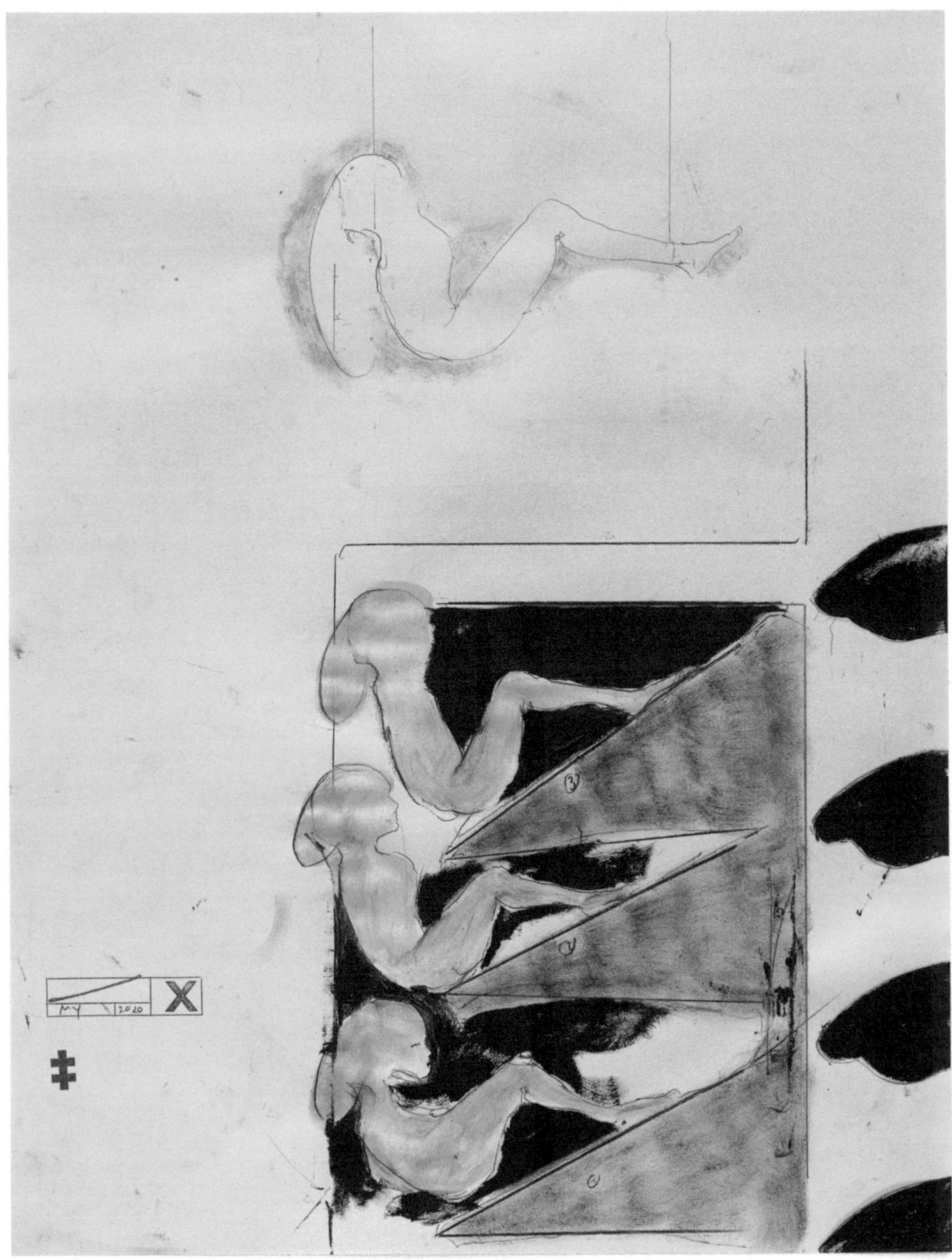

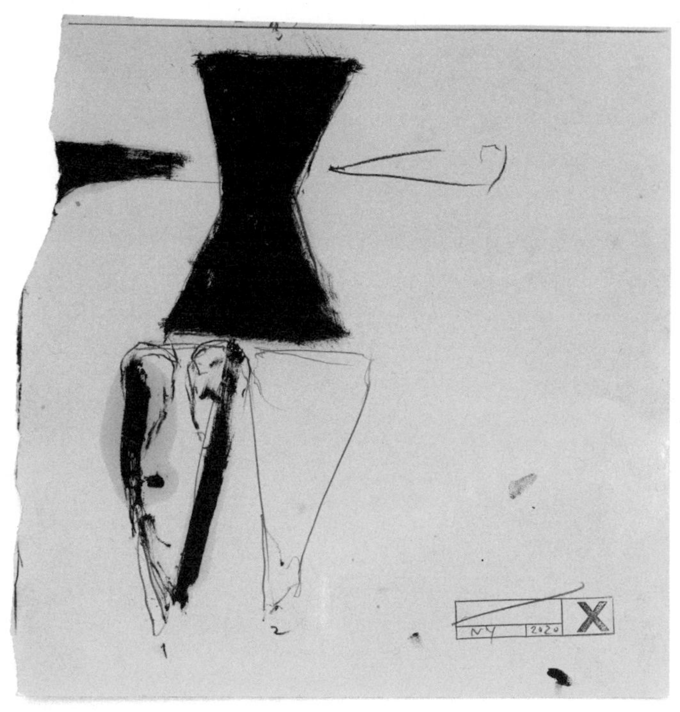
X
NY
2020

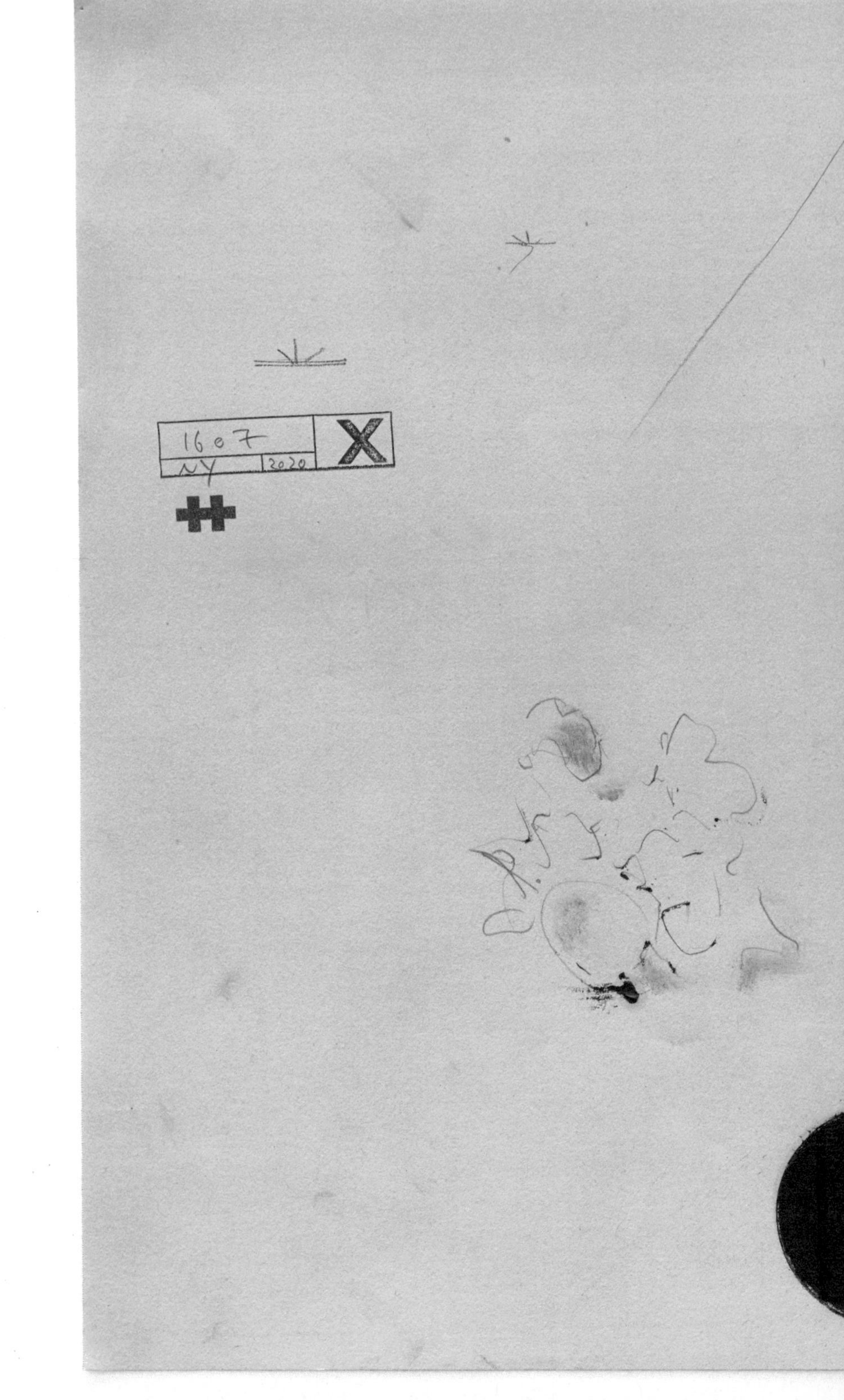
X
NY
2020

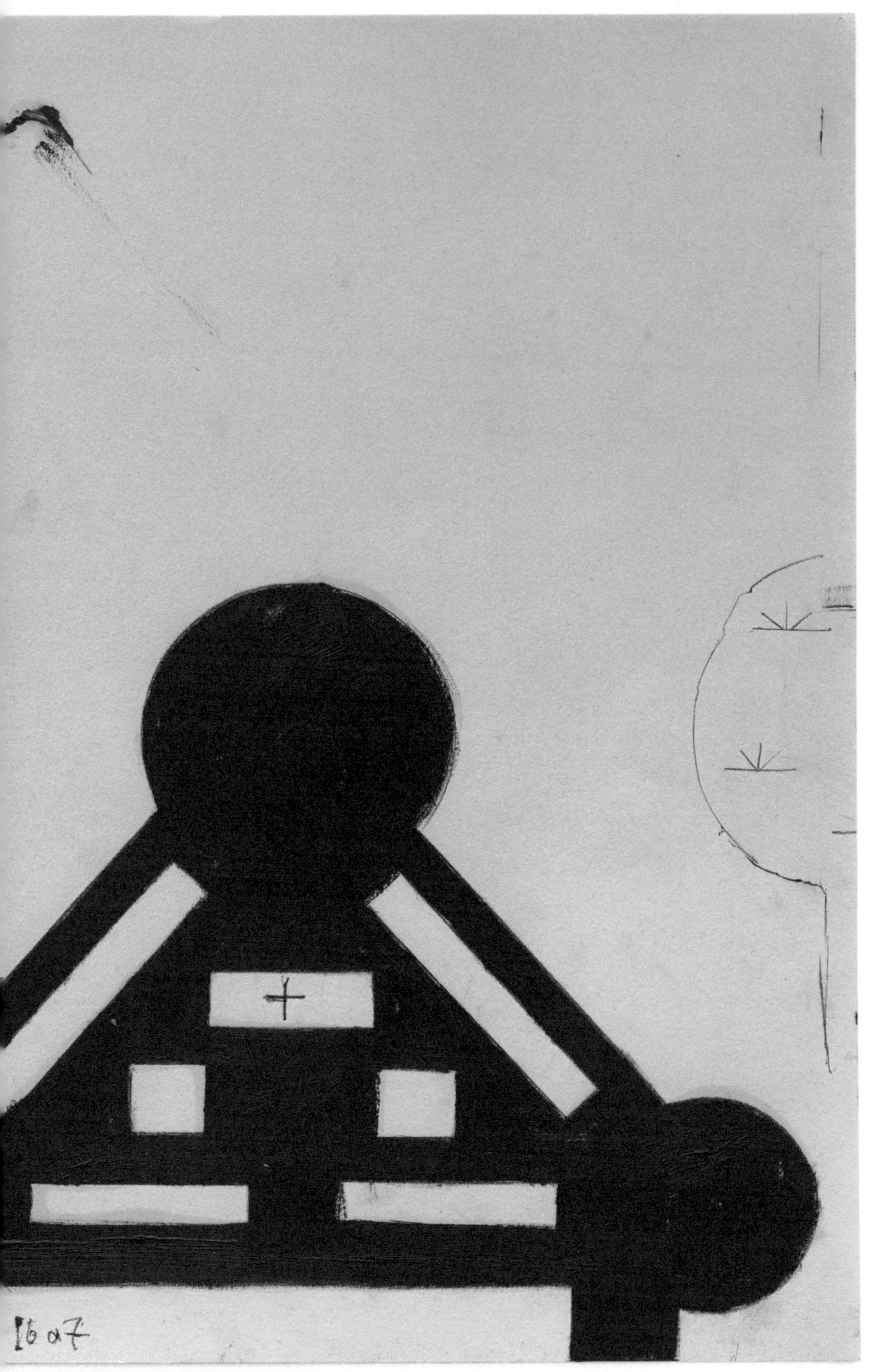

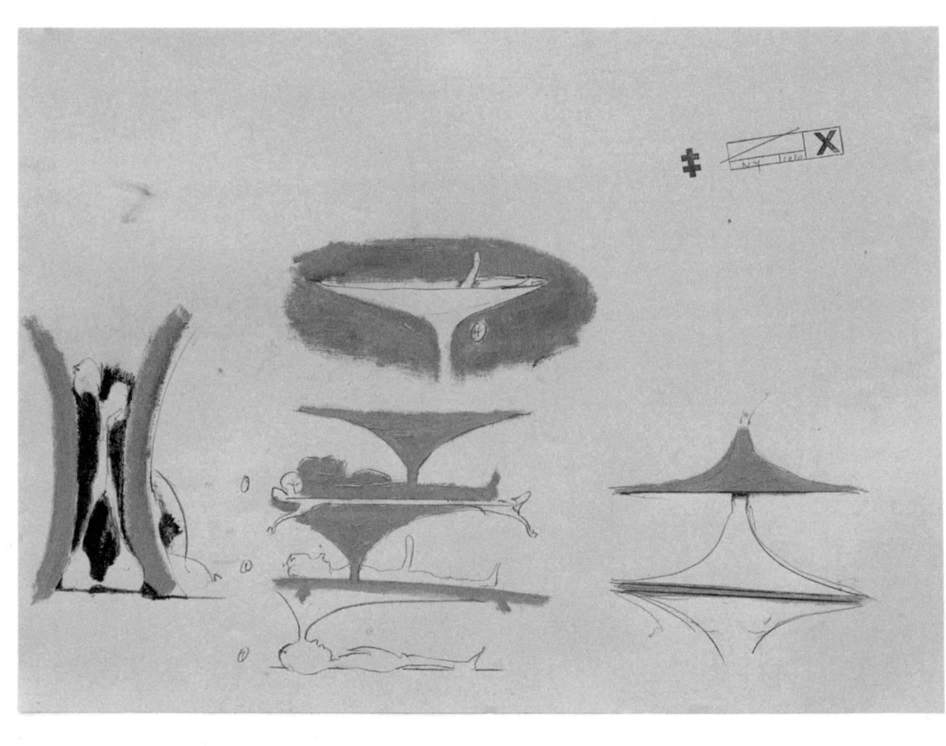

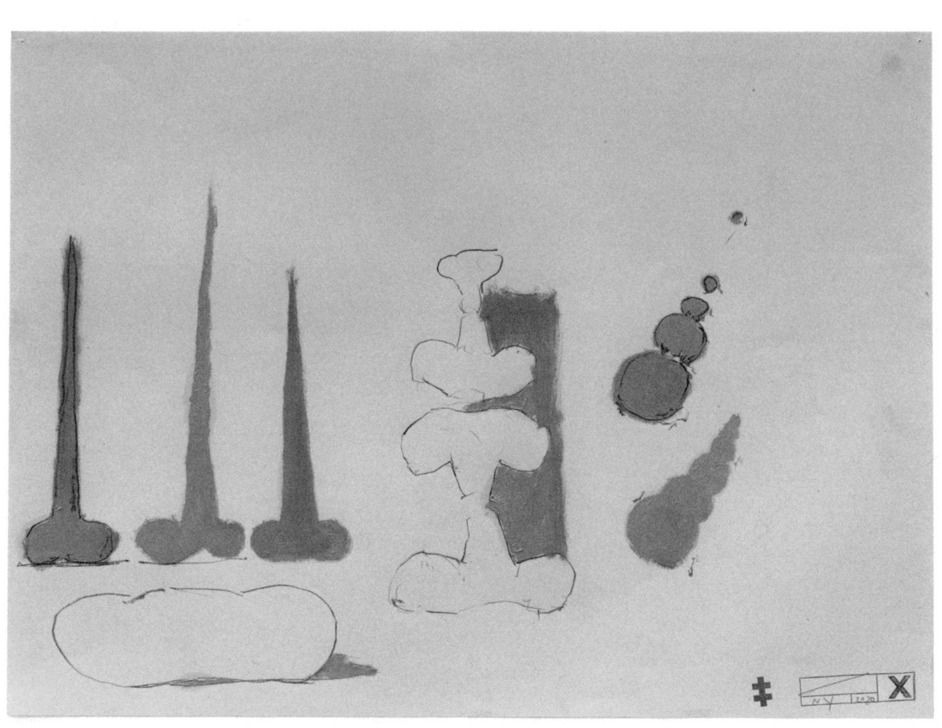

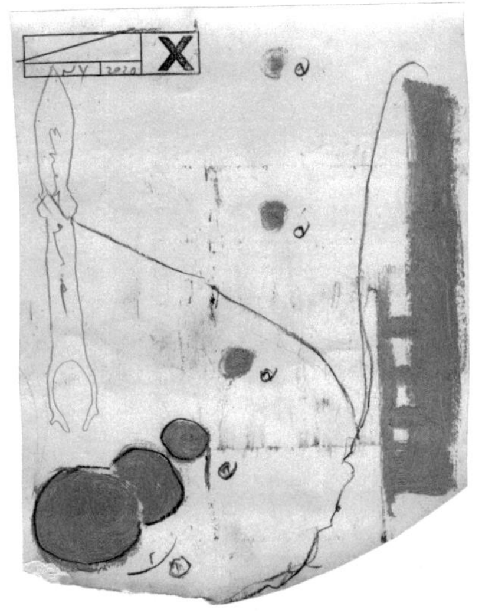

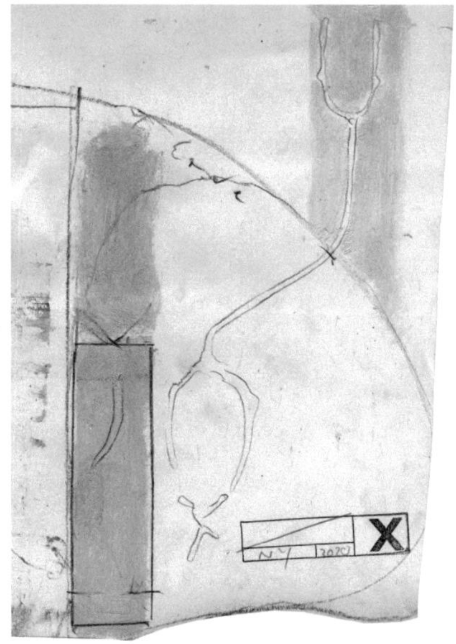

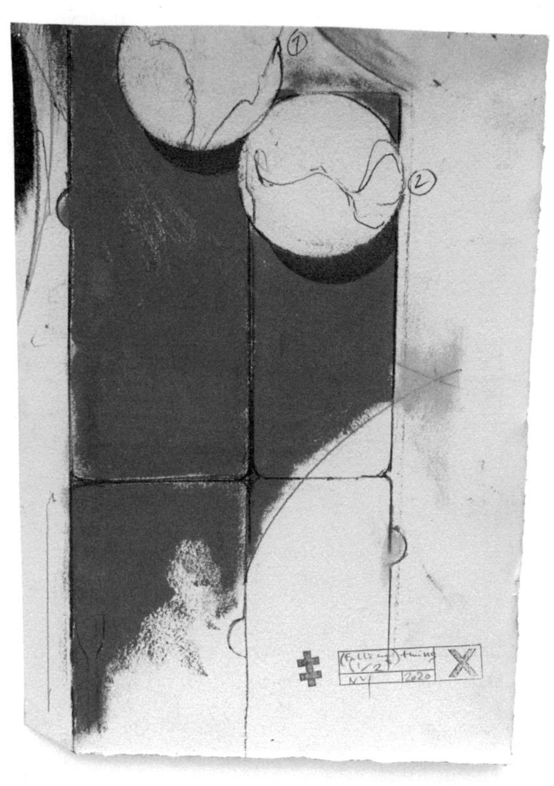

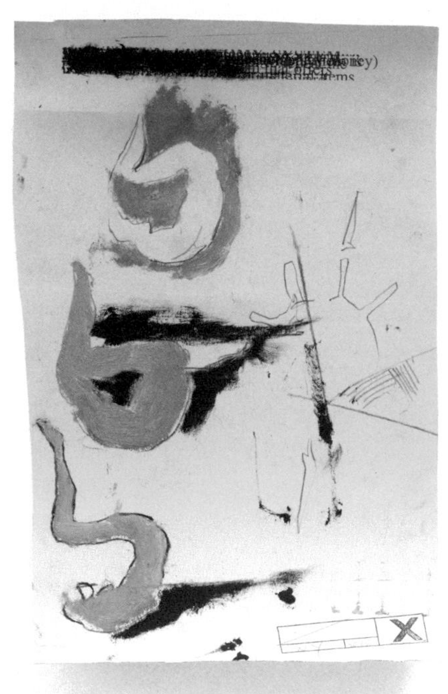

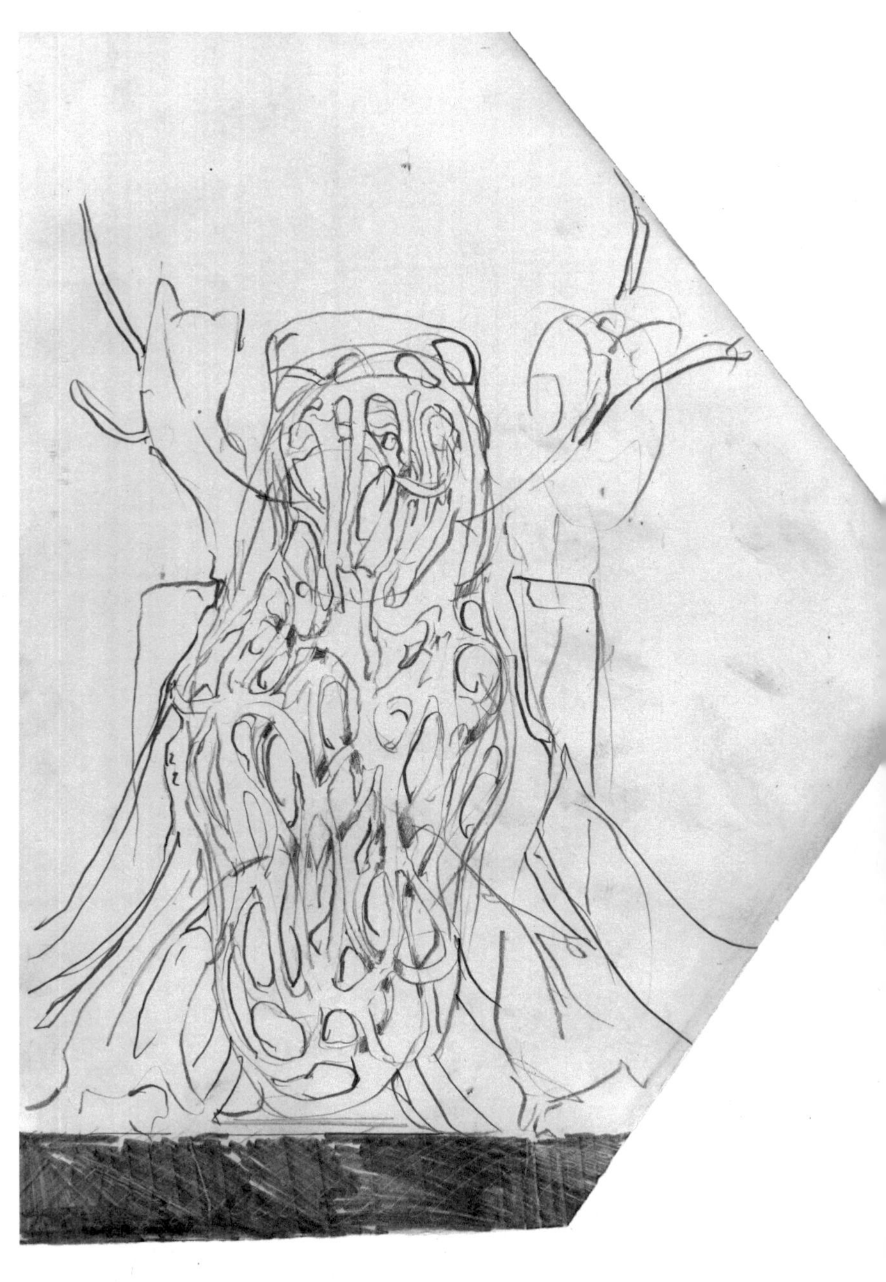

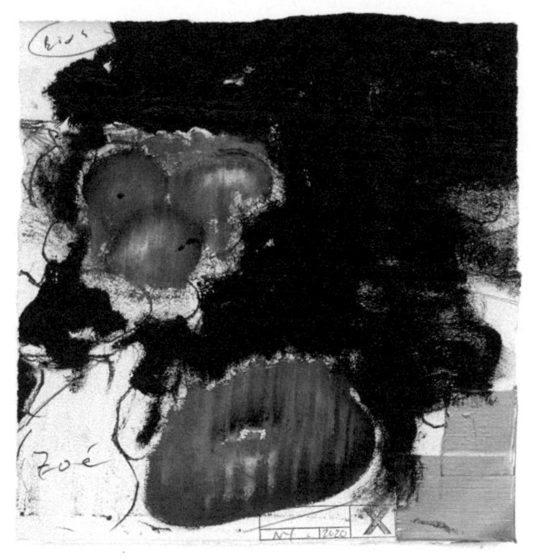
Zoé

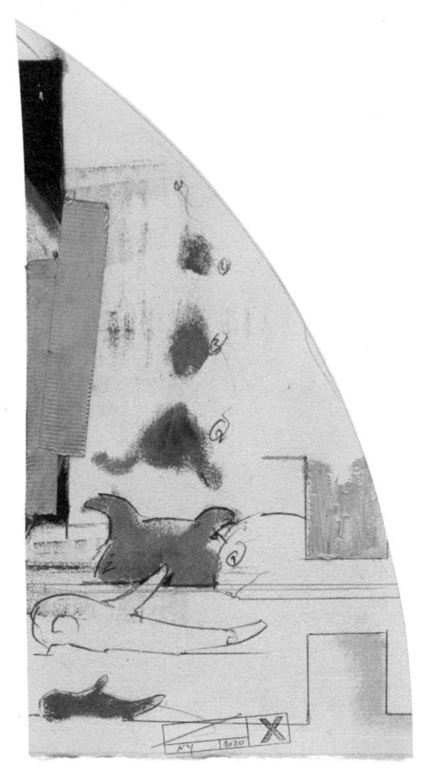

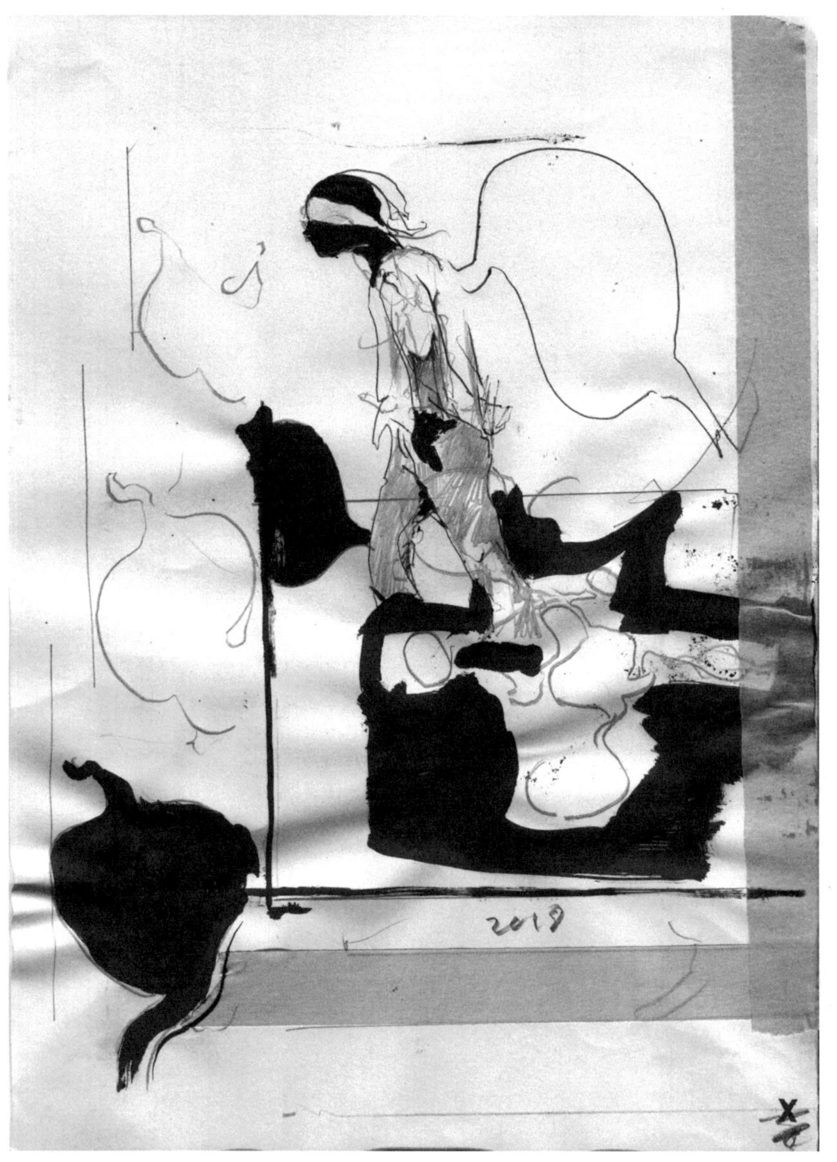

7

Breathing Pneuma

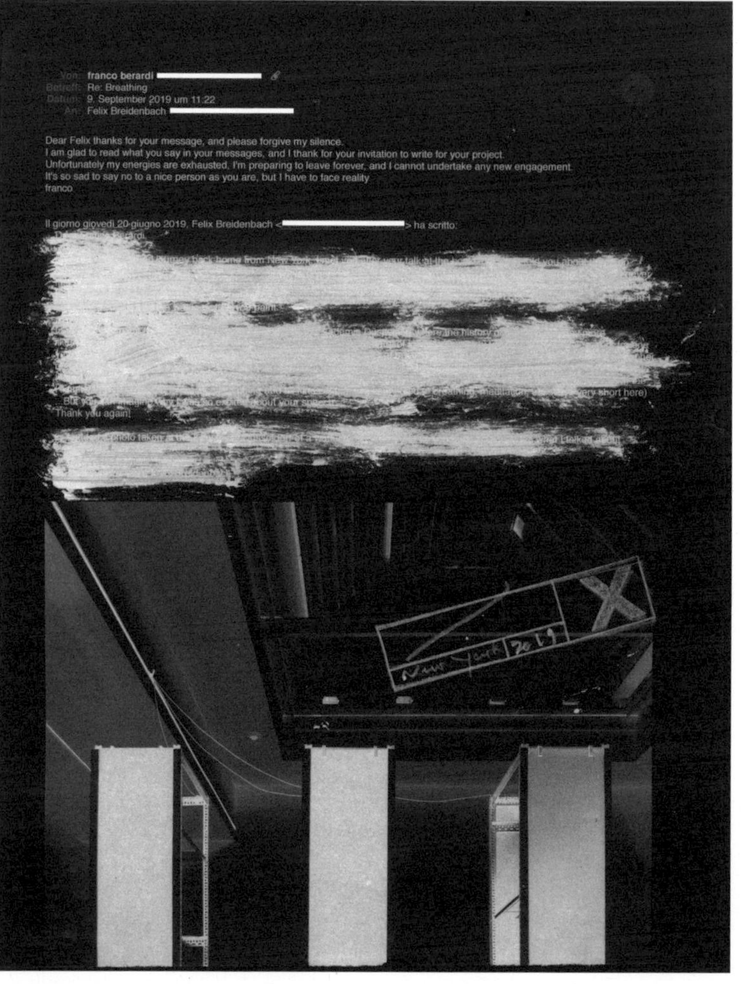

Von: **franco berardi**
Betreff: Re: Breathing
Datum: 9. September 2019 um 11:22
An: Felix Breidenbach

Dear Felix thanks for your message, and please forgive my silence.
I am glad to read what you say in your messages, and I thank for your invitation to write for your project.
Unfortunately my energies are exhausted, I'm preparing to leave forever, and I cannot undertake any new engagement.
It's so sad to say no to a nice person as you are, but I have to face reality
franco

Il giorno giovedì 20 giugno 2019, Felix Breidenbach <> ha scritto:

Thank you again!

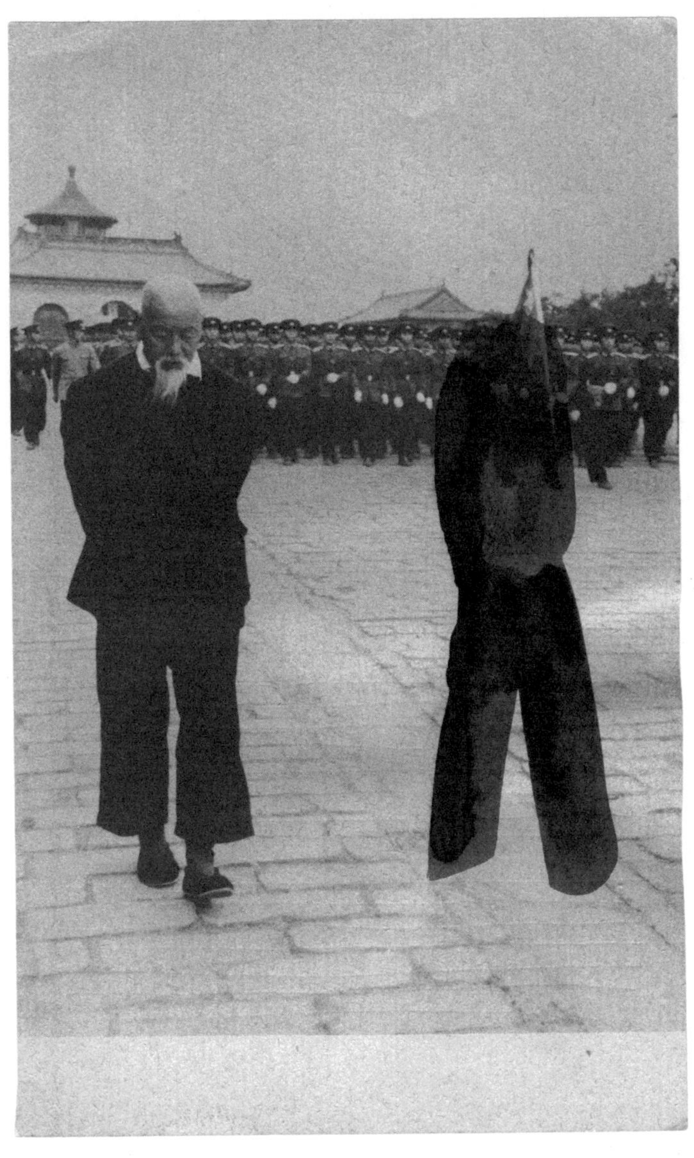

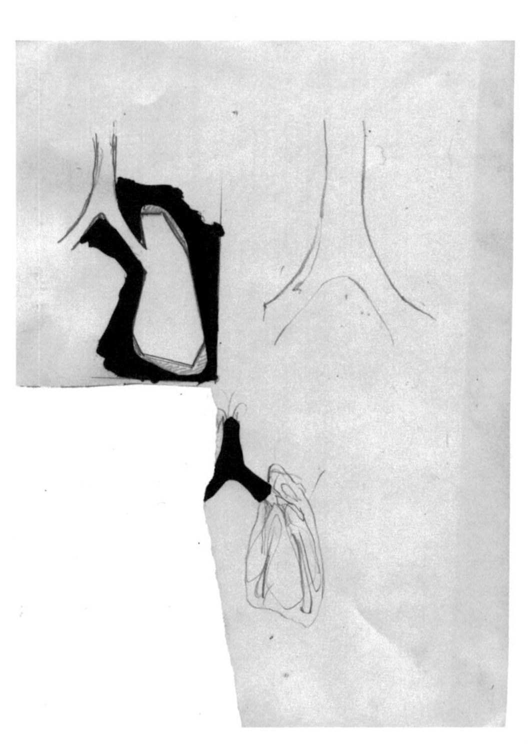

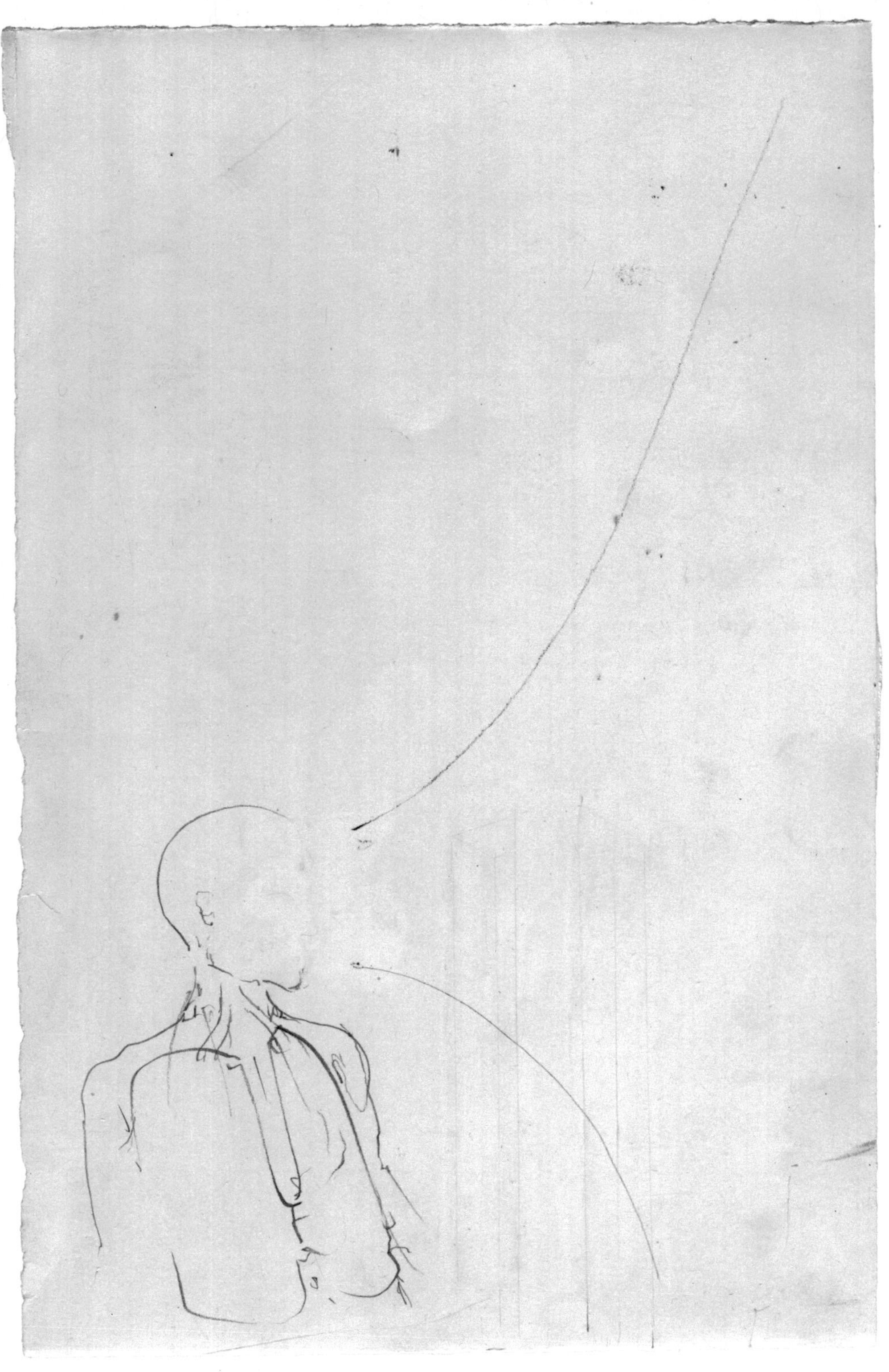

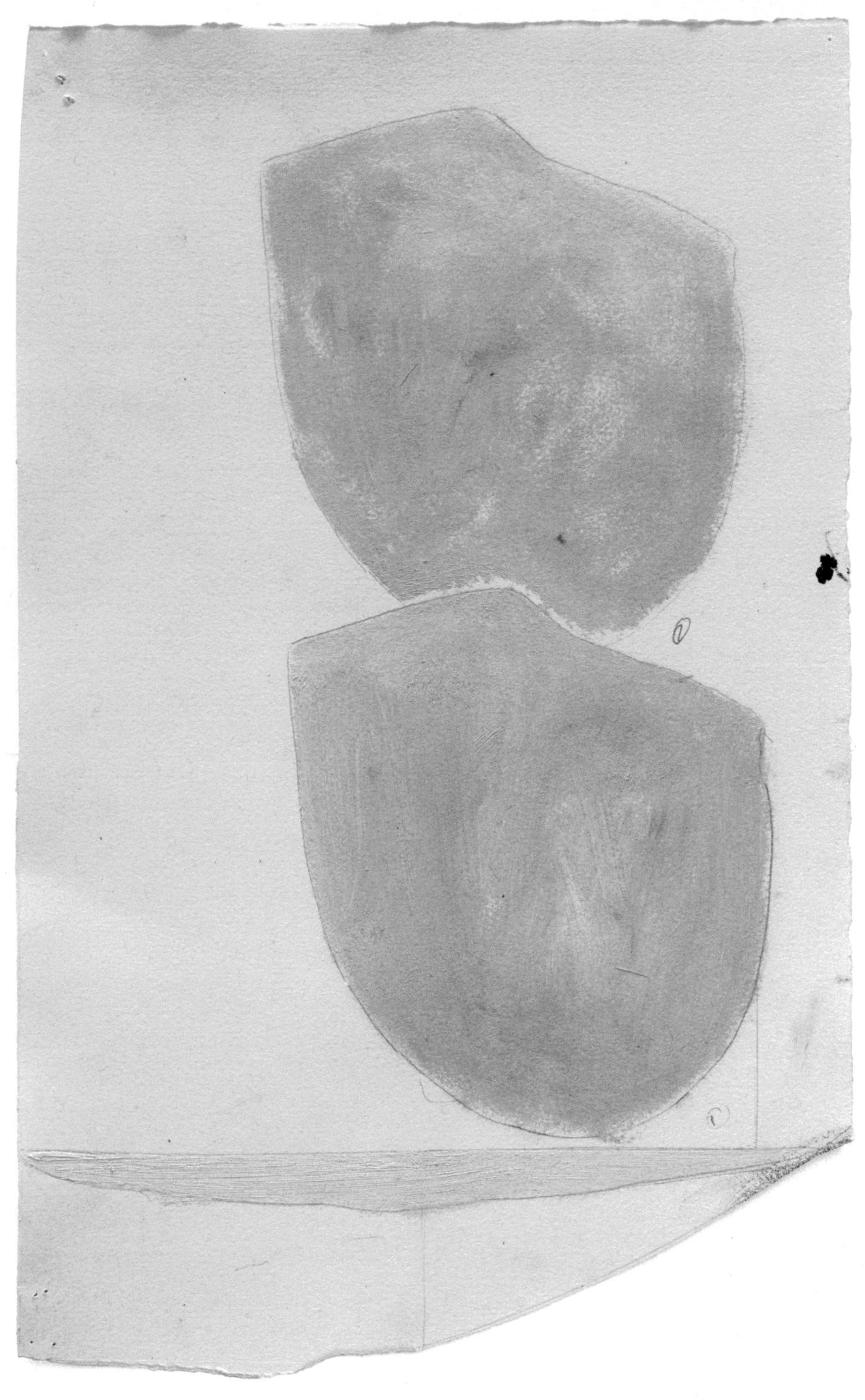

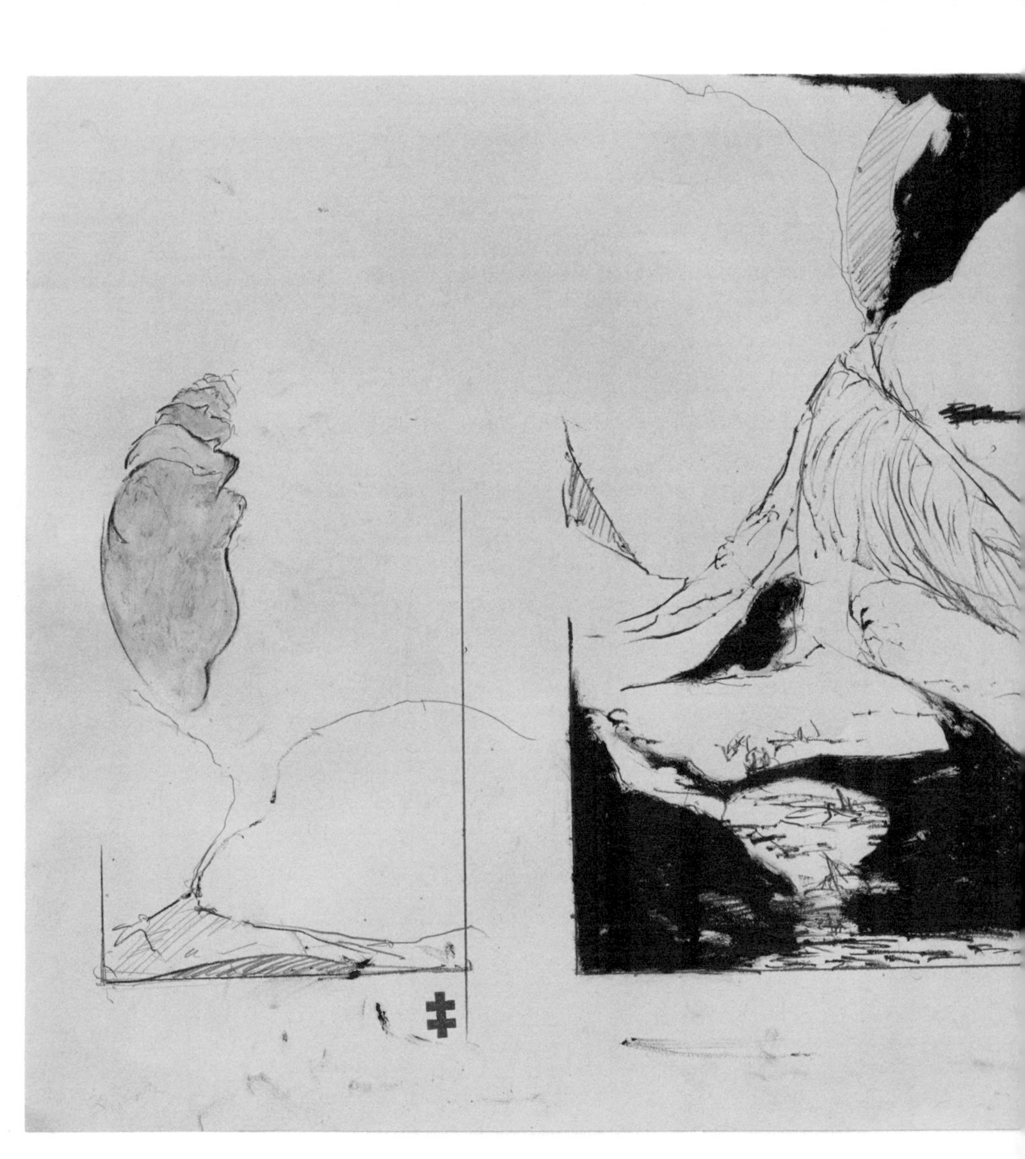

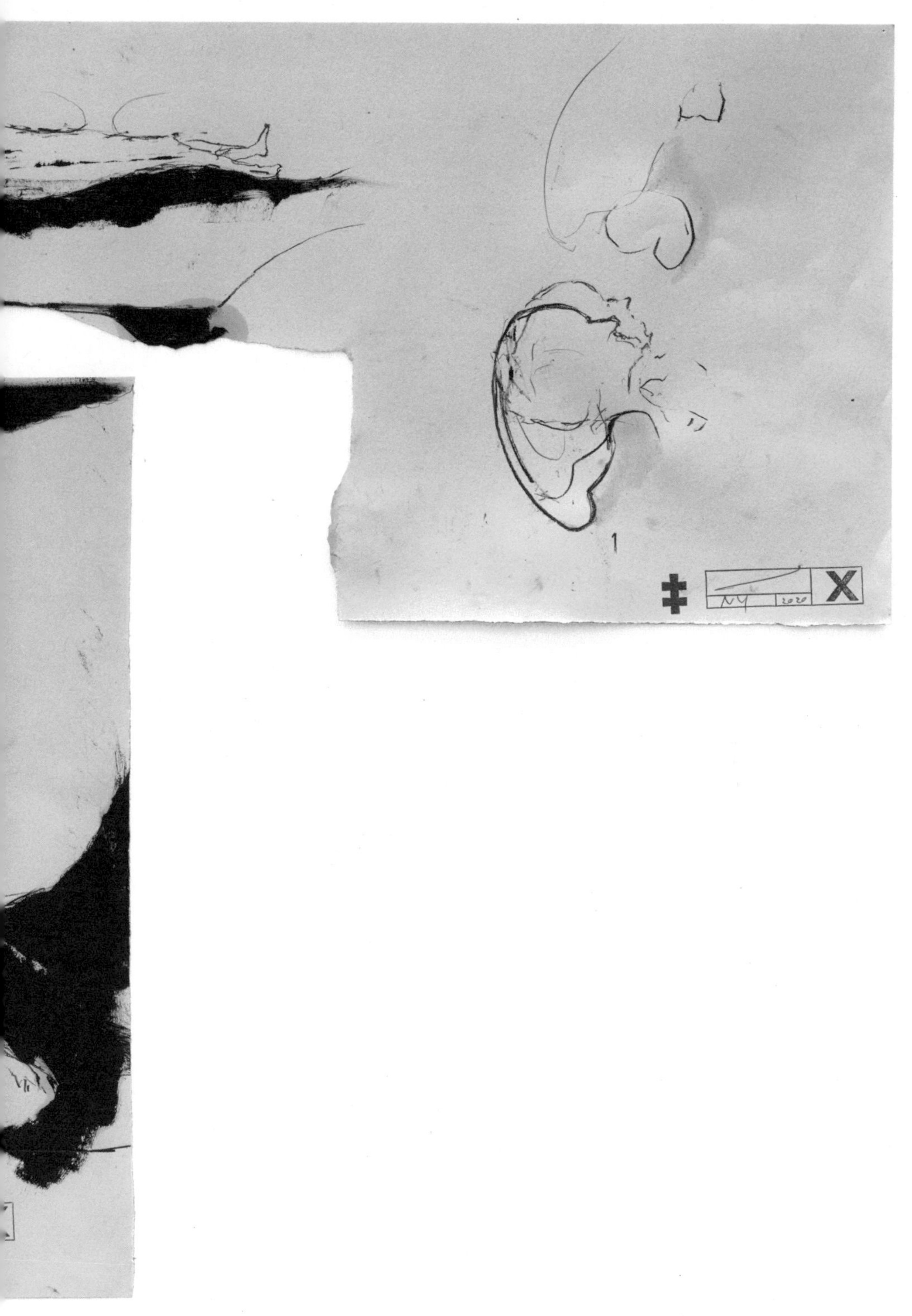

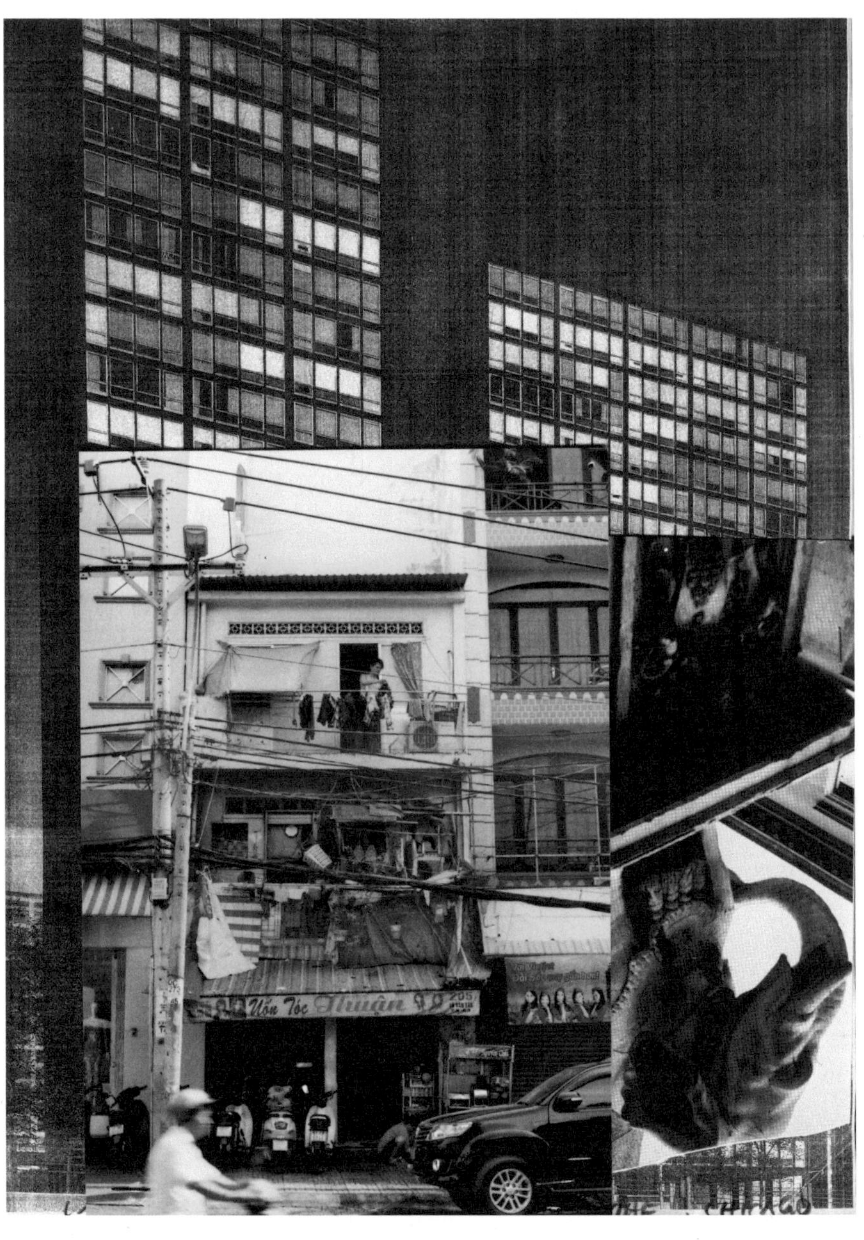

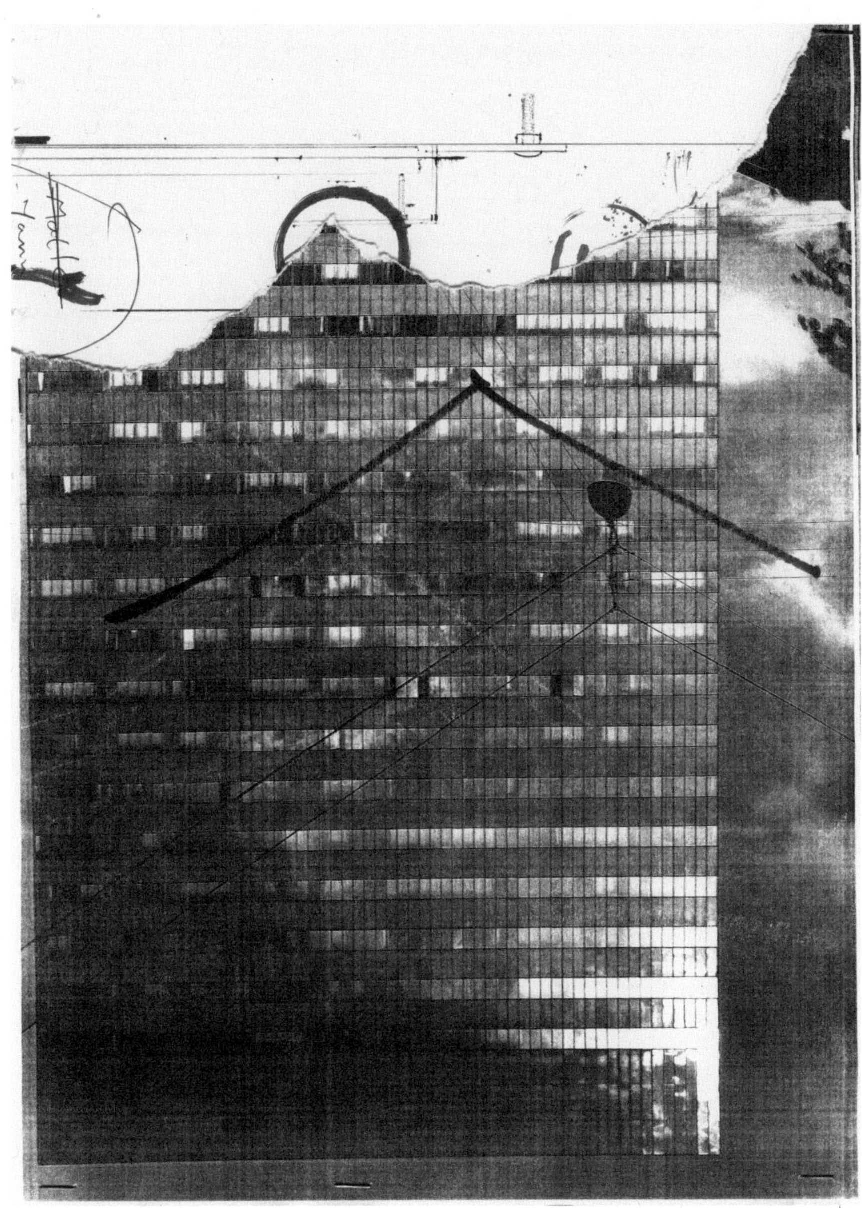

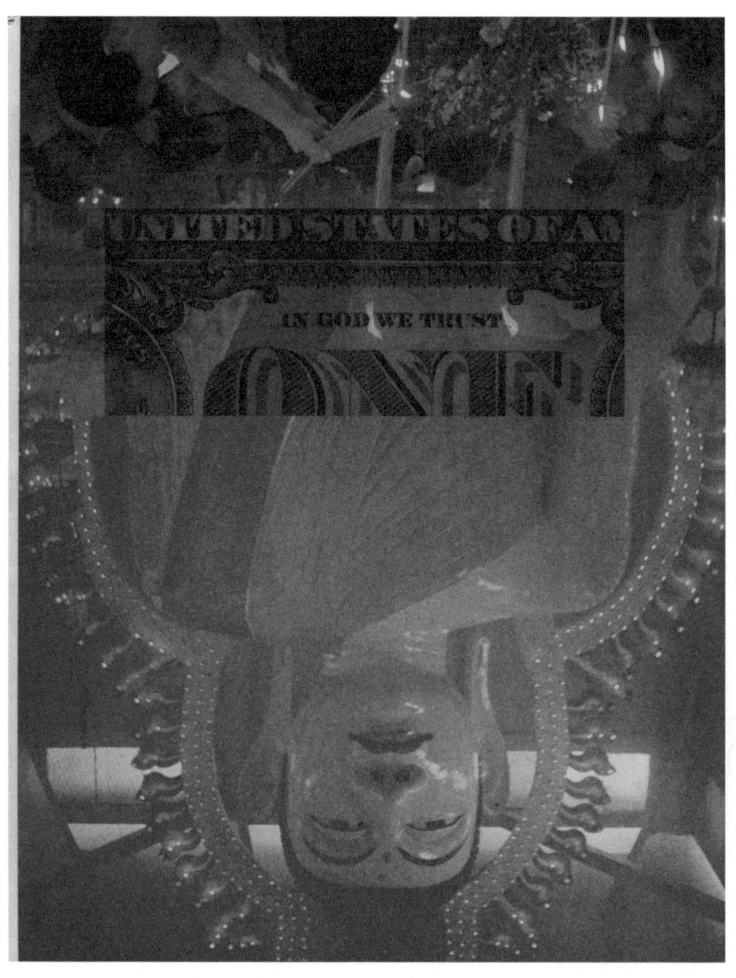
UNITED STATES OF A
IN GOD WE TRUST

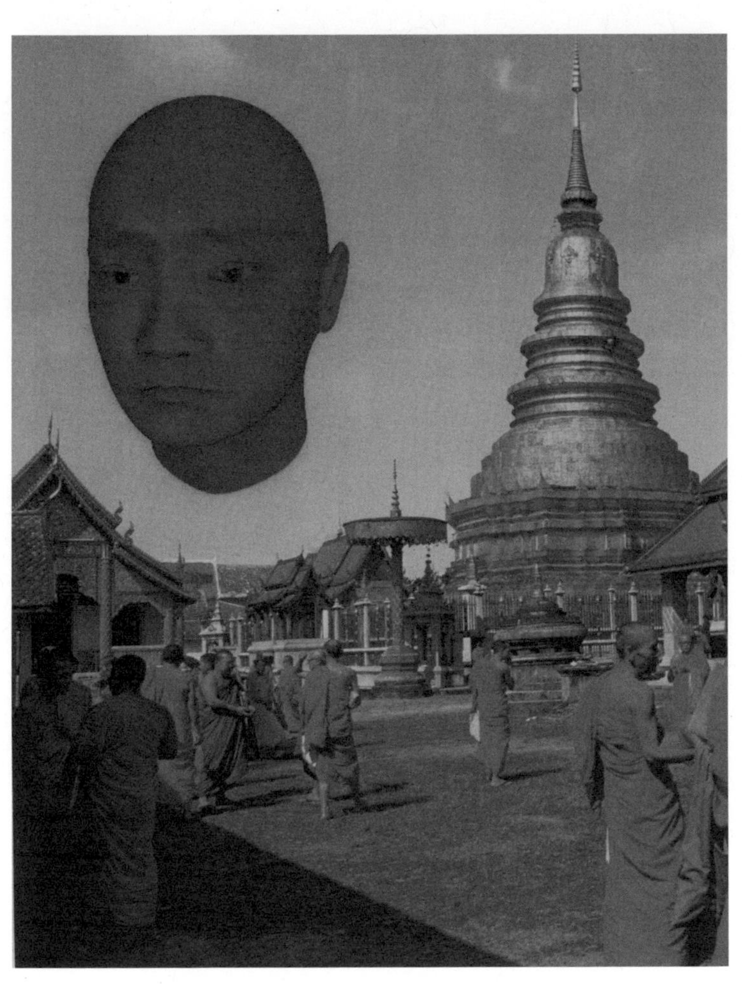

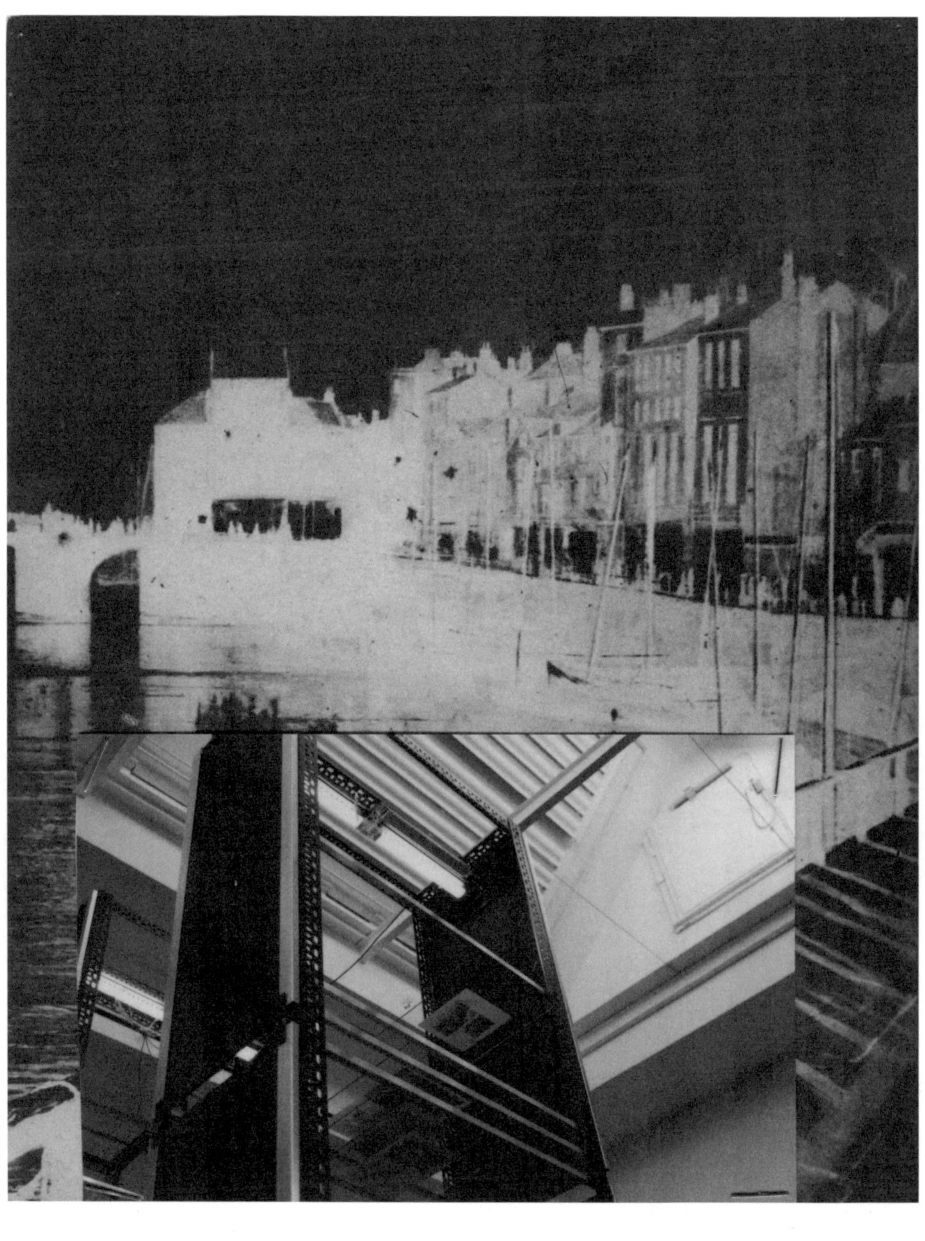

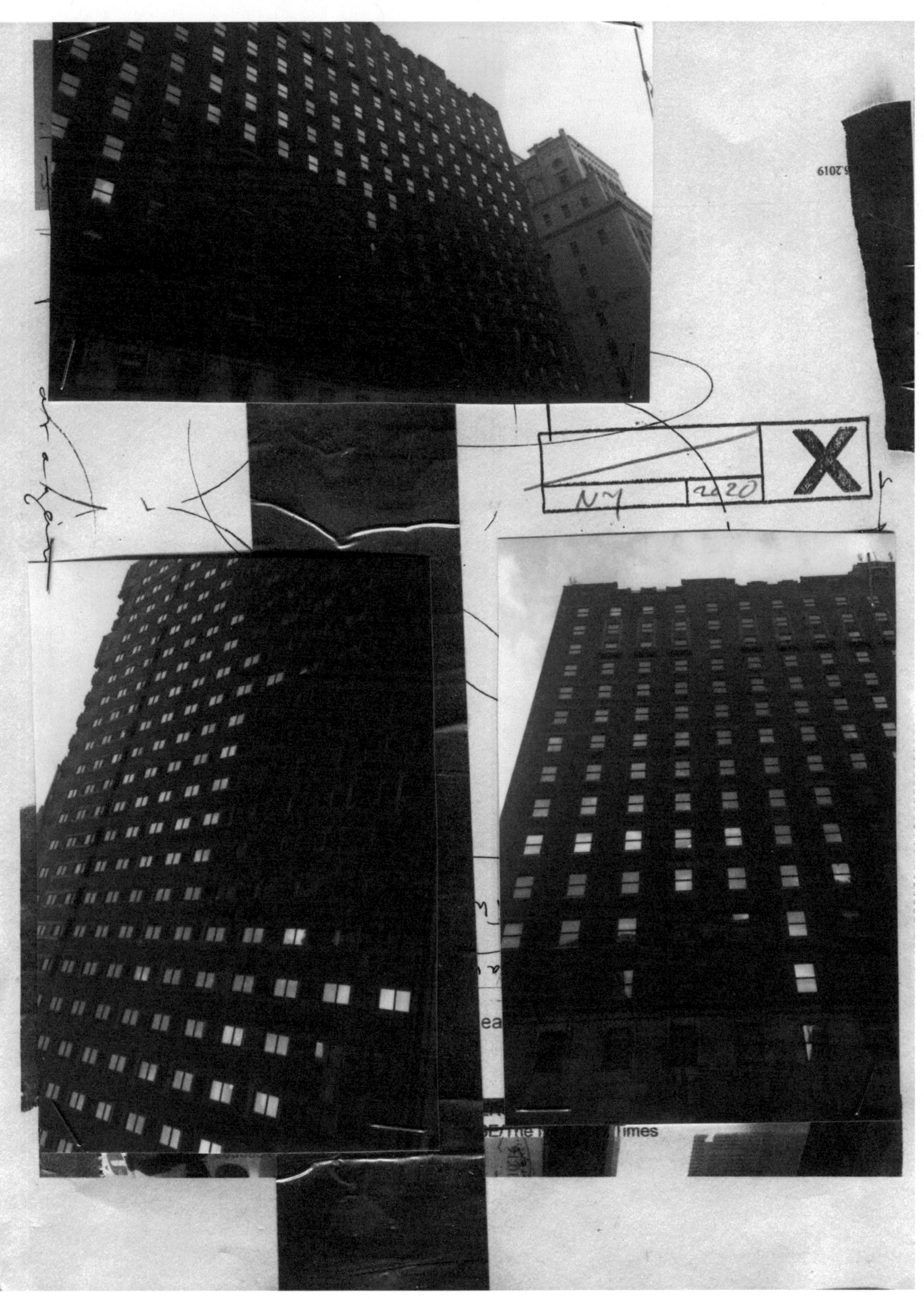

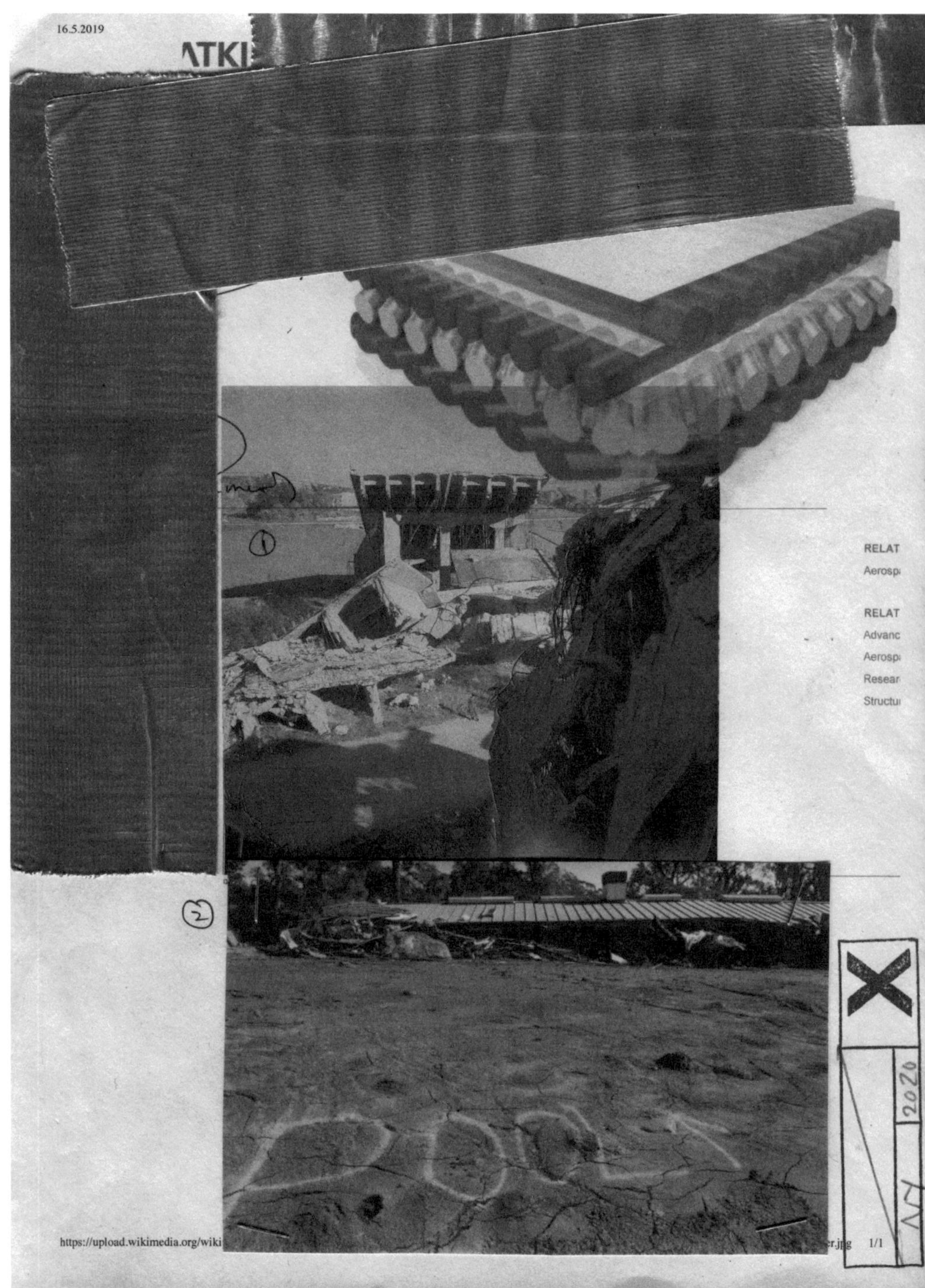
16.5.2019
ATKI
RELAT
Aerosp
RELAT
Advanc
Aerosp
Resear
Structu
https://upload.wikimedia.org/wiki
er.jpg 1/1
2020

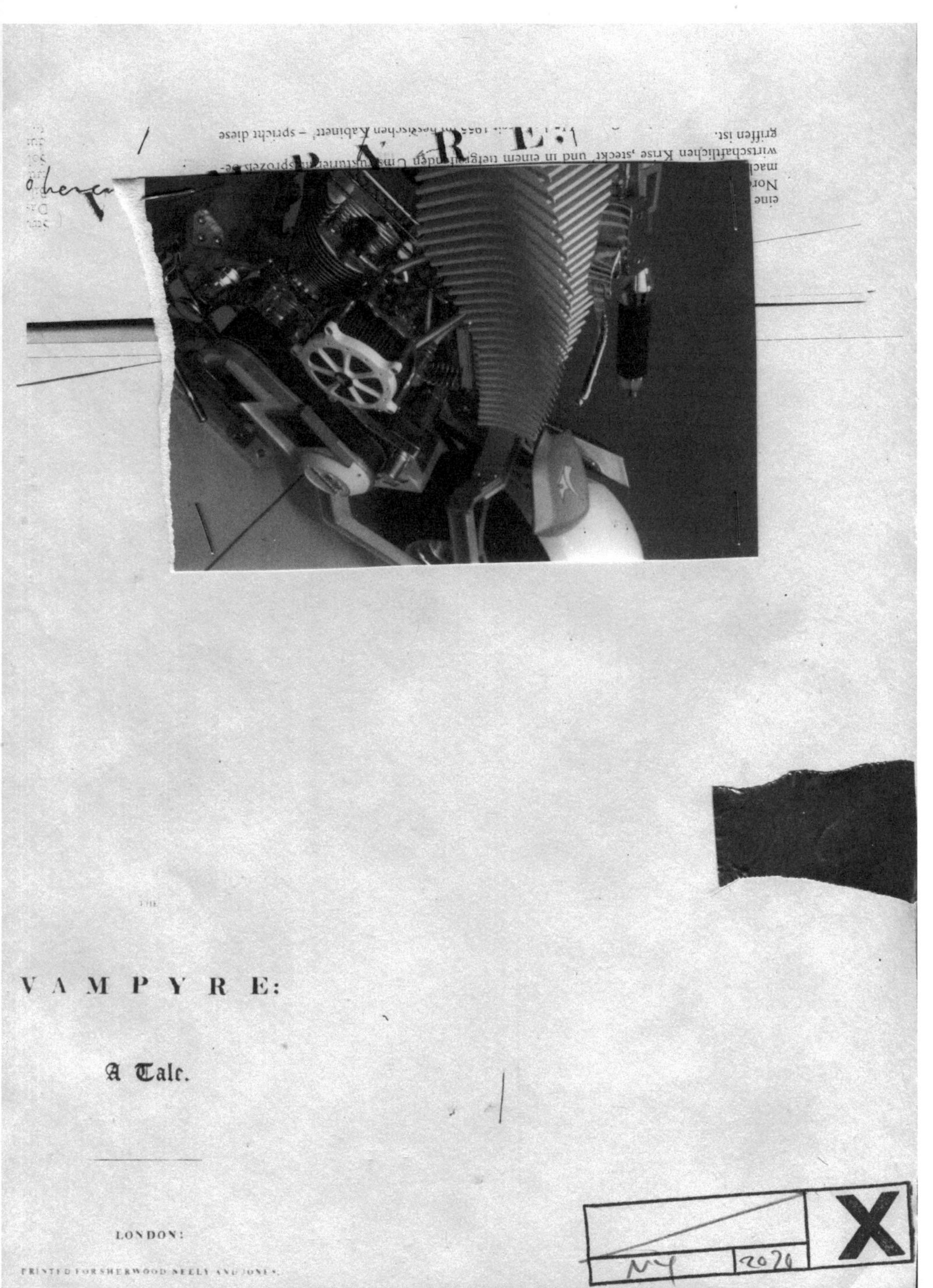
THE
VAMPYRE:
A Tale.
LONDON:
PRINTED FOR SHERWOOD, NEELY, AND JONES.
NY
2020
X

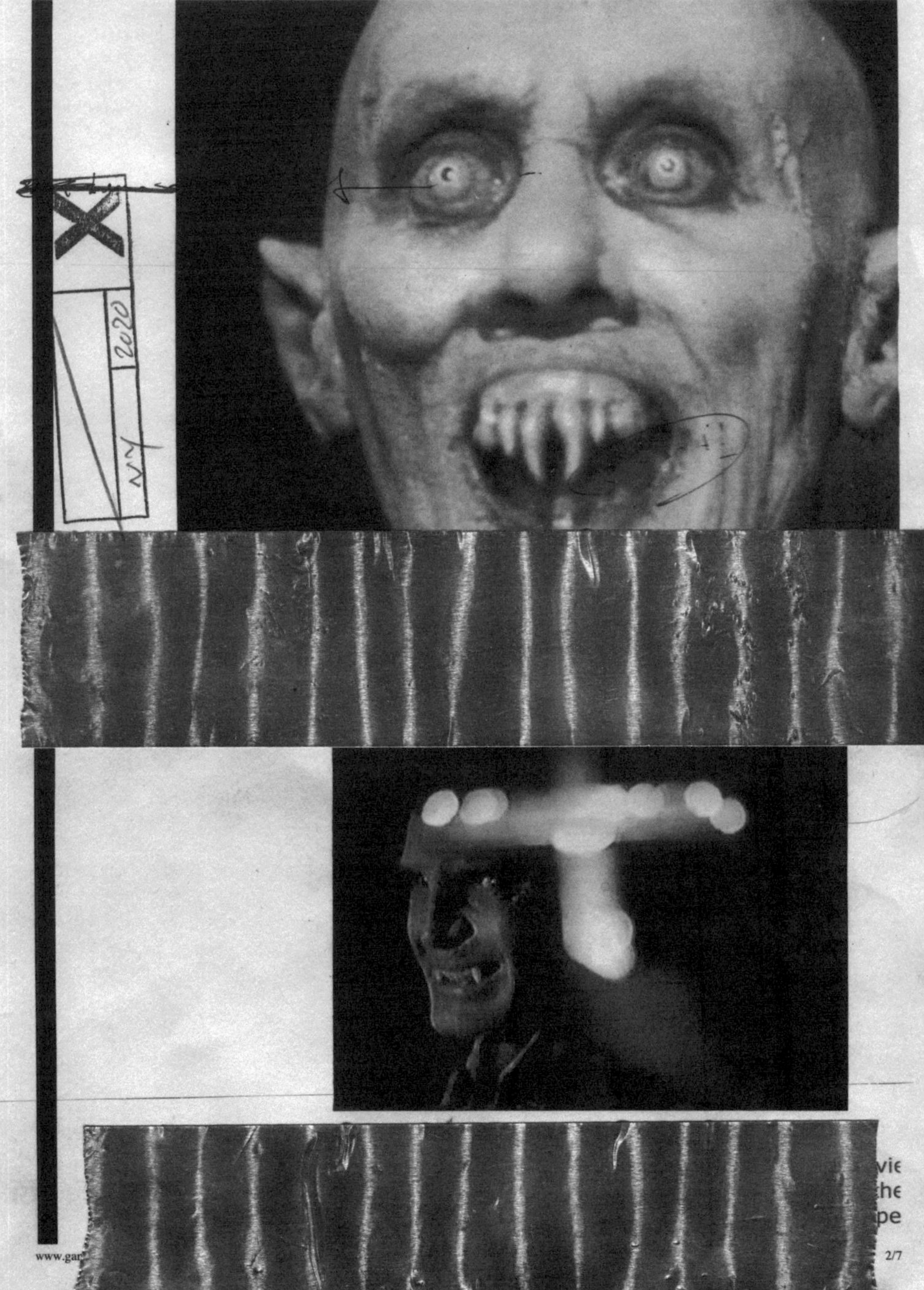

vie
the
pe

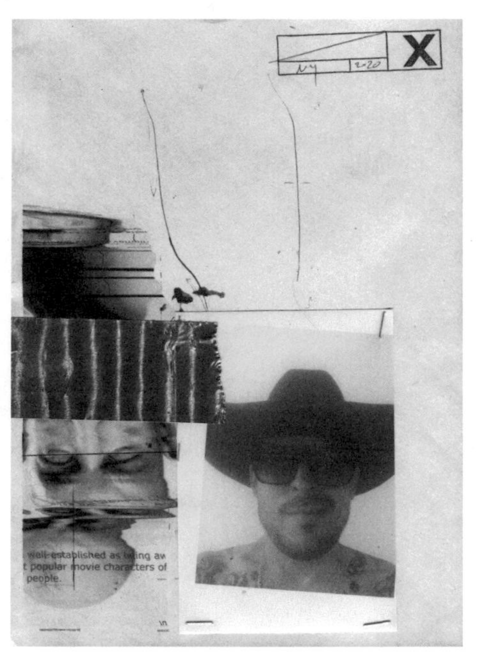
X
NY
2020
well-established as
popular movie characters of
people.

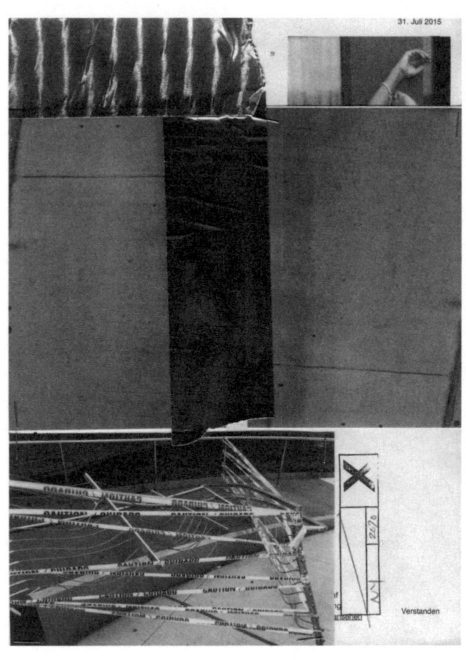
31. Juli 2015
CAUTION
X
2020
NY
Verstanden

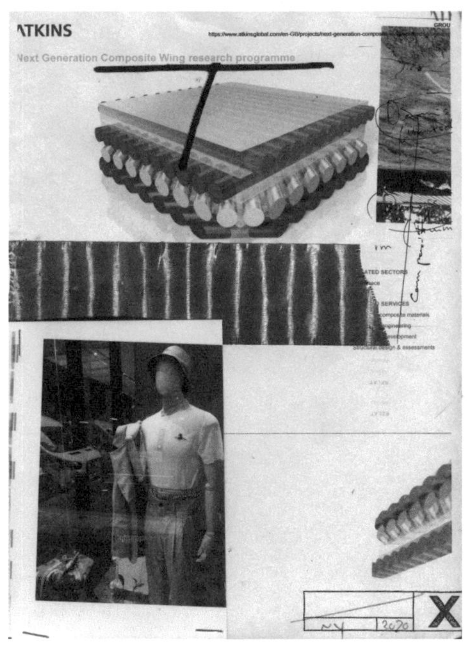
ATKINS
Next Generation Composite Wing research programme
structural design & assessments
X
NY
2020

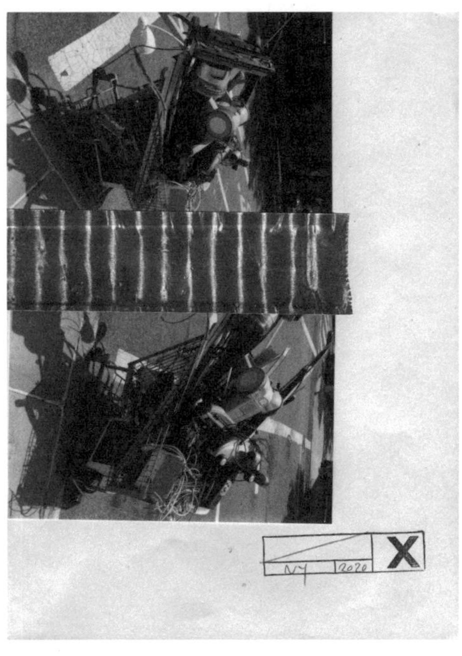
X
NY
2020

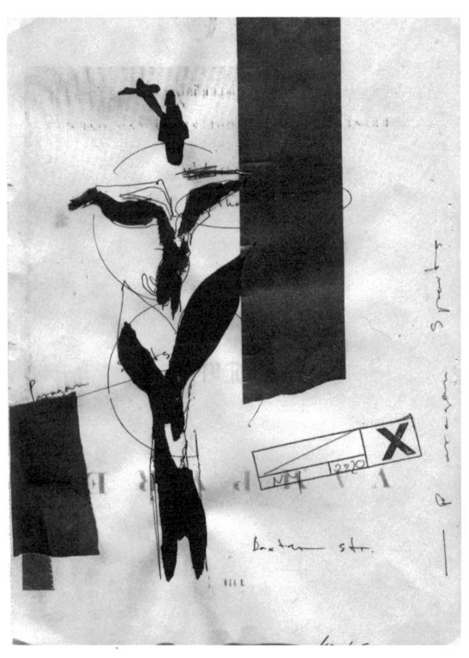
X
NY
2020

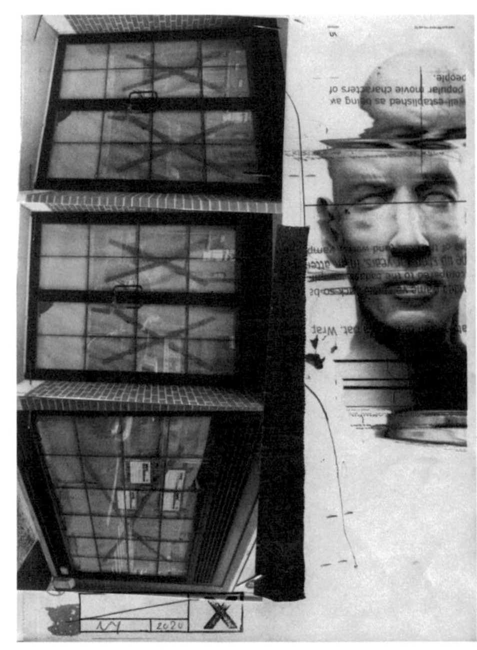
X
NY
2020

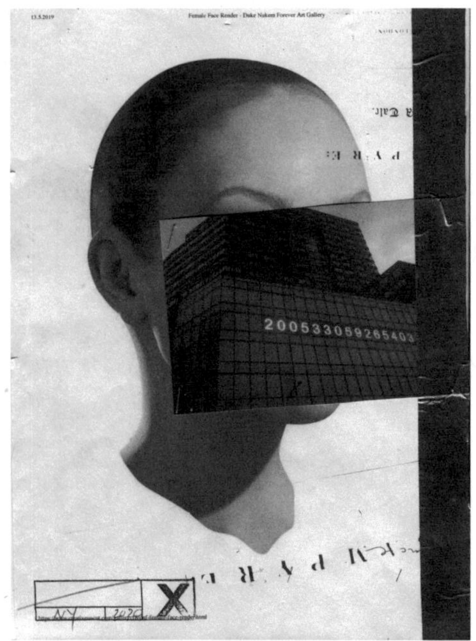
13.5.2019
Female Face Render · Duke Nukem Forever Art Gallery
200533059265403
X
NY
2020

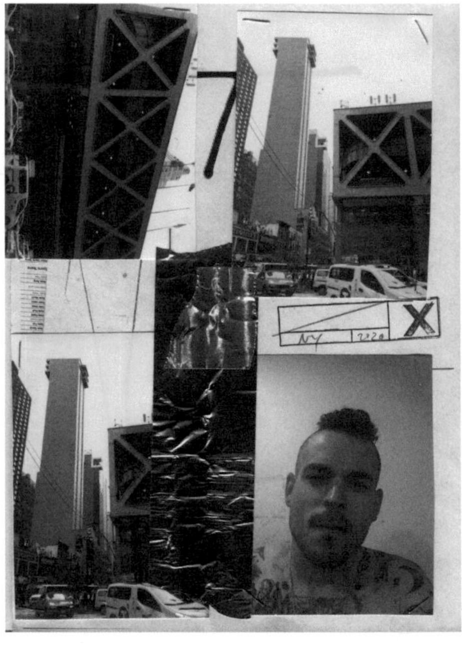
X
NY
2020

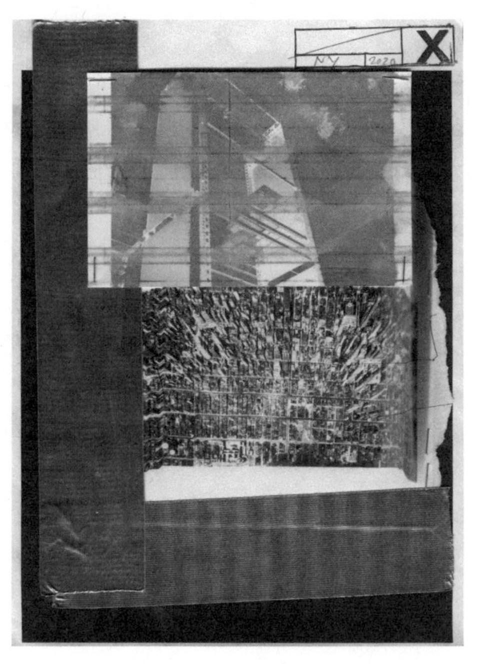

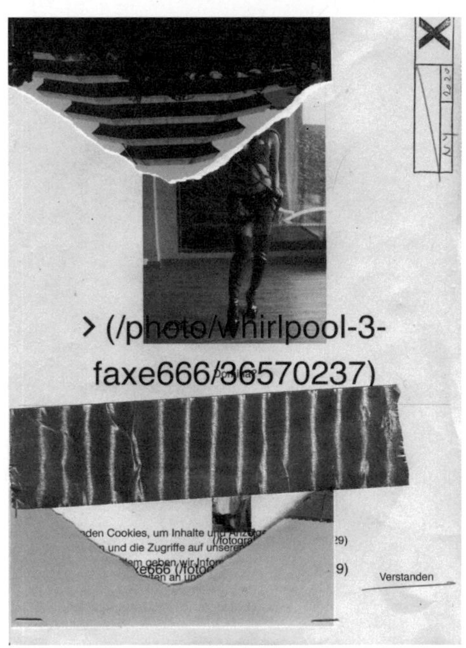

> (/photo/whirlpool-3-
faxe666/36570237)
Verstanden

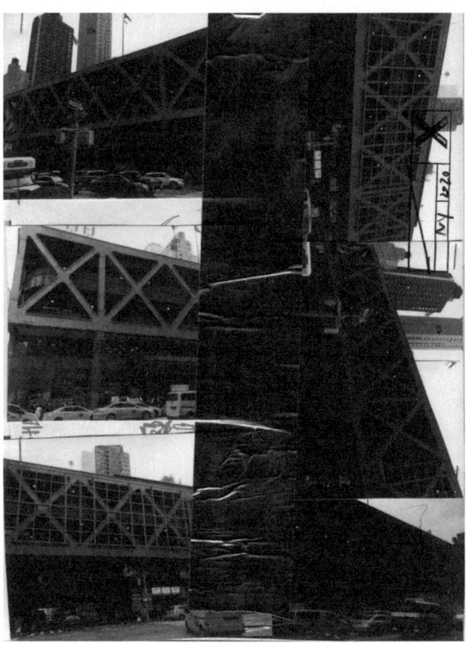

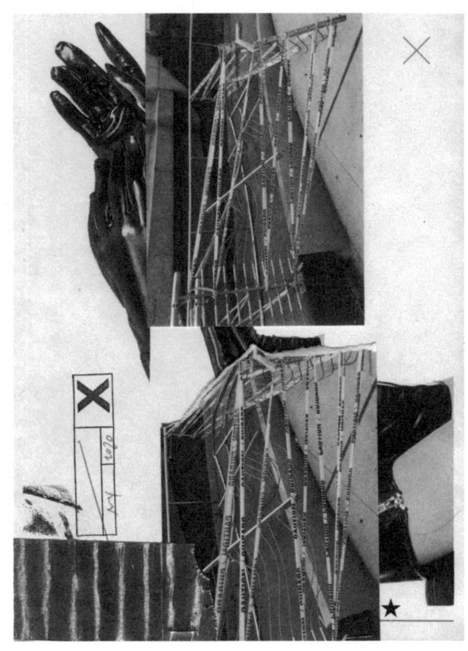

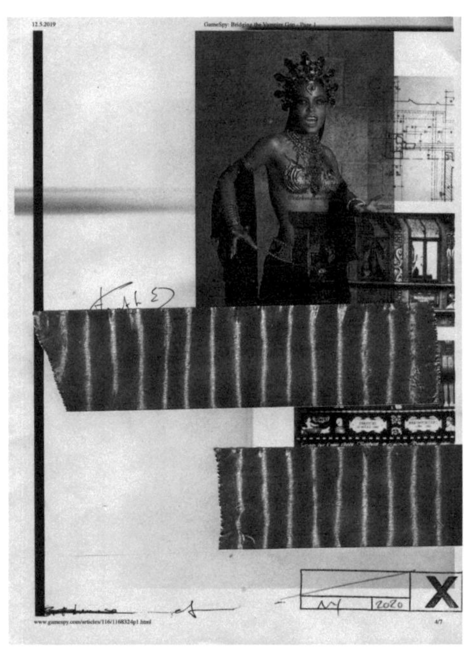
12.5.2019
NY
2020
X
www.gamespy.com/articles/116/1168324p1.html
4/7

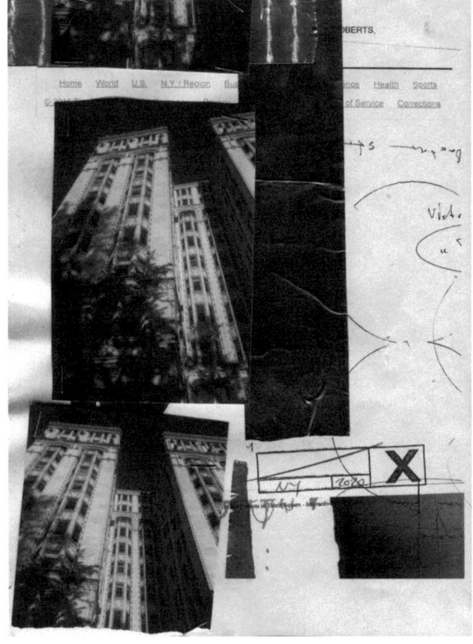
Home World U.S. N.Y. / Region
Health Sports
of Service Corrections
NY
2020
X

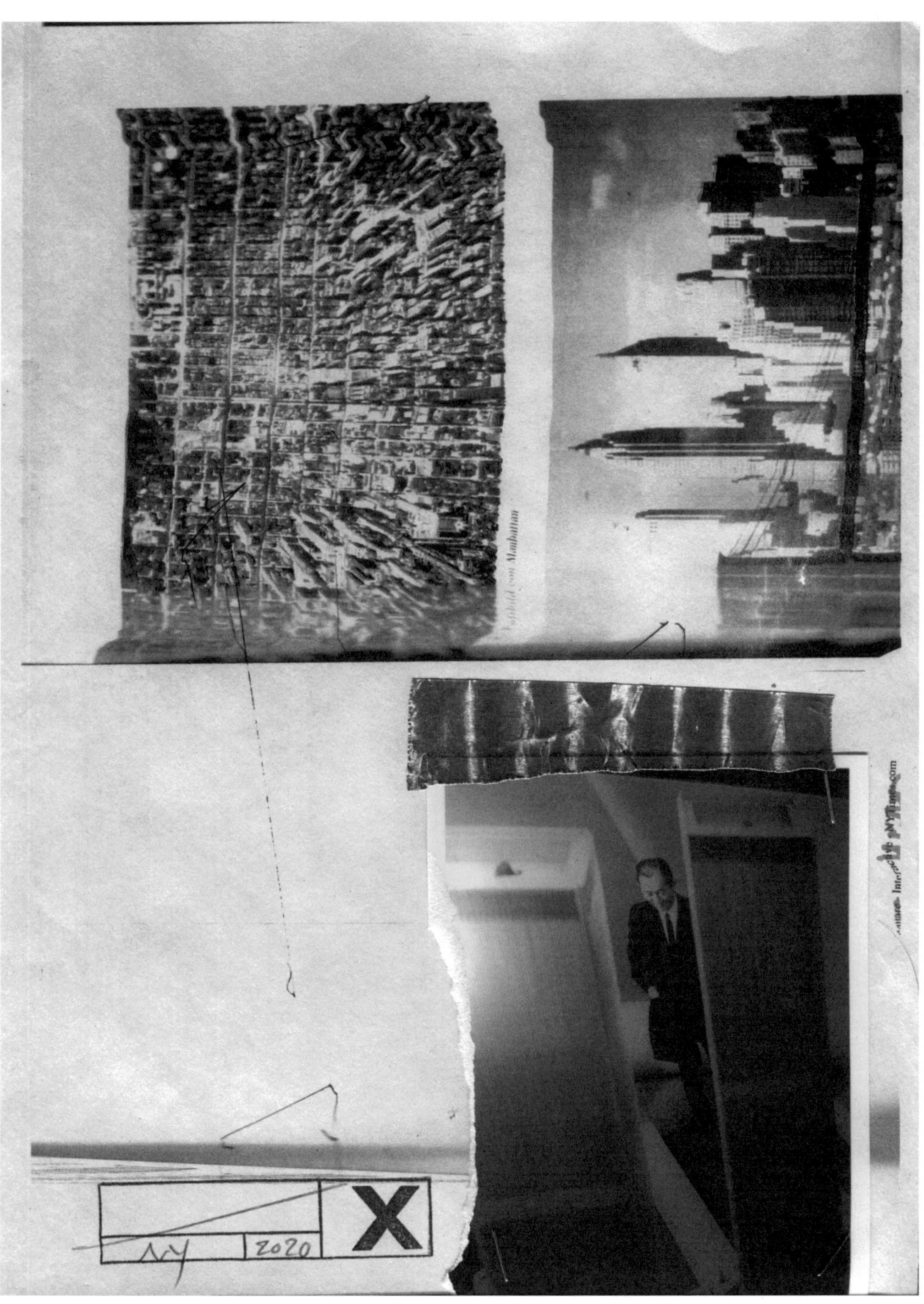
X
NY
2020

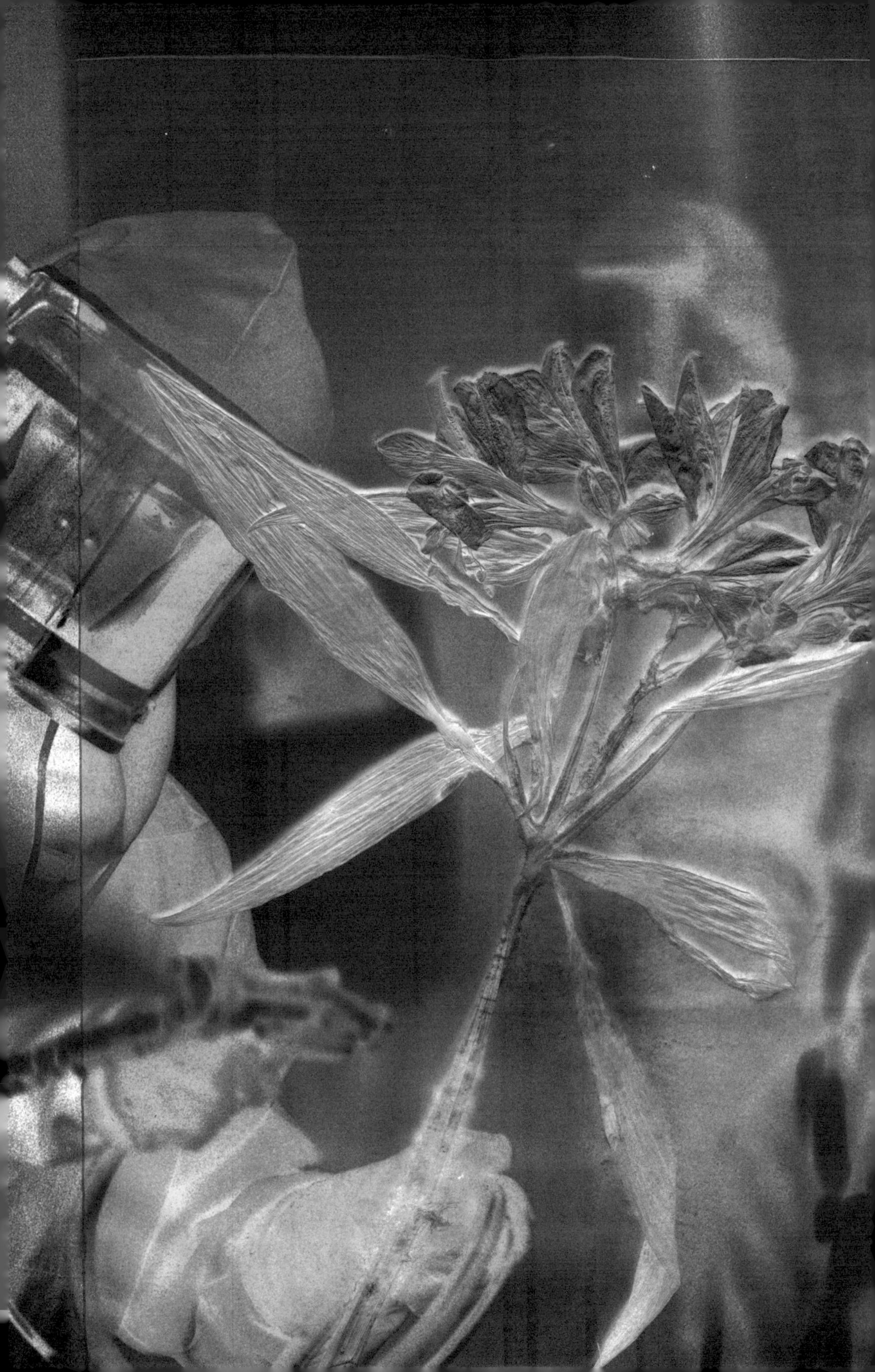

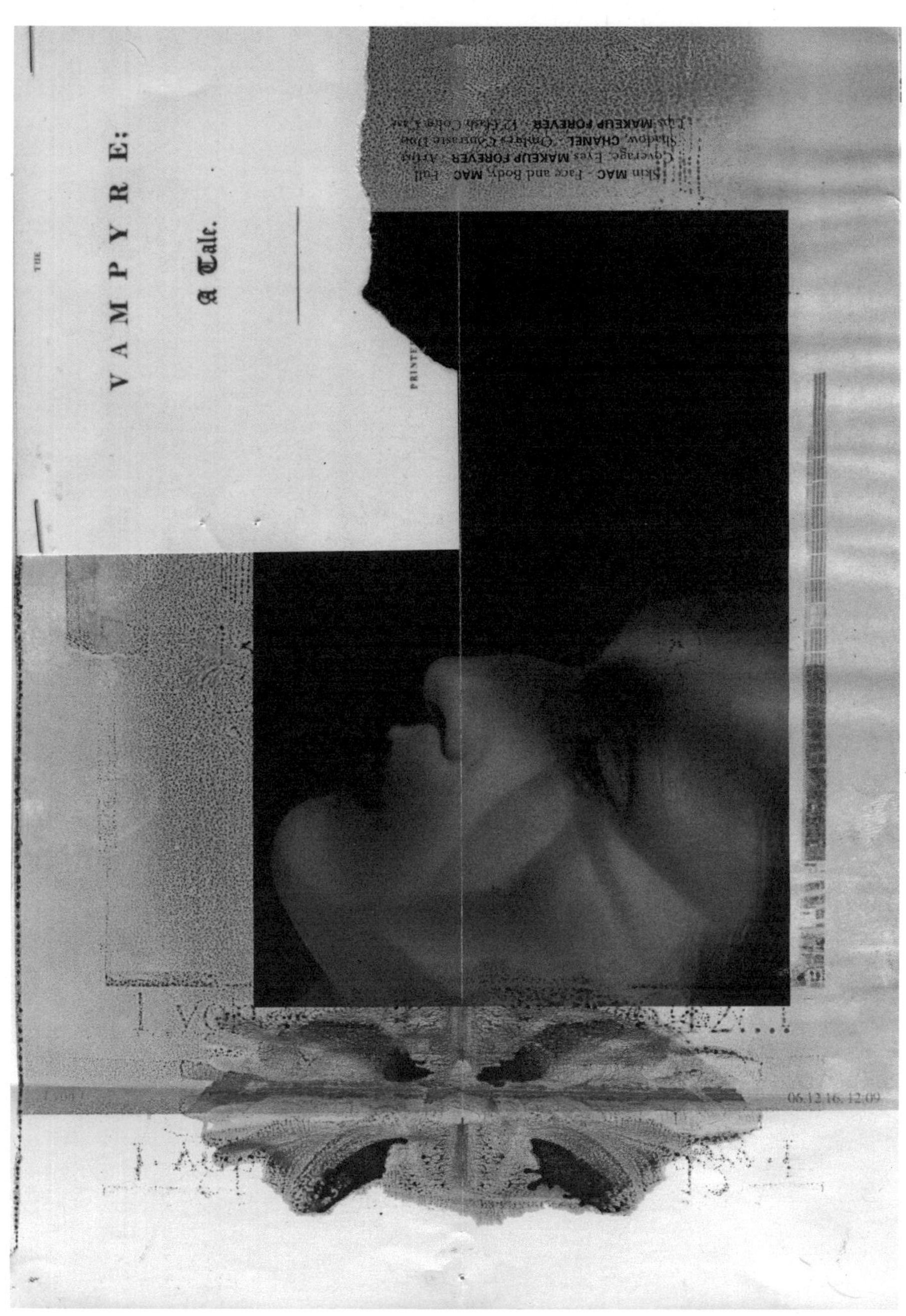
THE
VAMPYRE:
A Tale.
06.12.16. 12:09

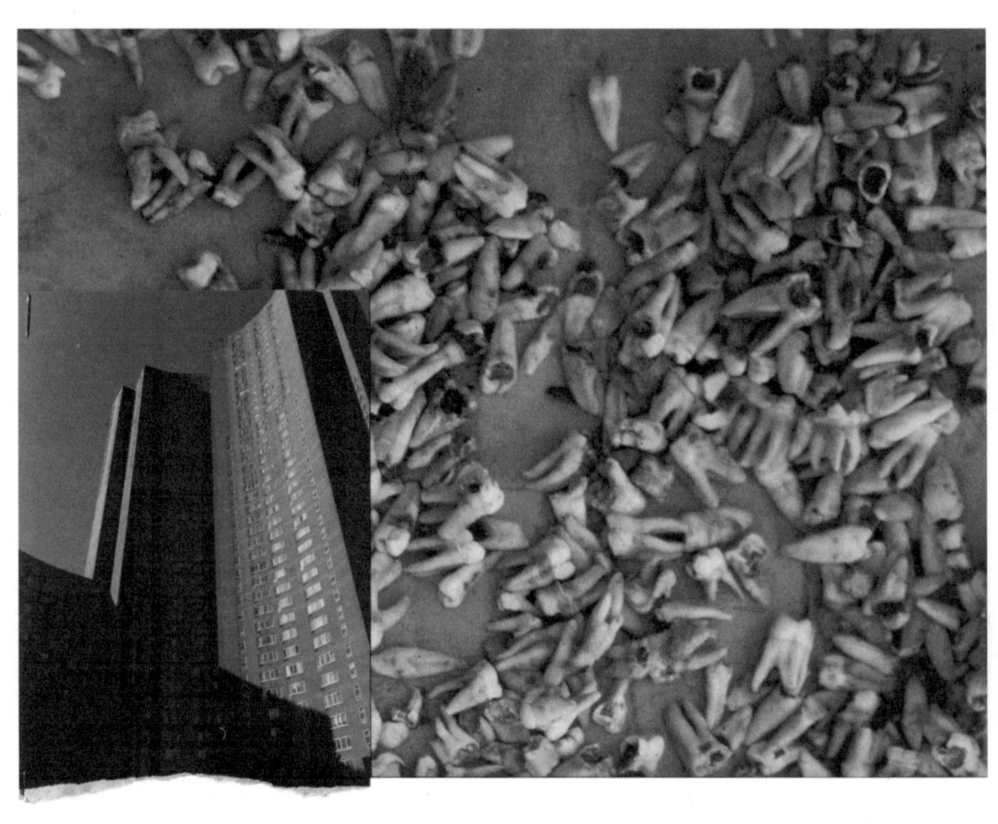

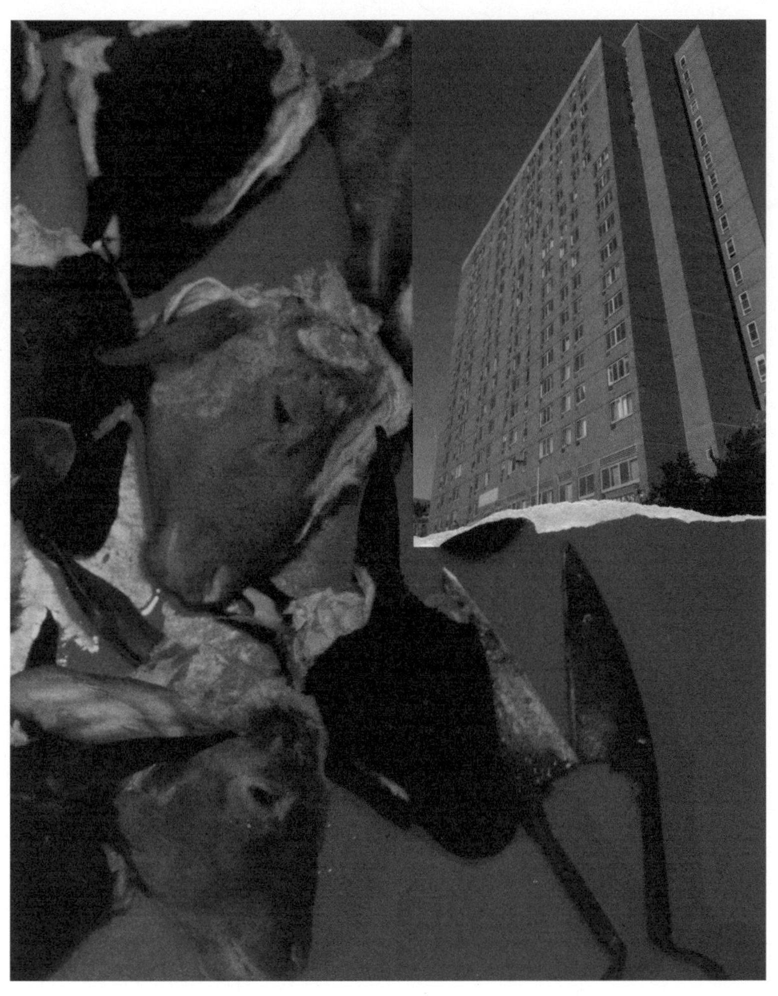

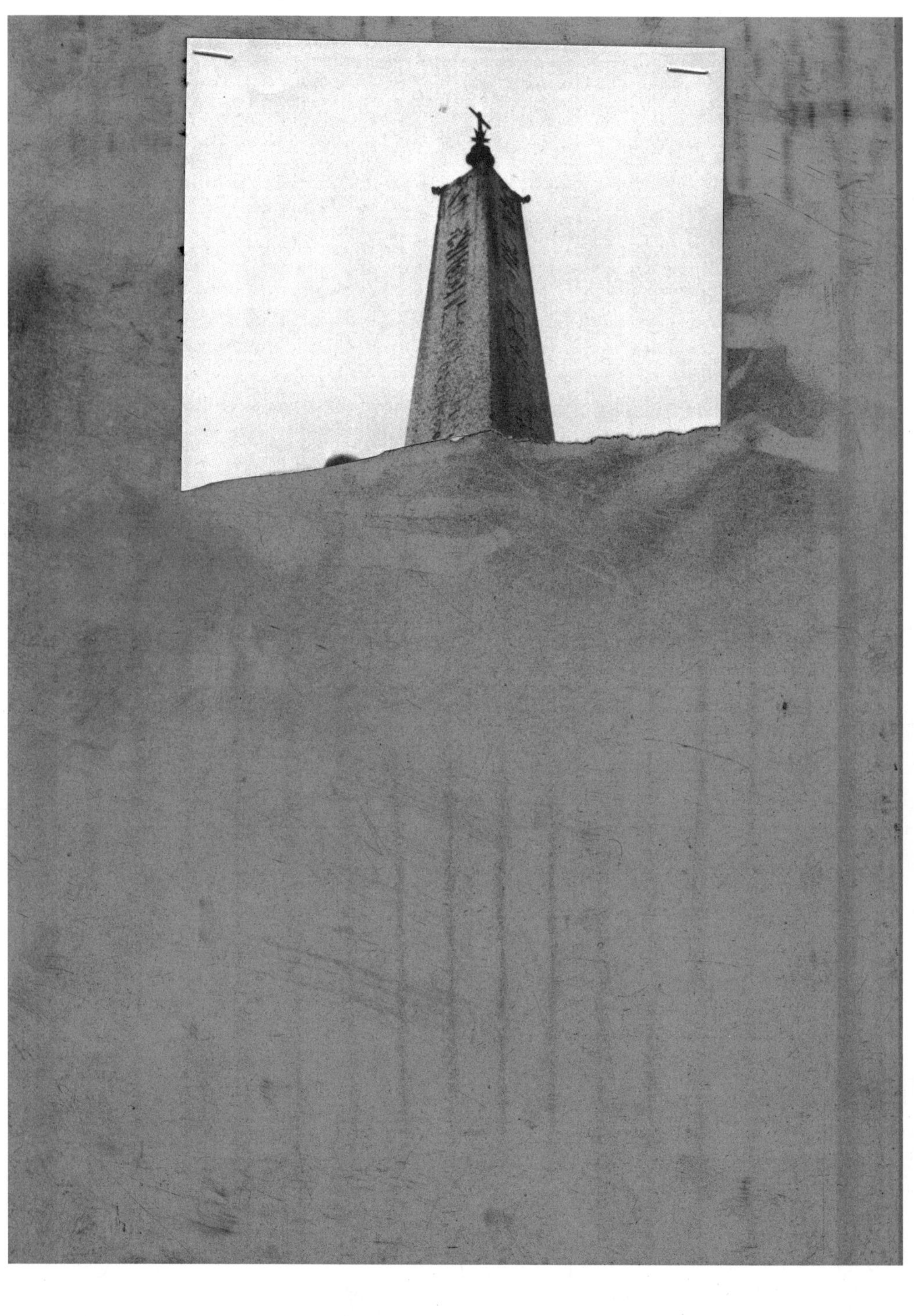

6

Fall
Abyss

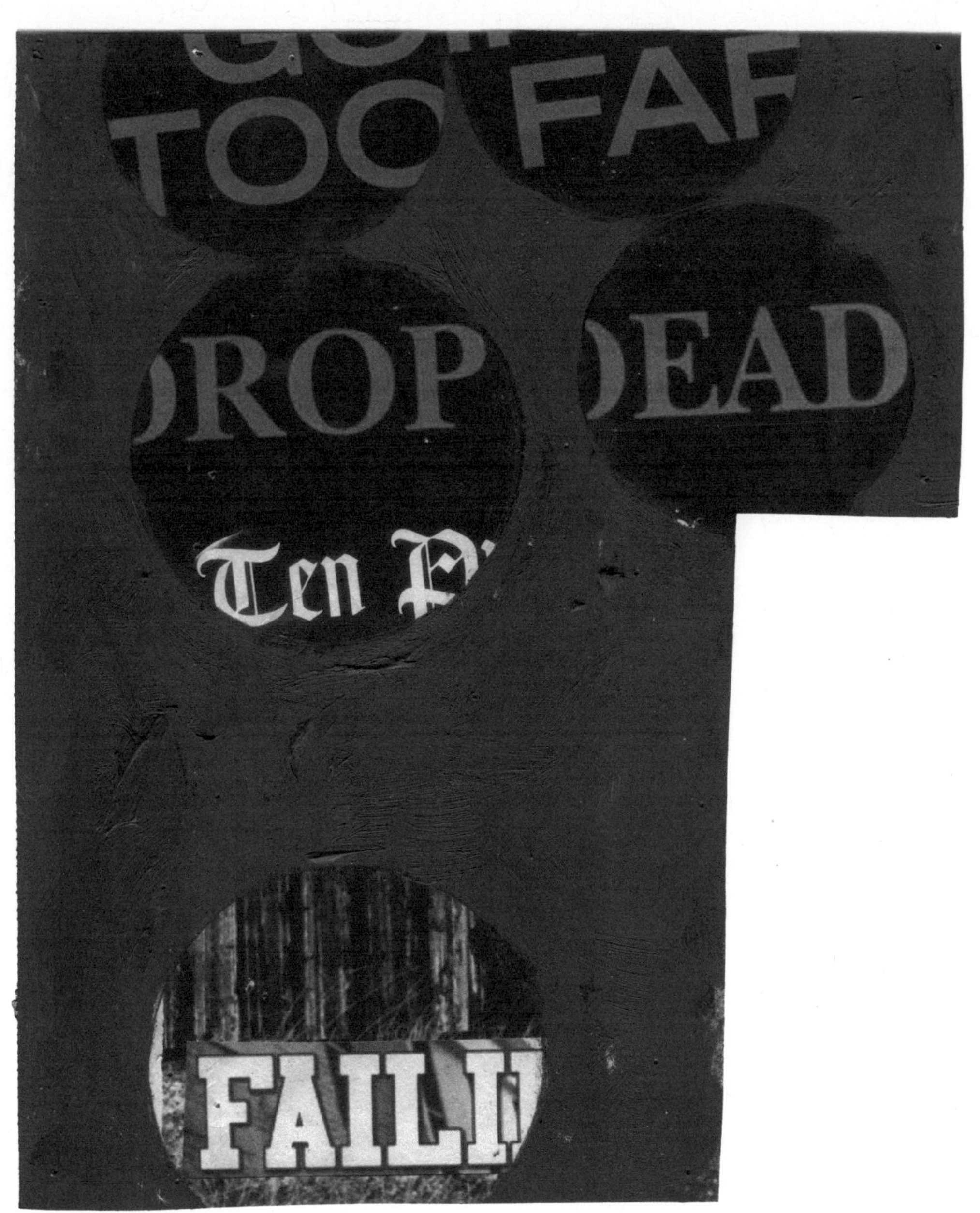
TOO FA
ROP
EAD
Ten
FAIL

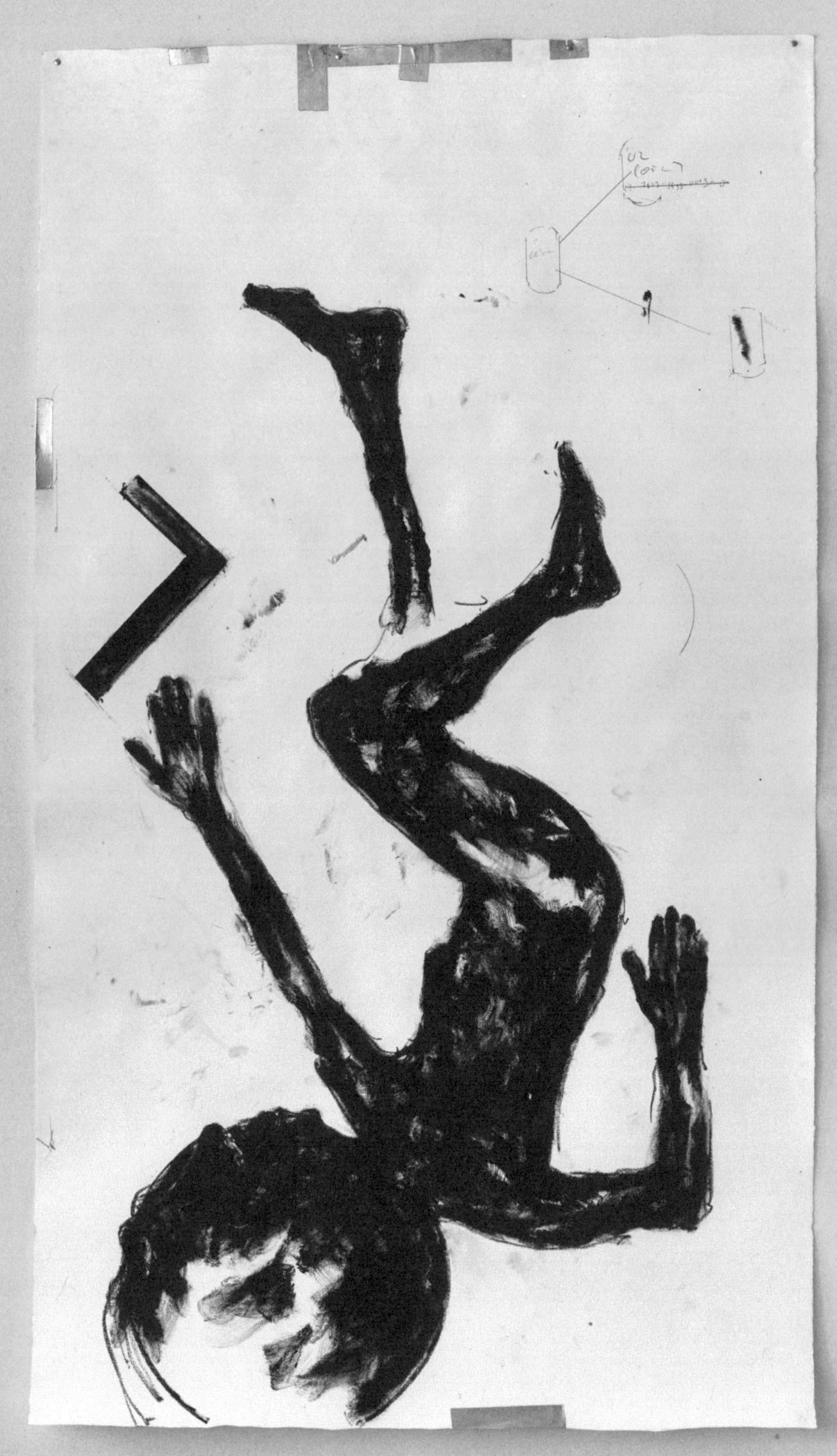

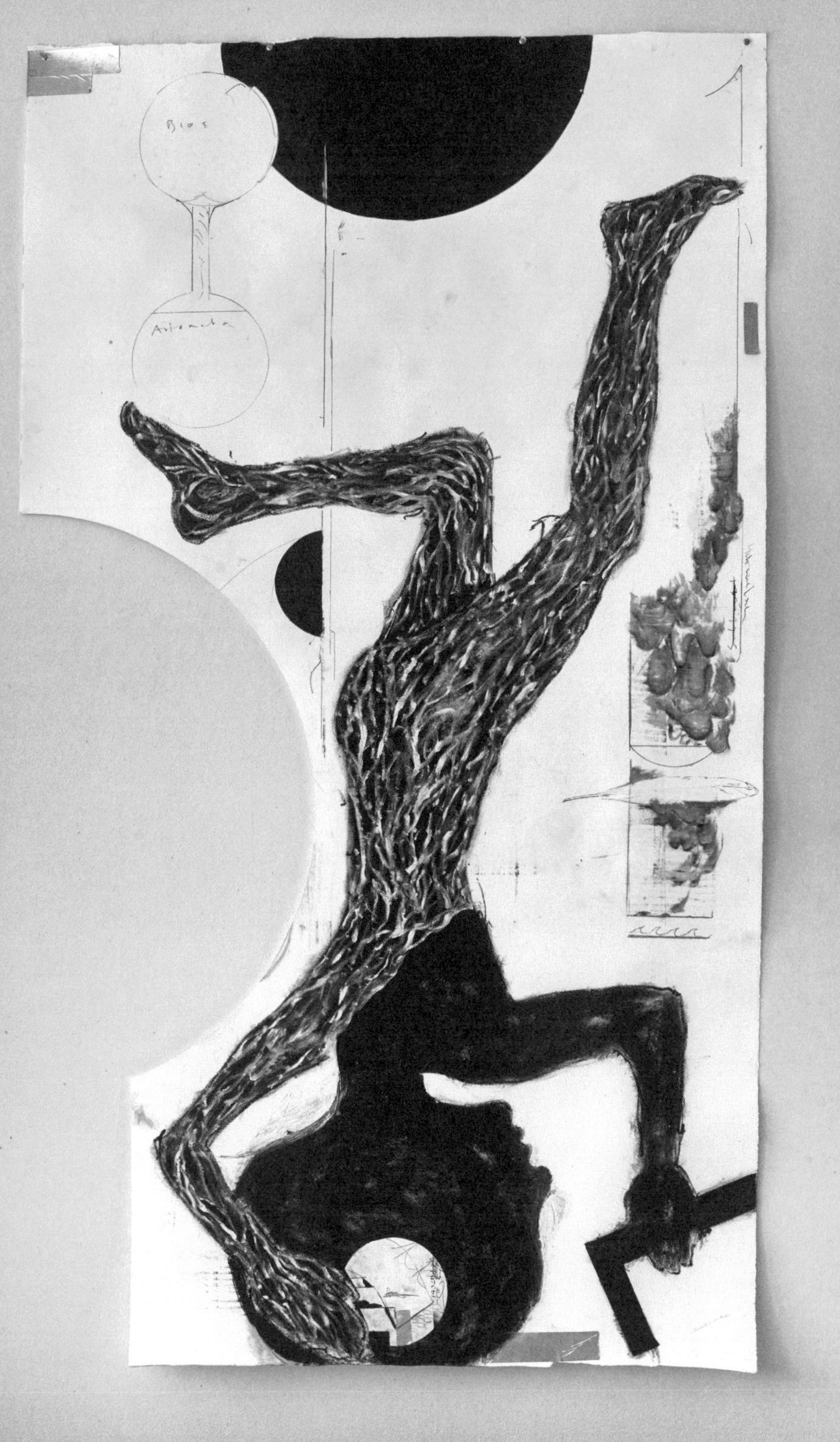
Bios
Automata

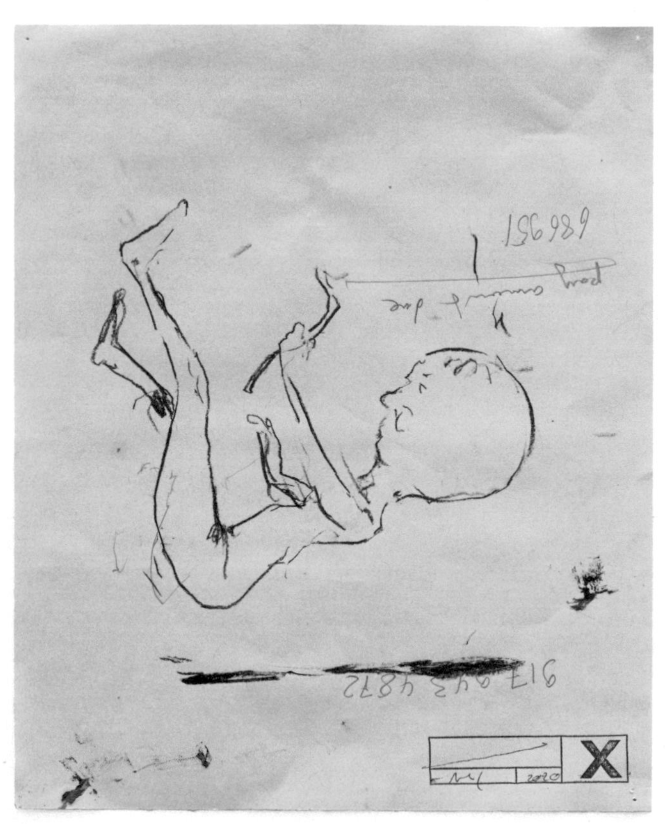

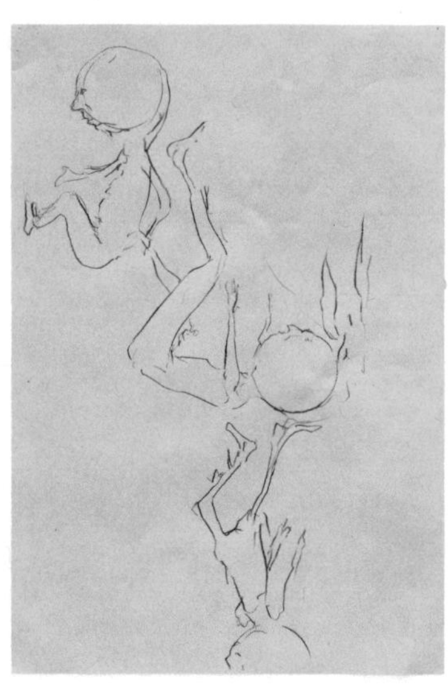

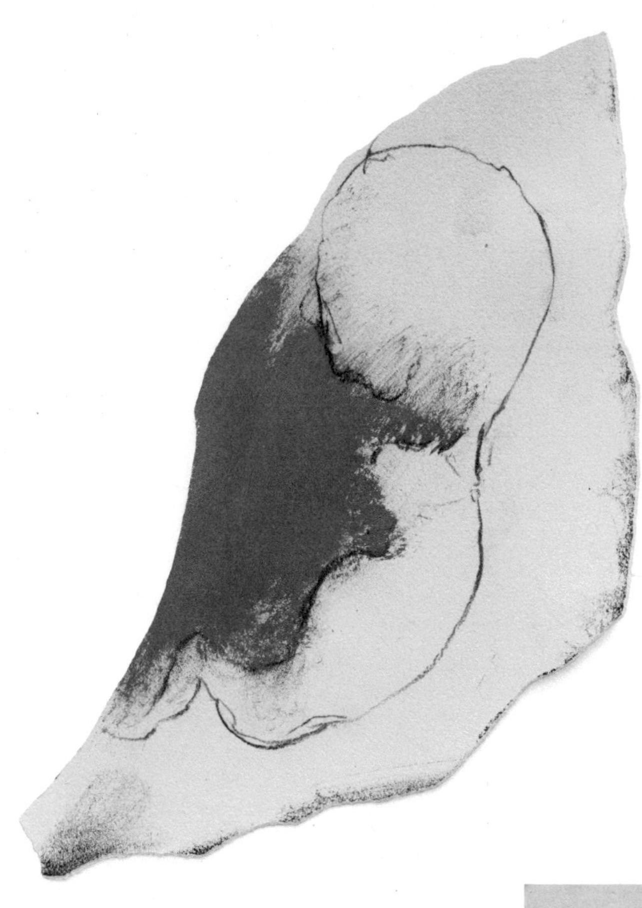

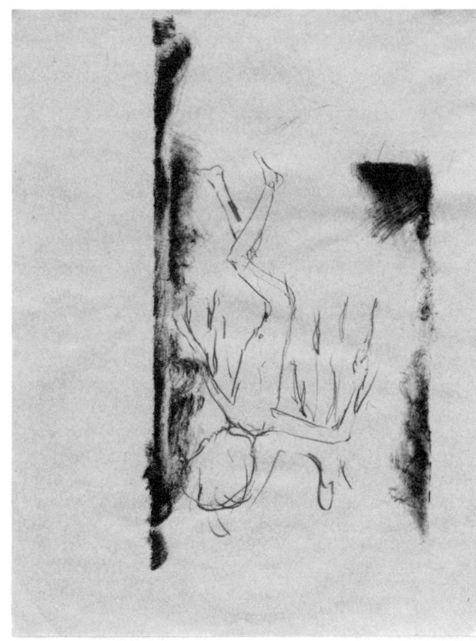

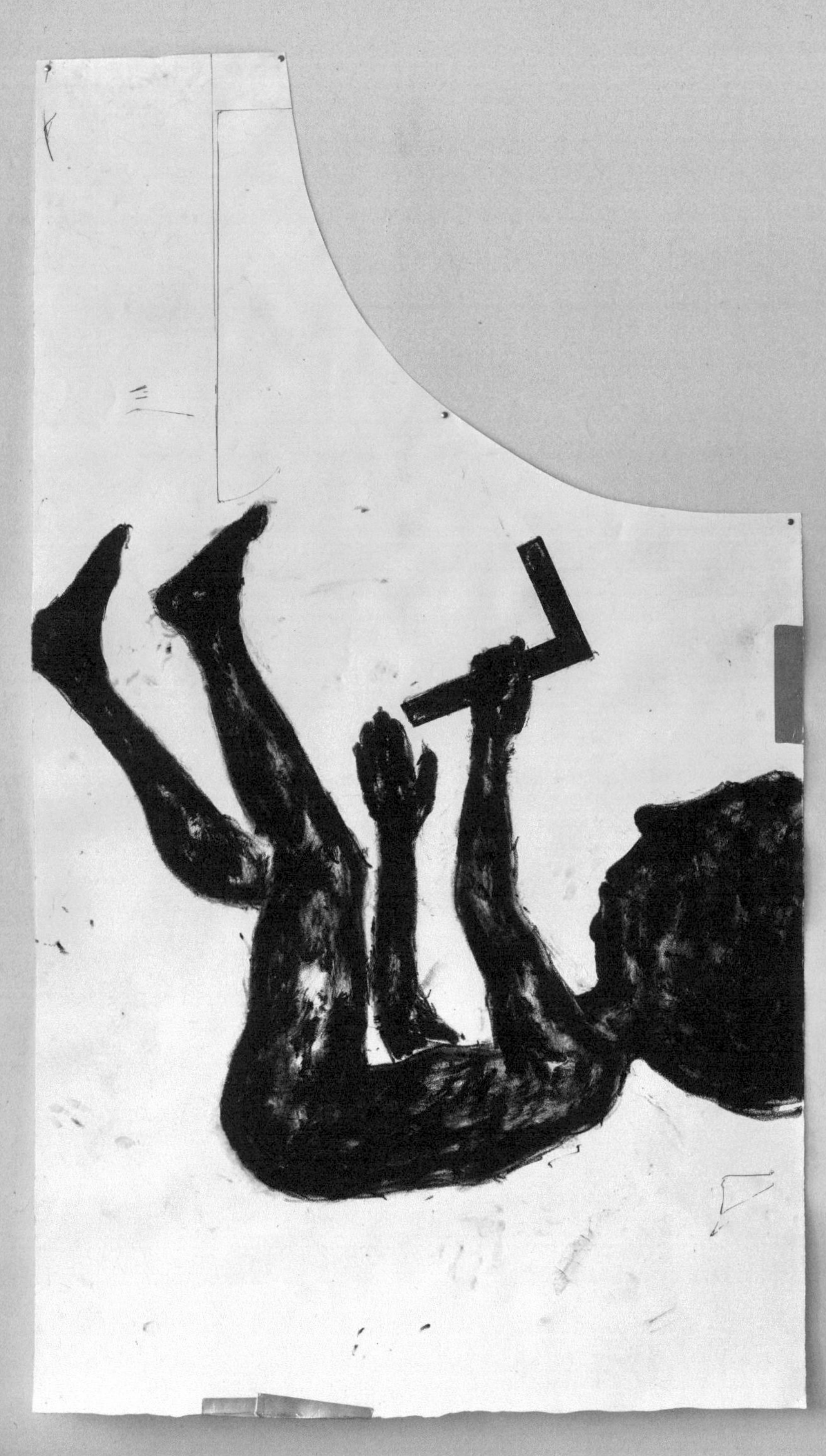

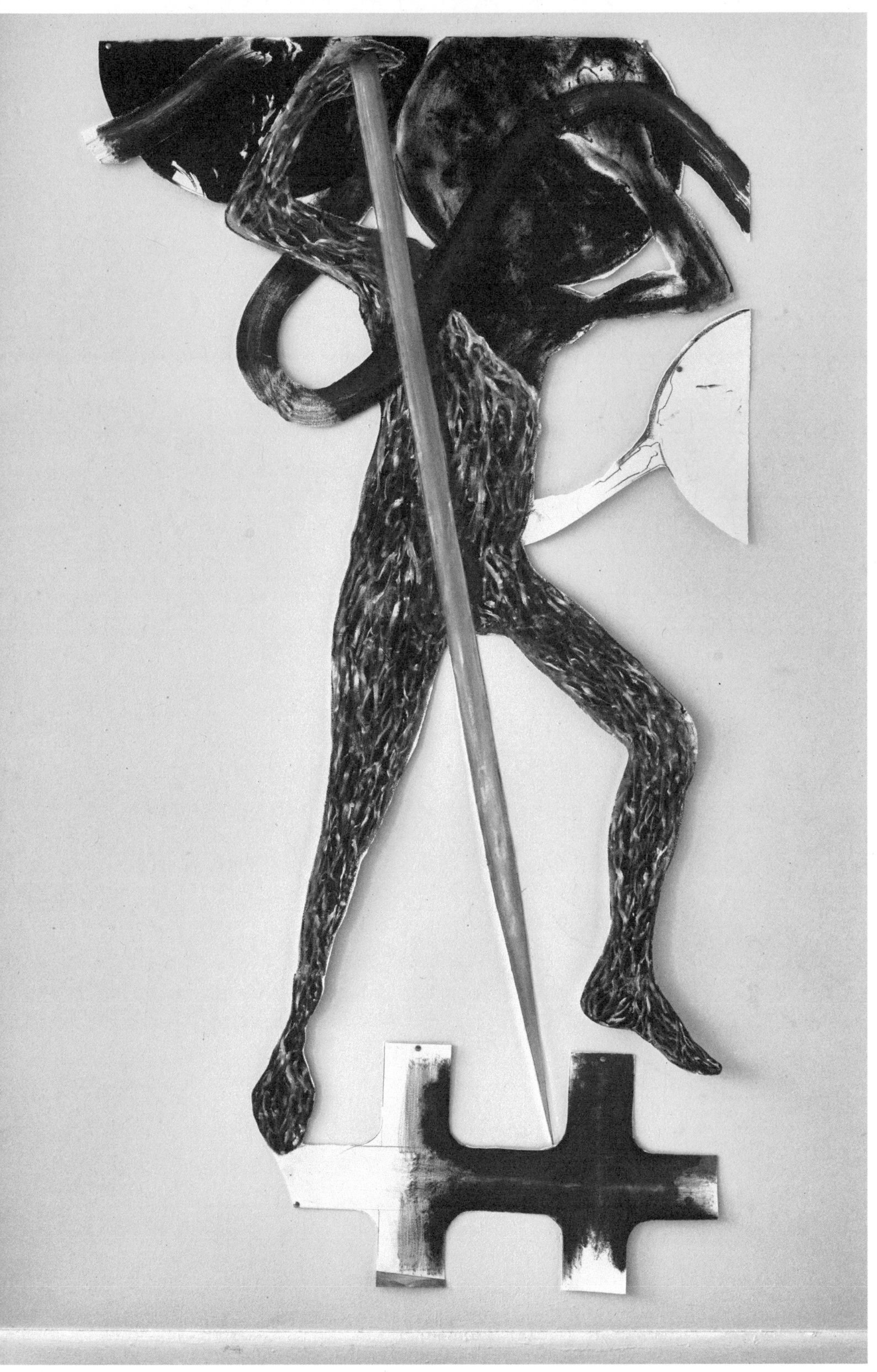

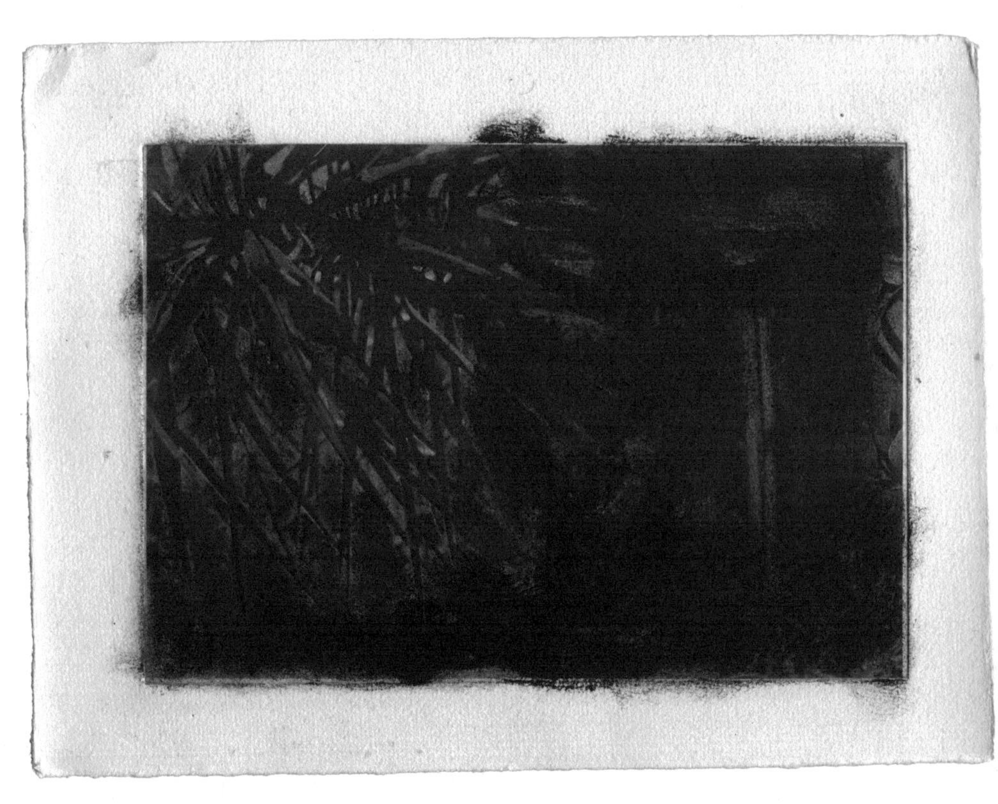

5

Violence

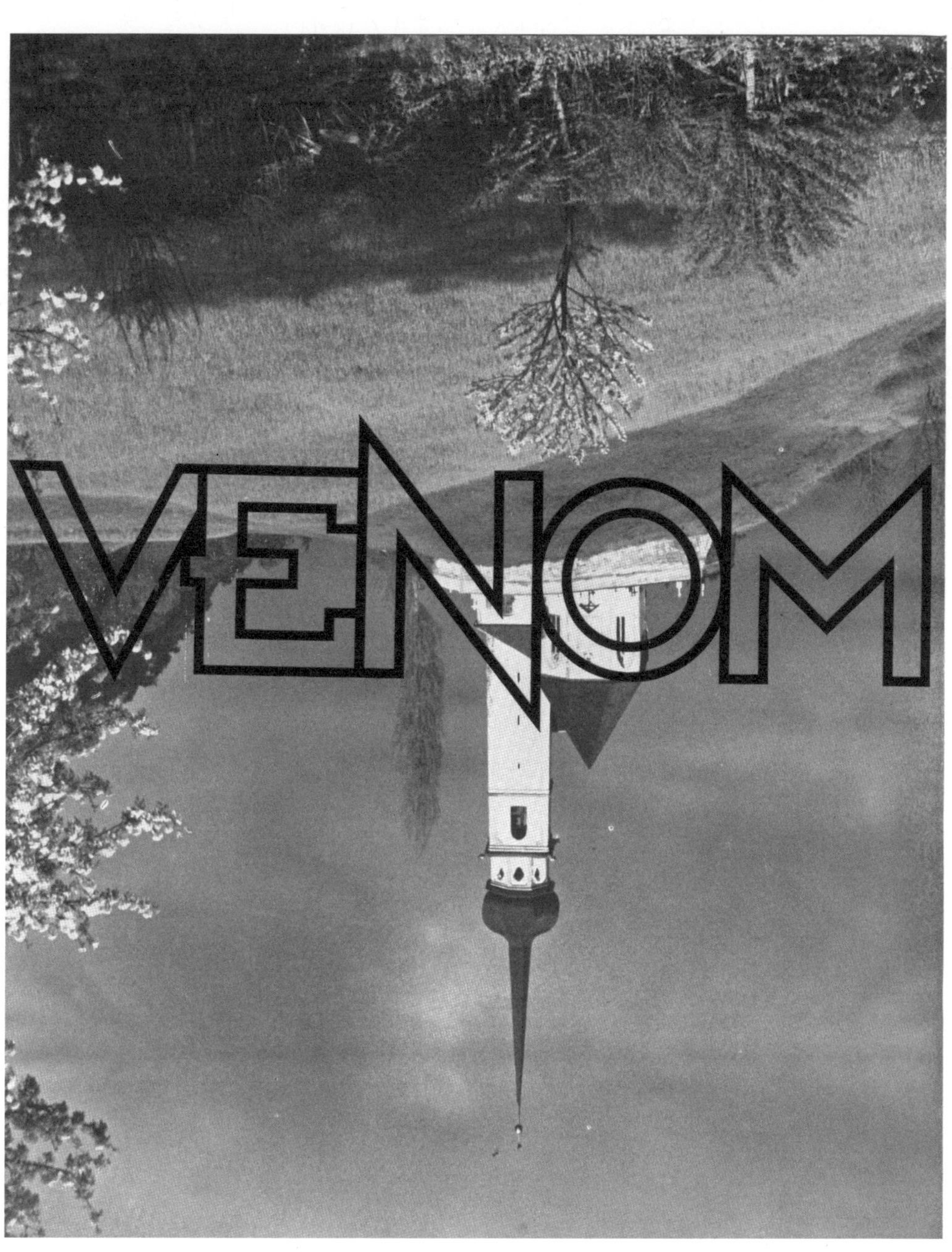
VENOM

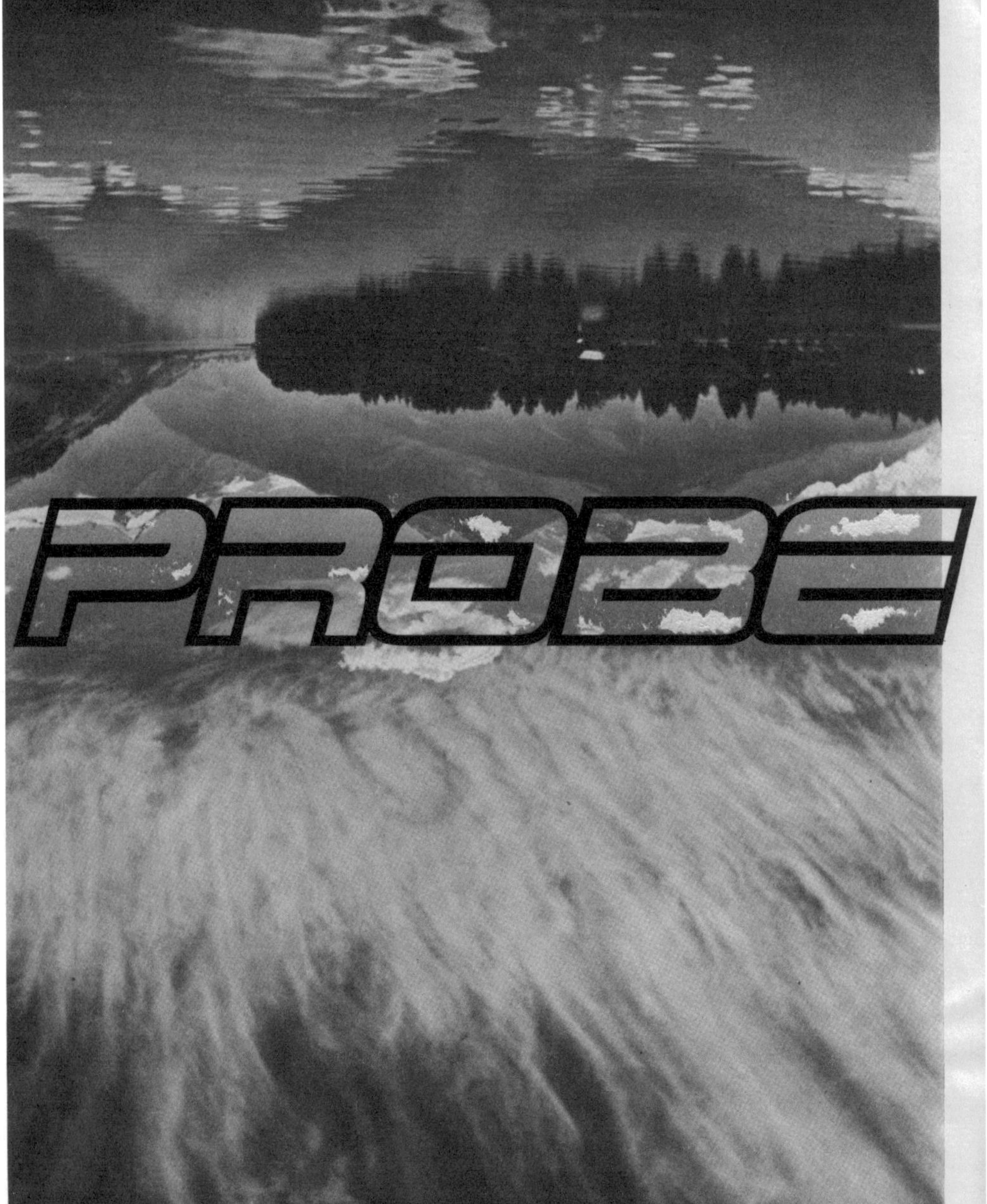
PROBE

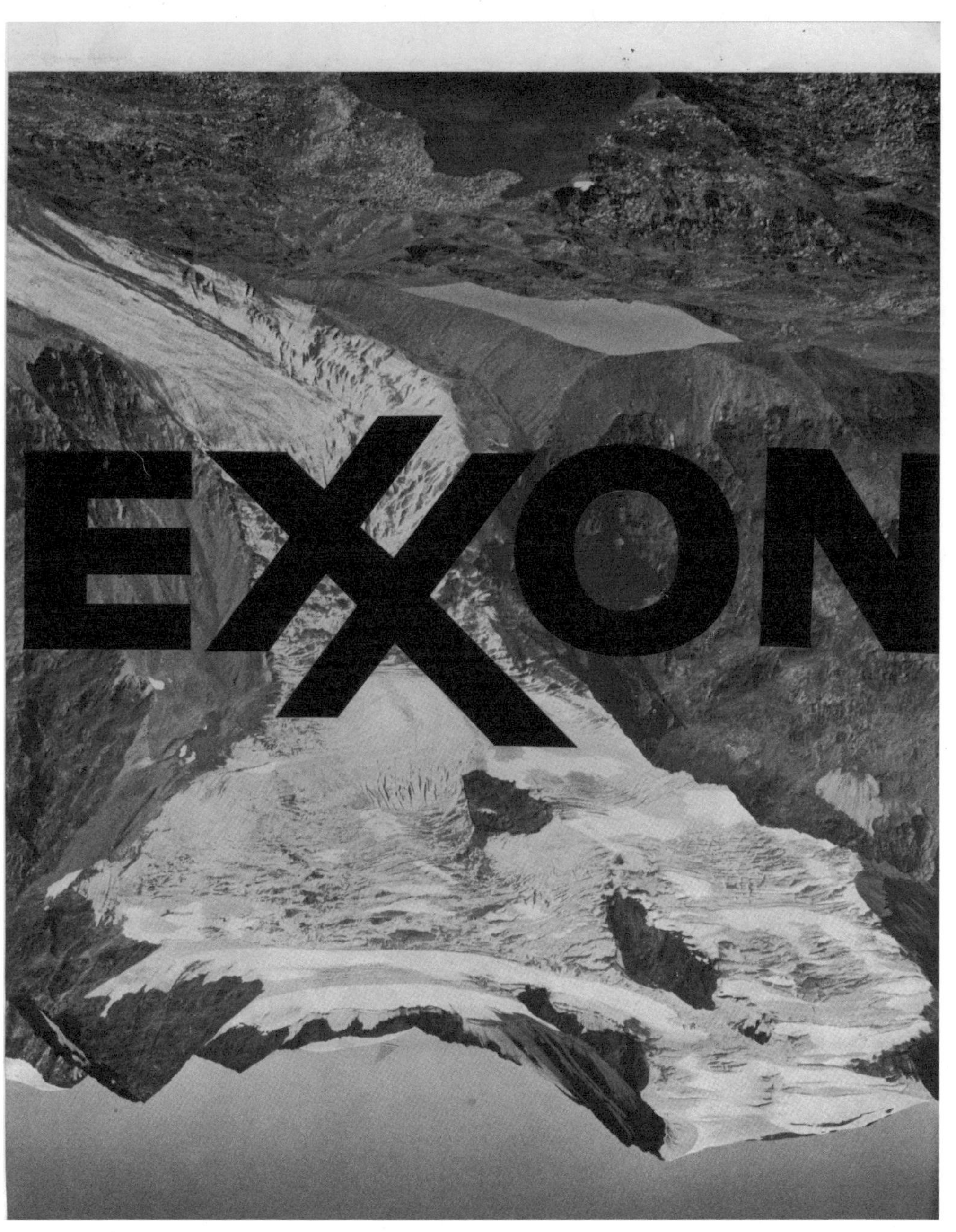
EXON

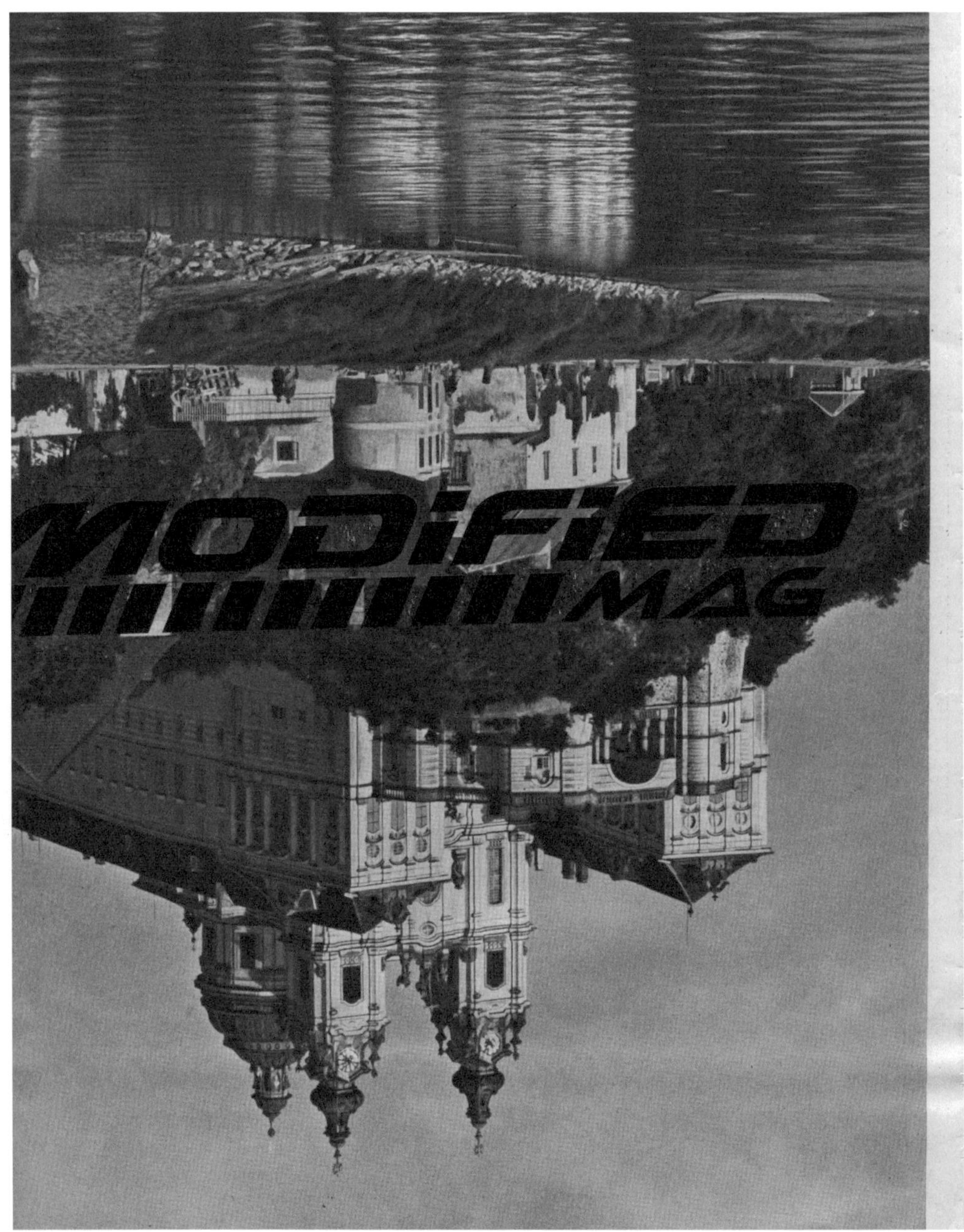
MODIFIED
MAG

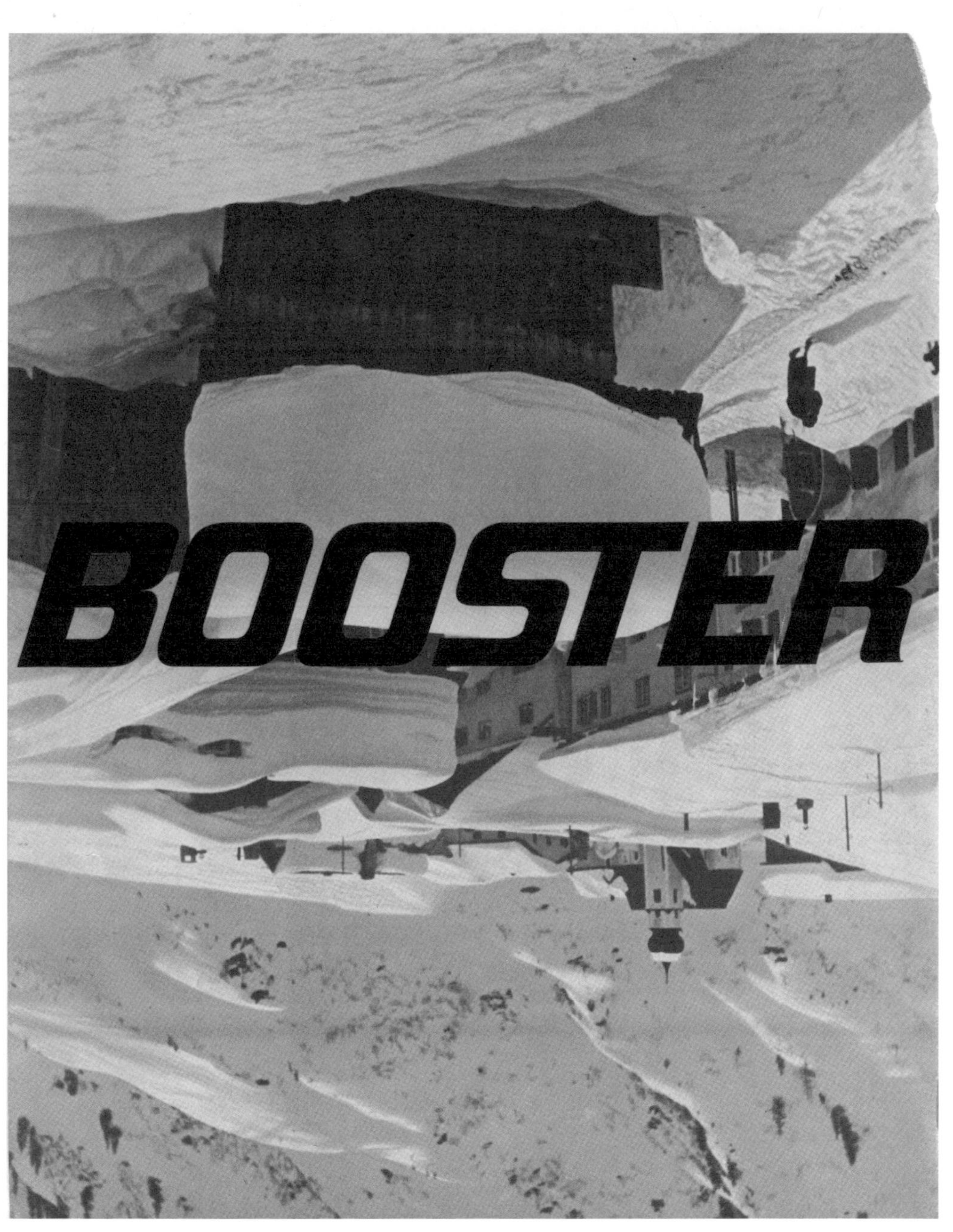
BOOSTER

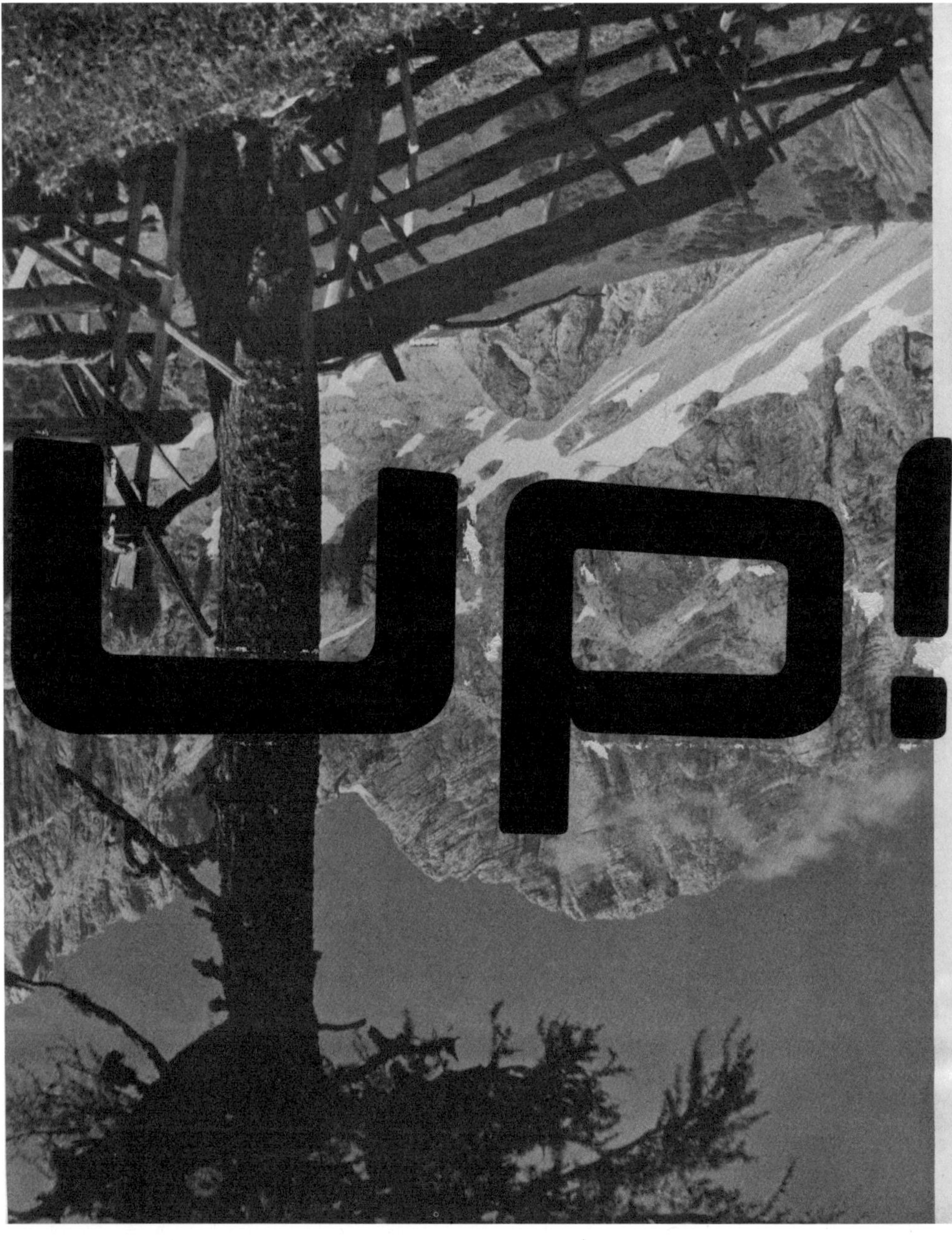
Up!

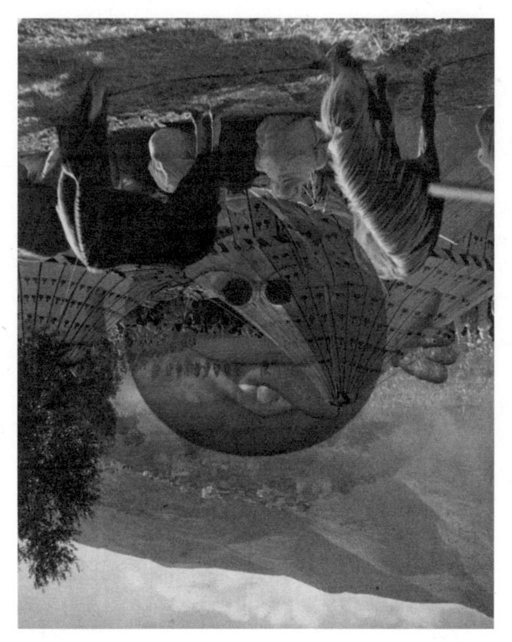

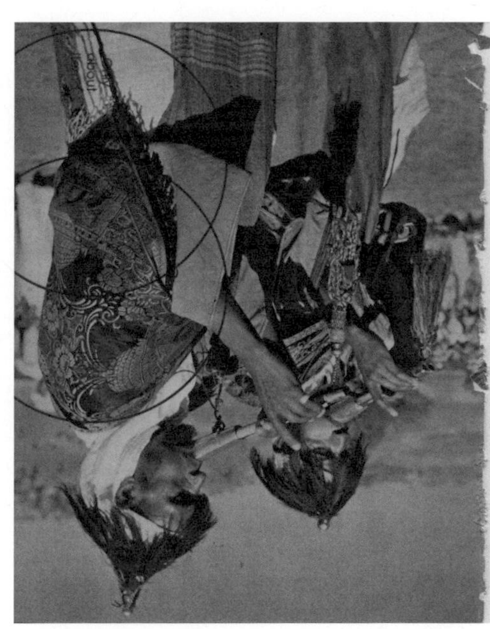

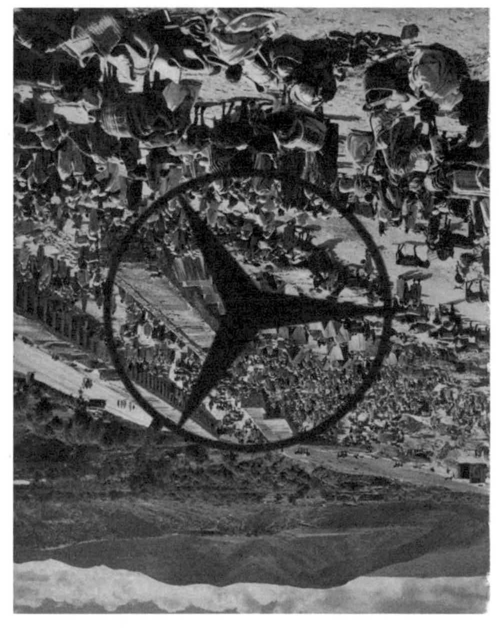

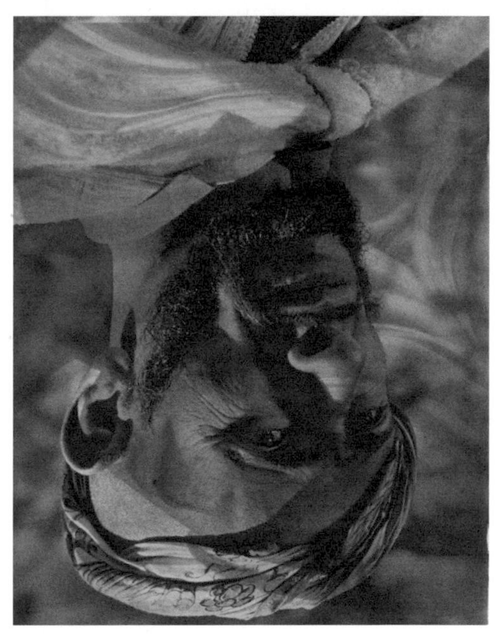

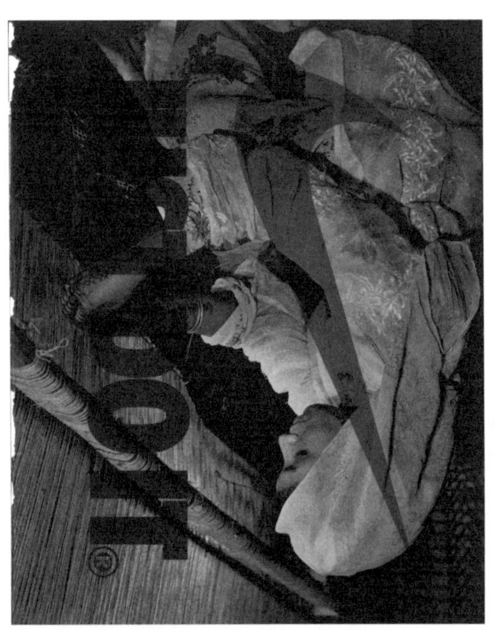

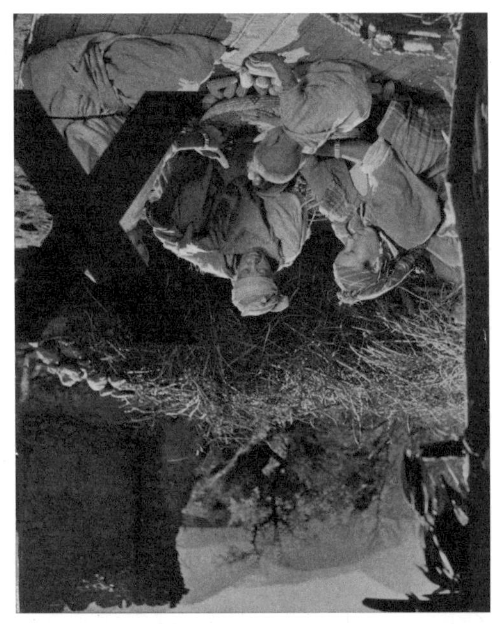

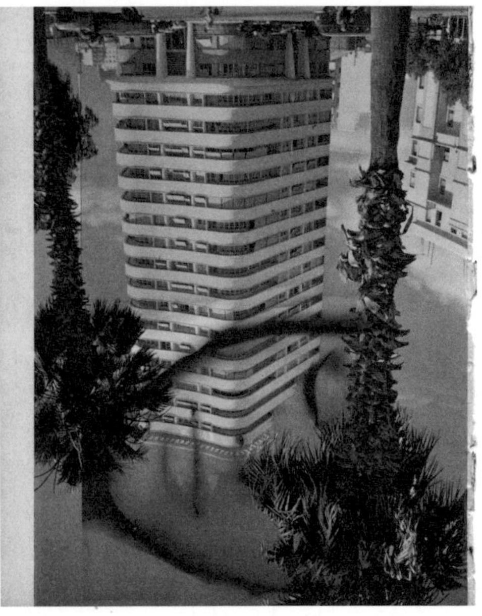

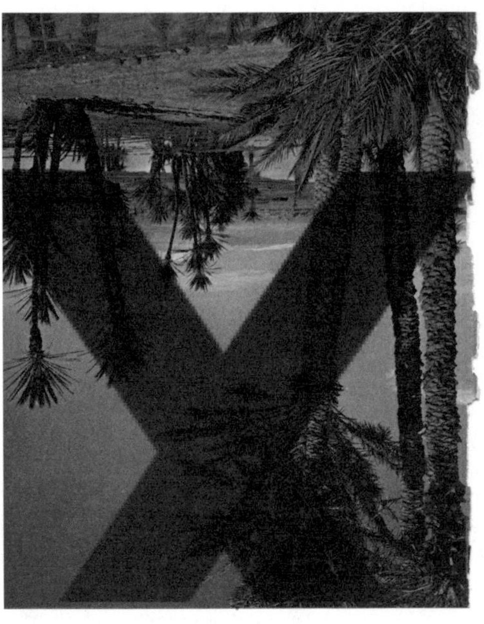

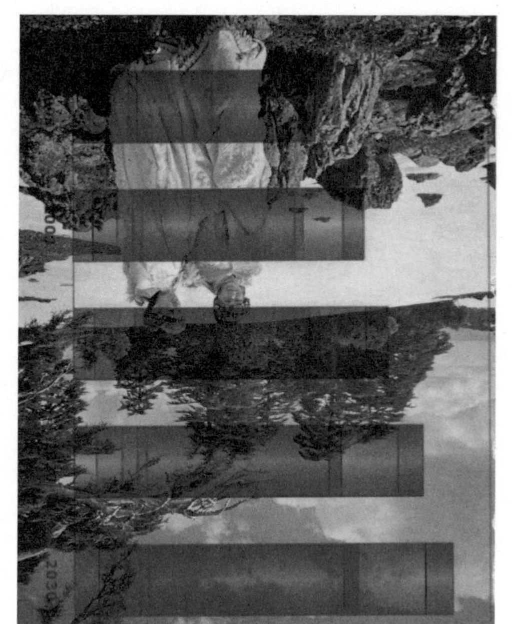

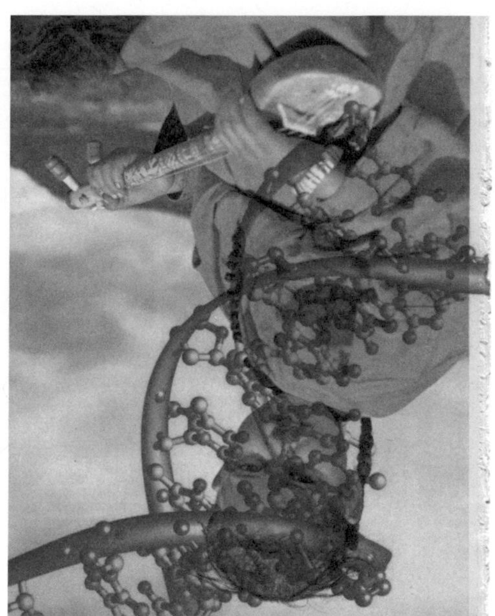

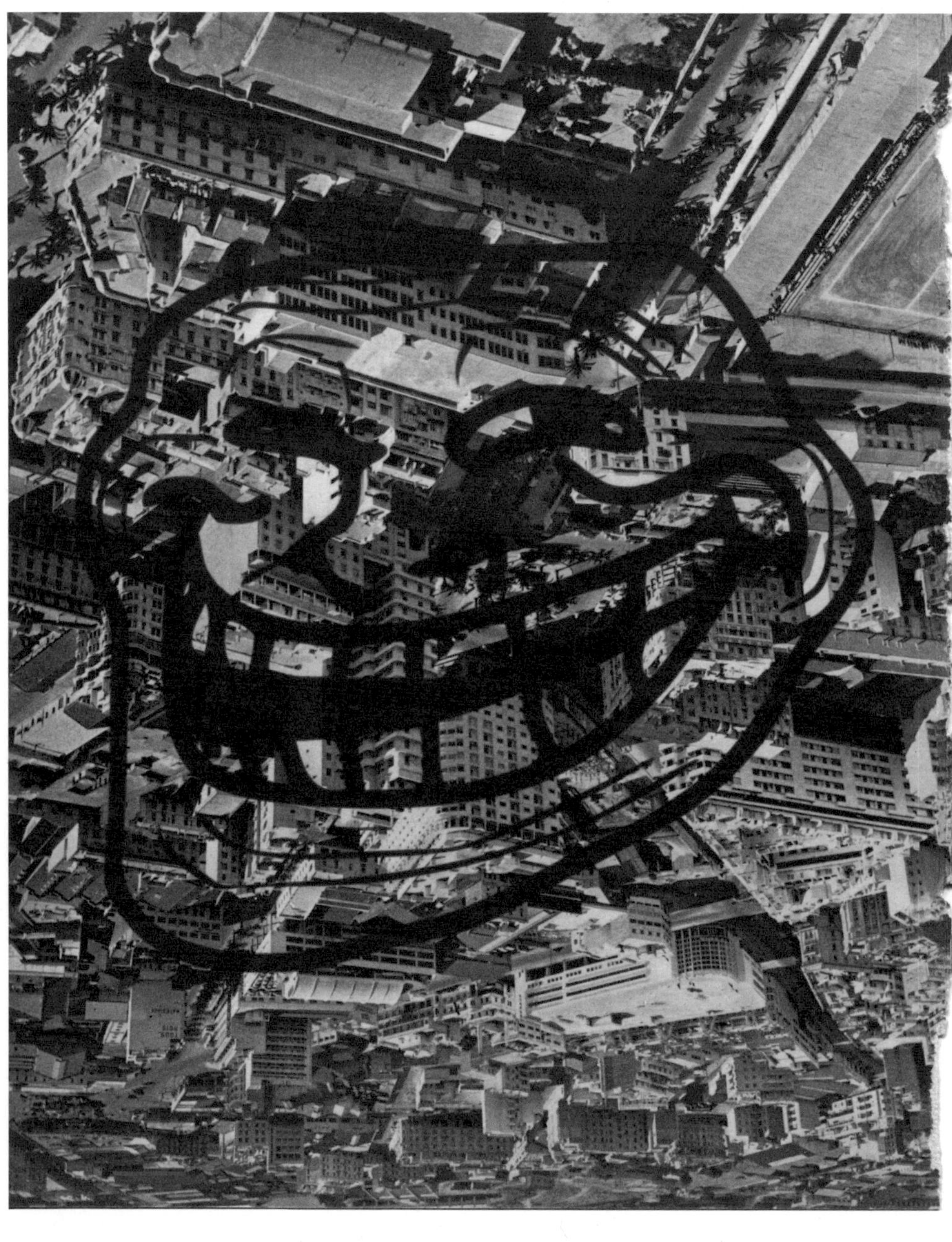

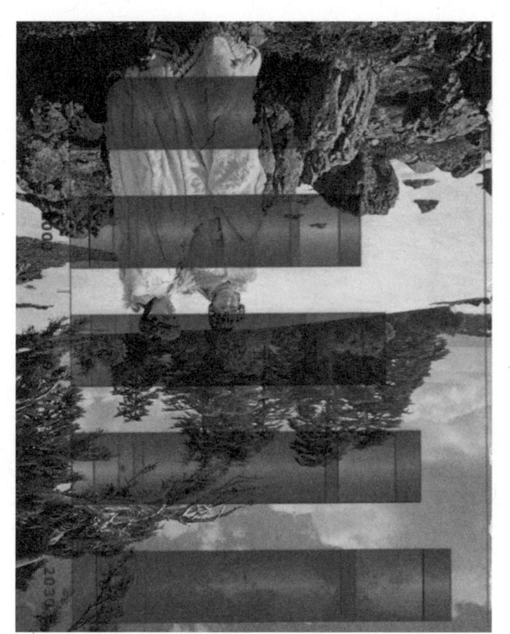

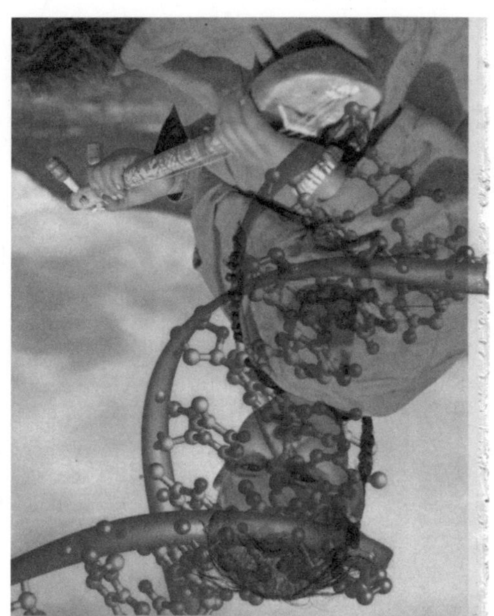

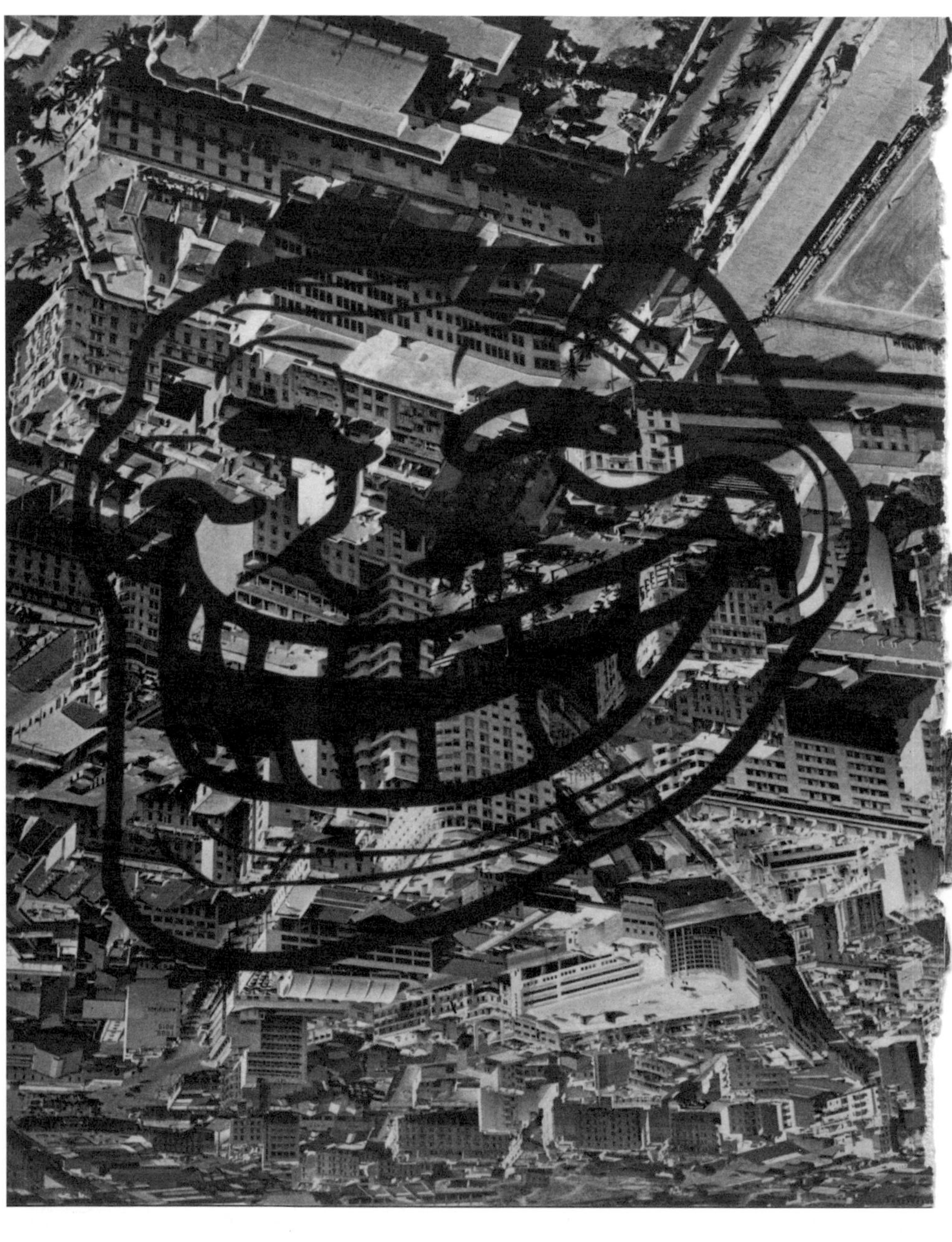

4

Grid (Paranoia)

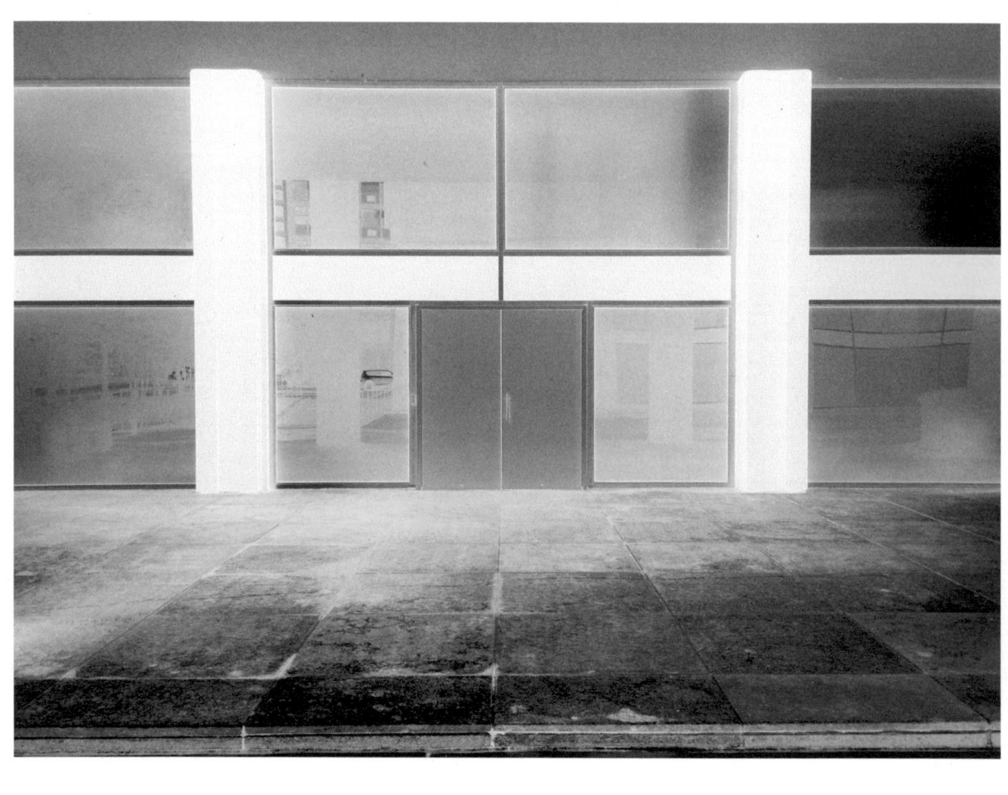

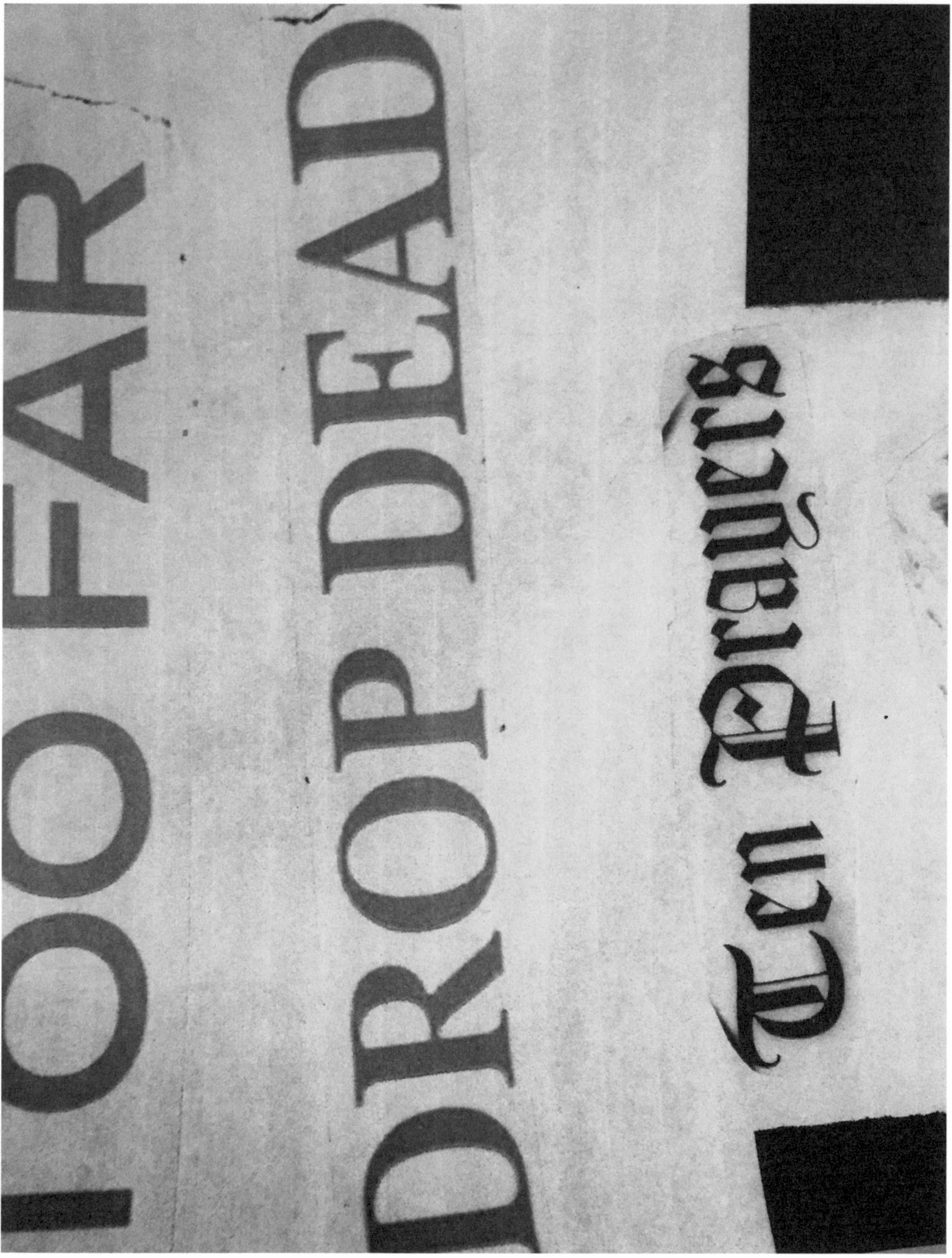

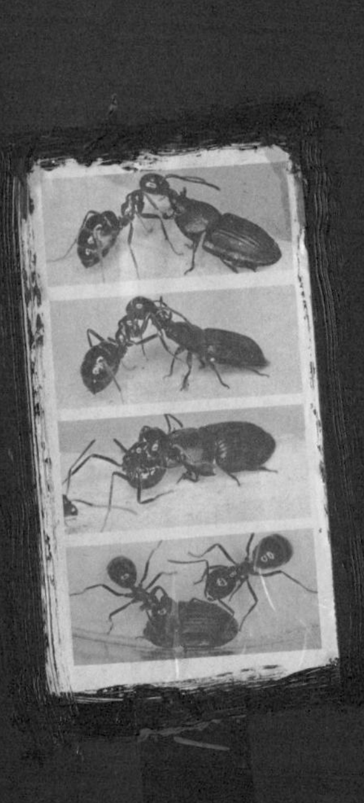
DROP DEAD

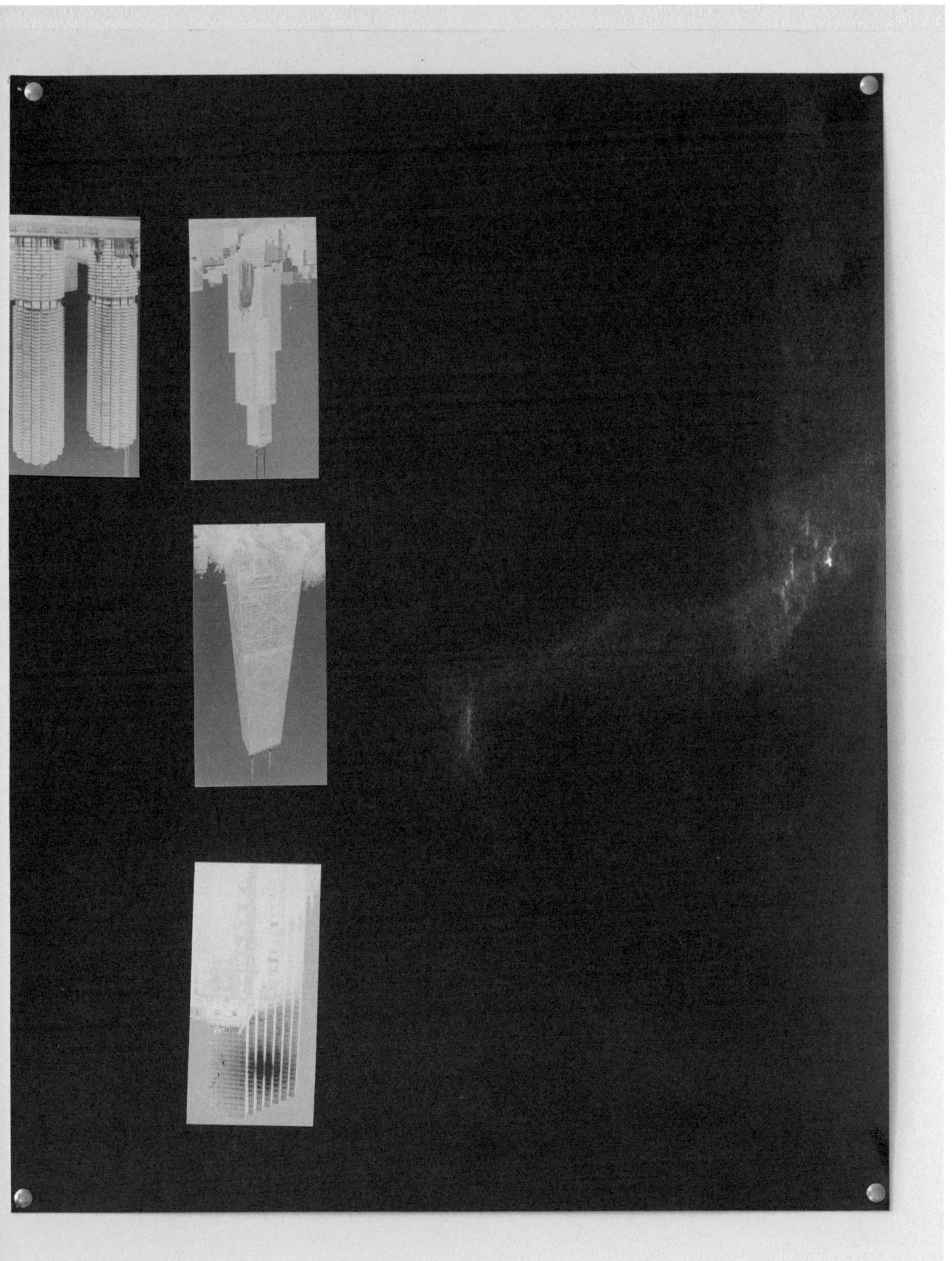

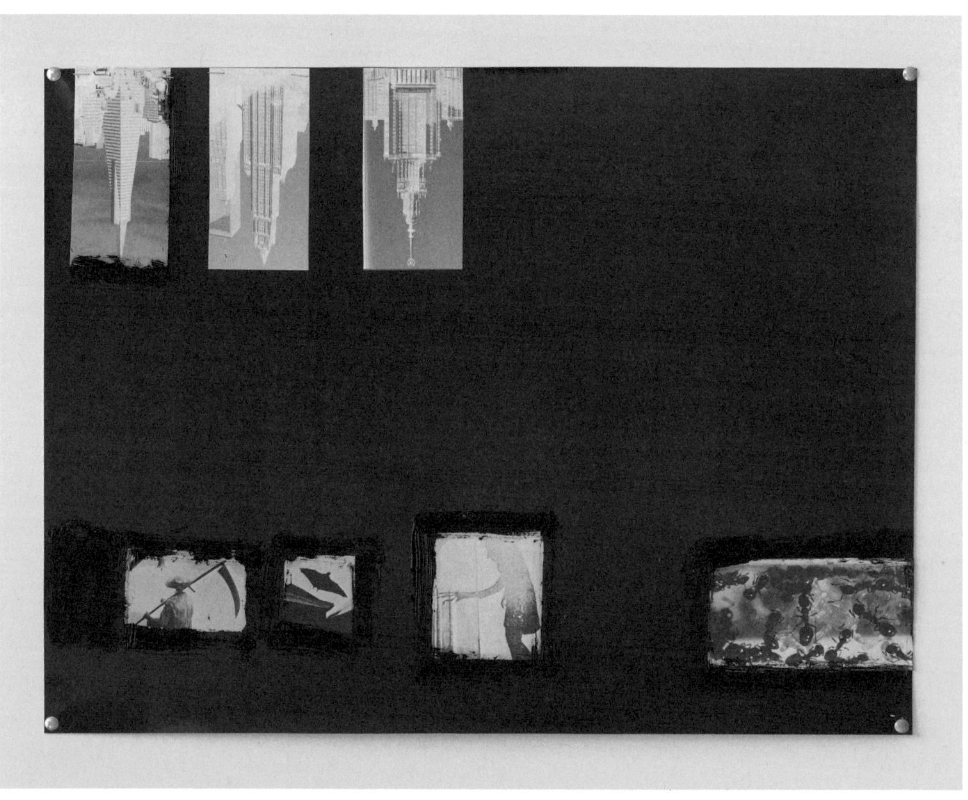

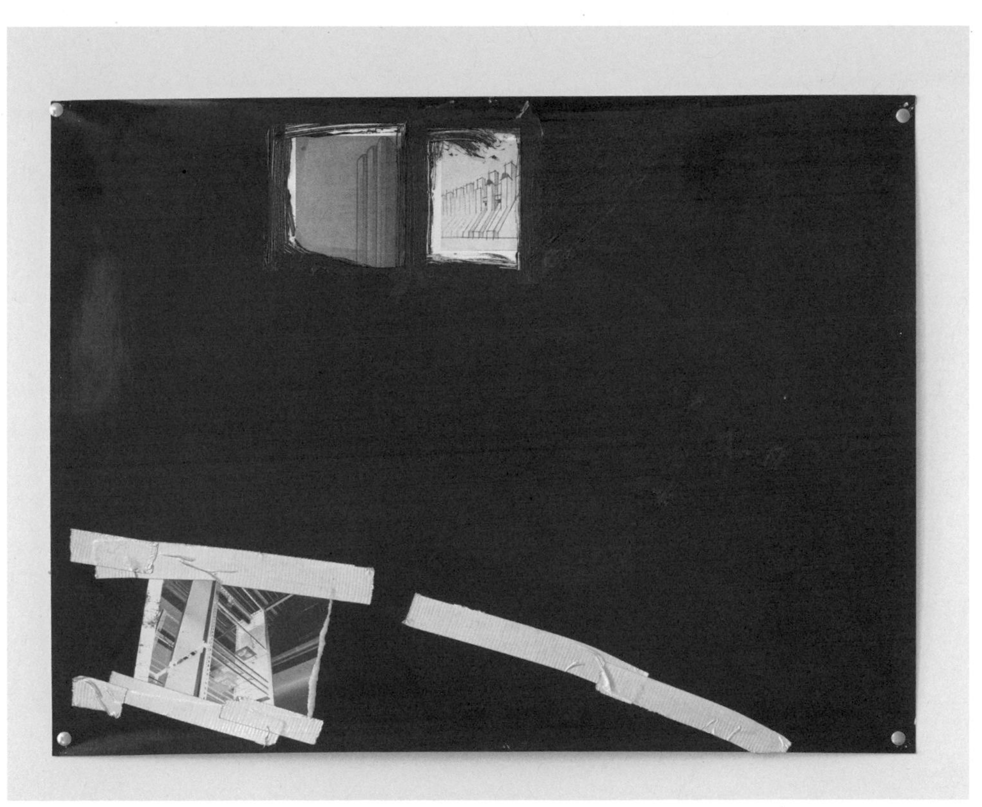

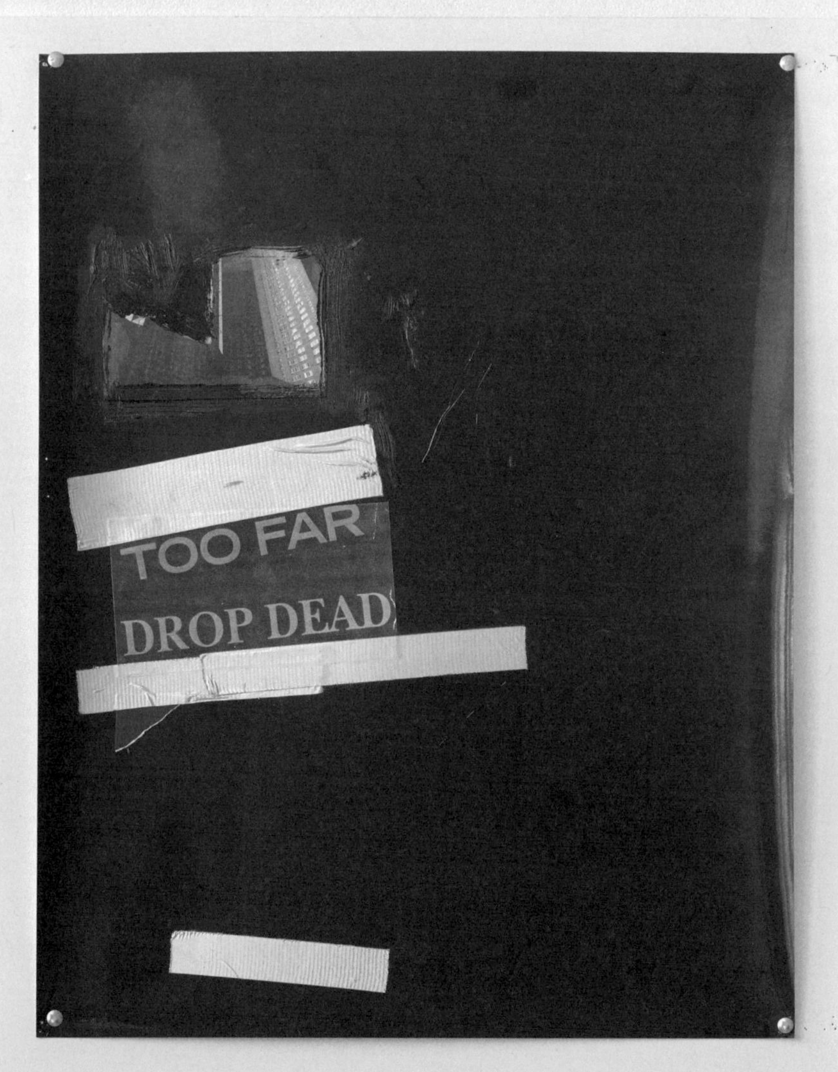
TOO FAR
DROP DEAD

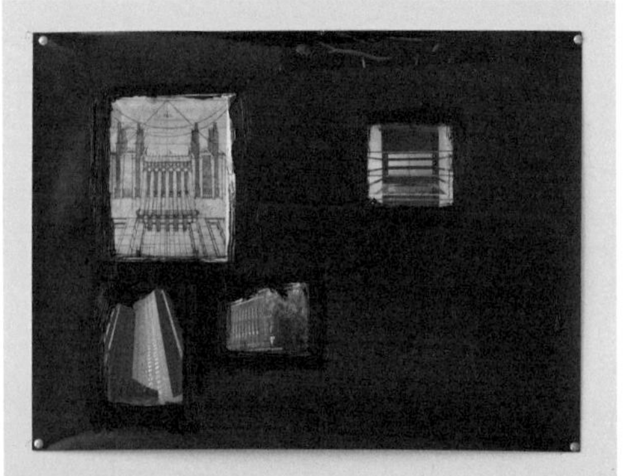

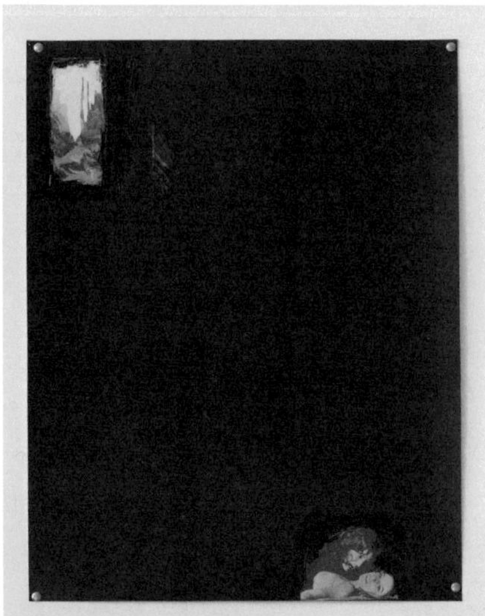

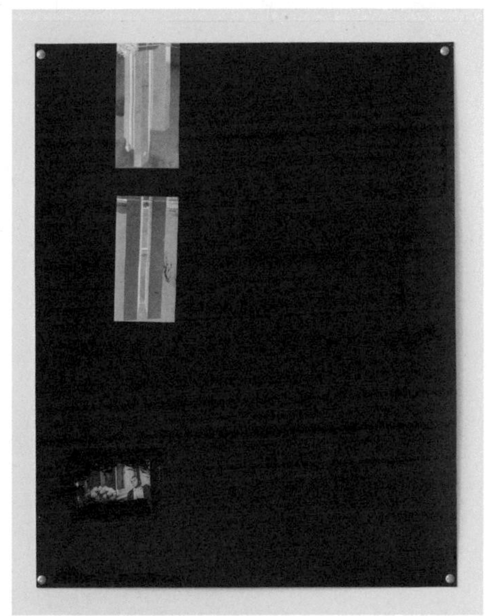

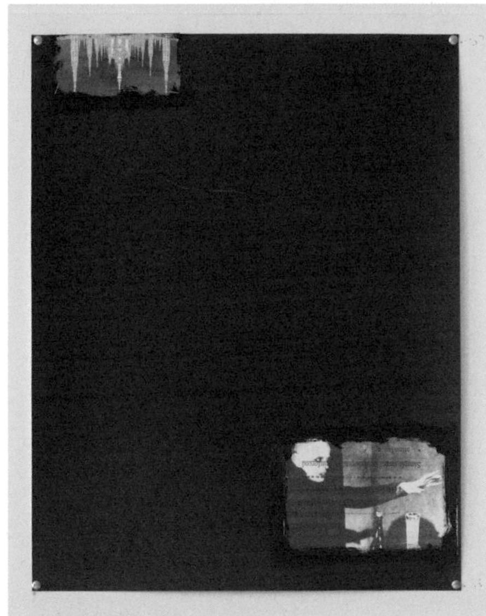

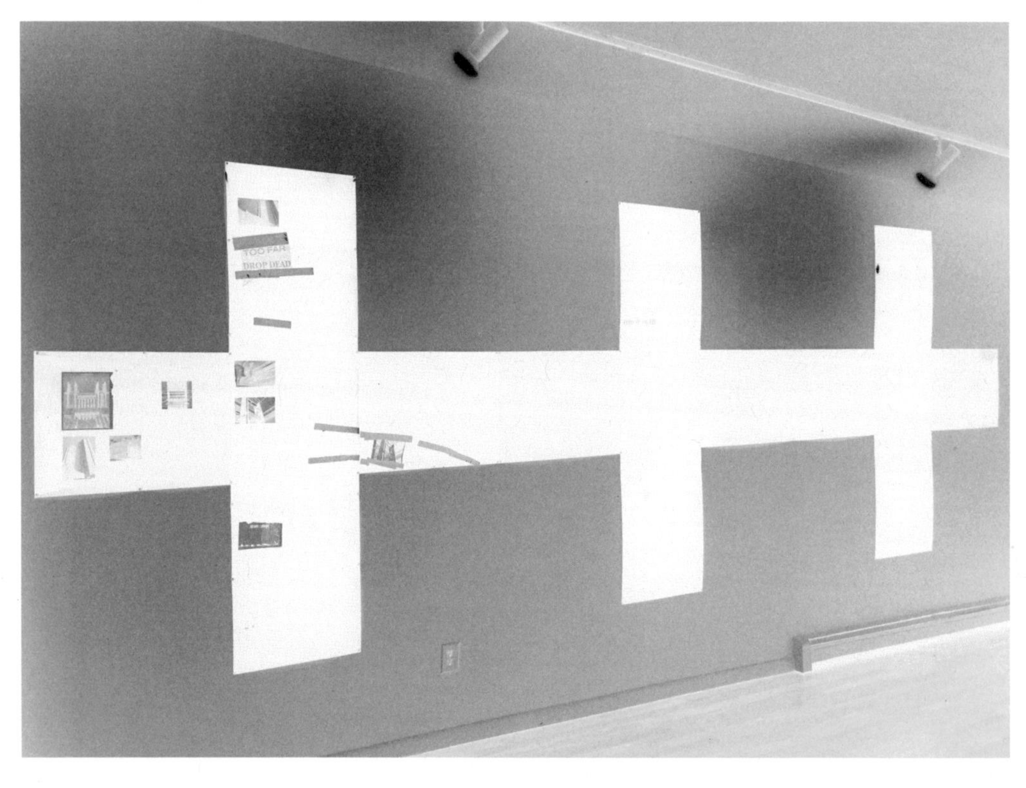
TOO FAR
DROP DEAD

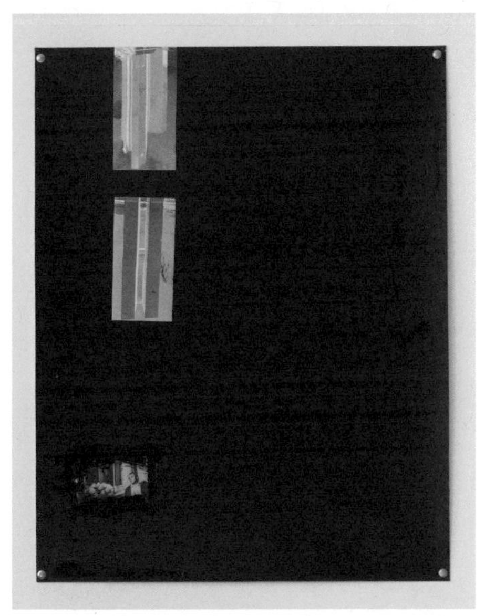

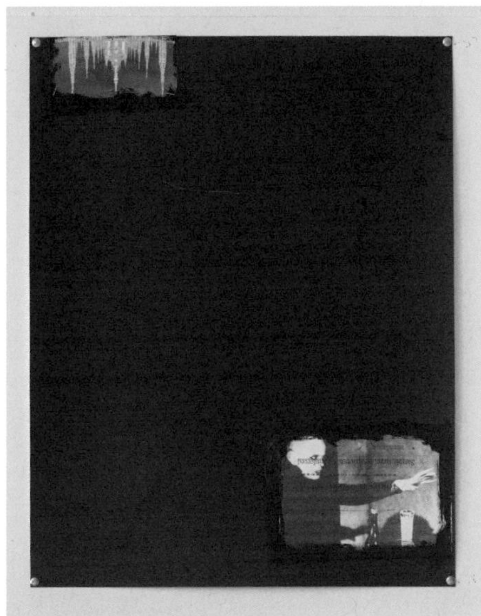

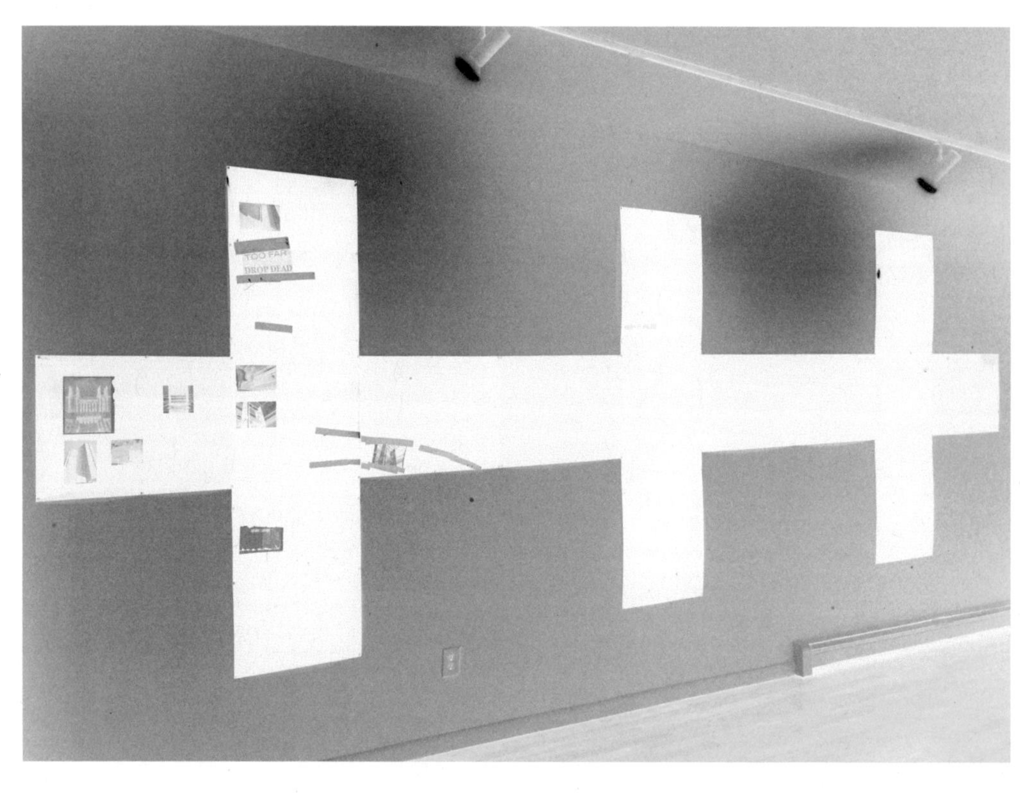
TOO FAR
DROP DEAD

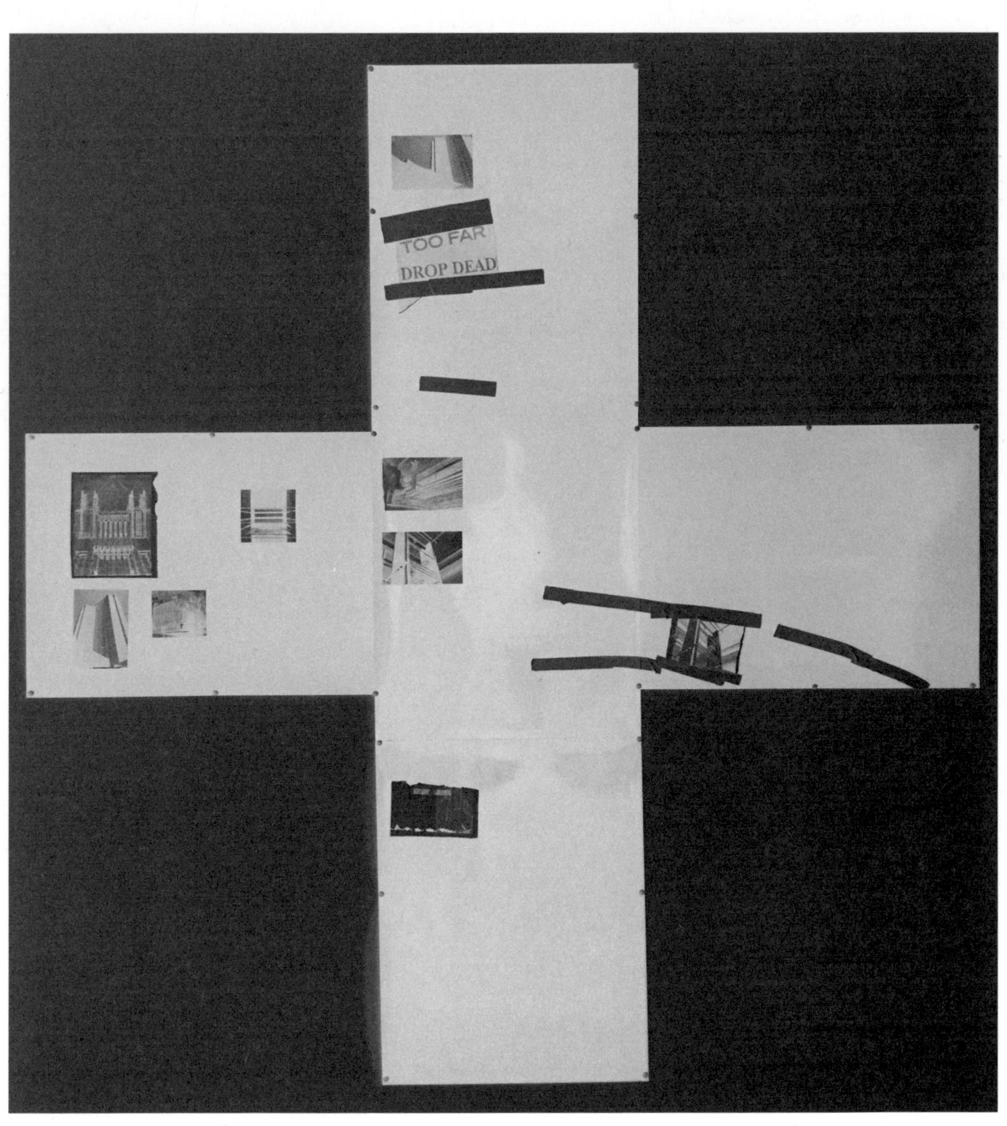
TOO FAR
DROP DEAD

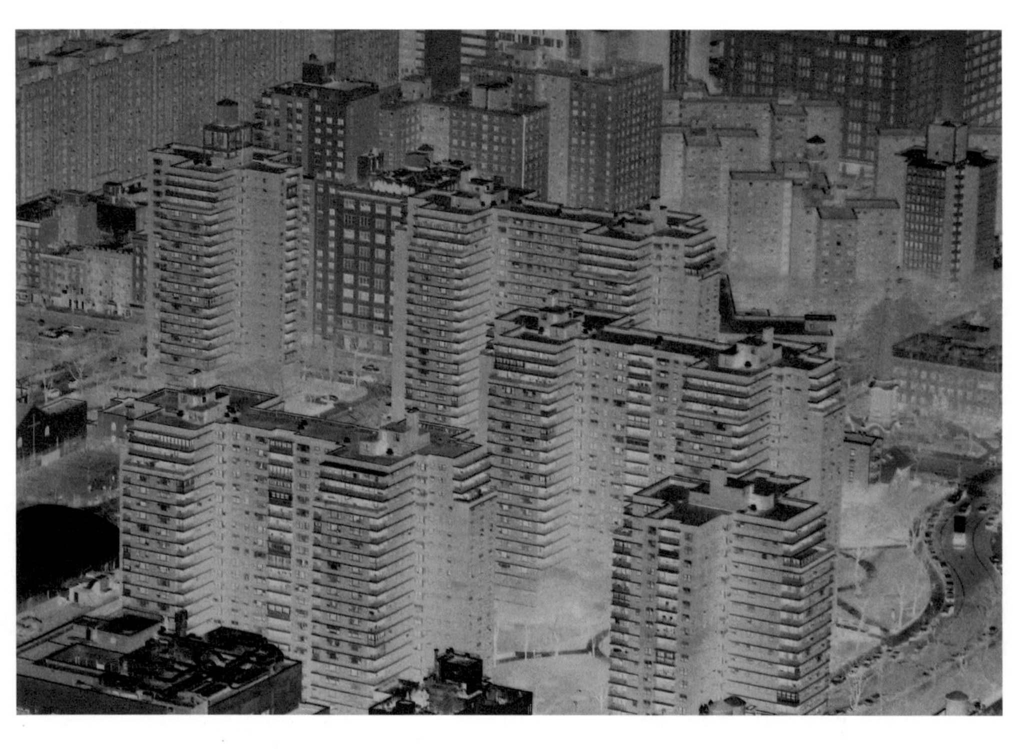

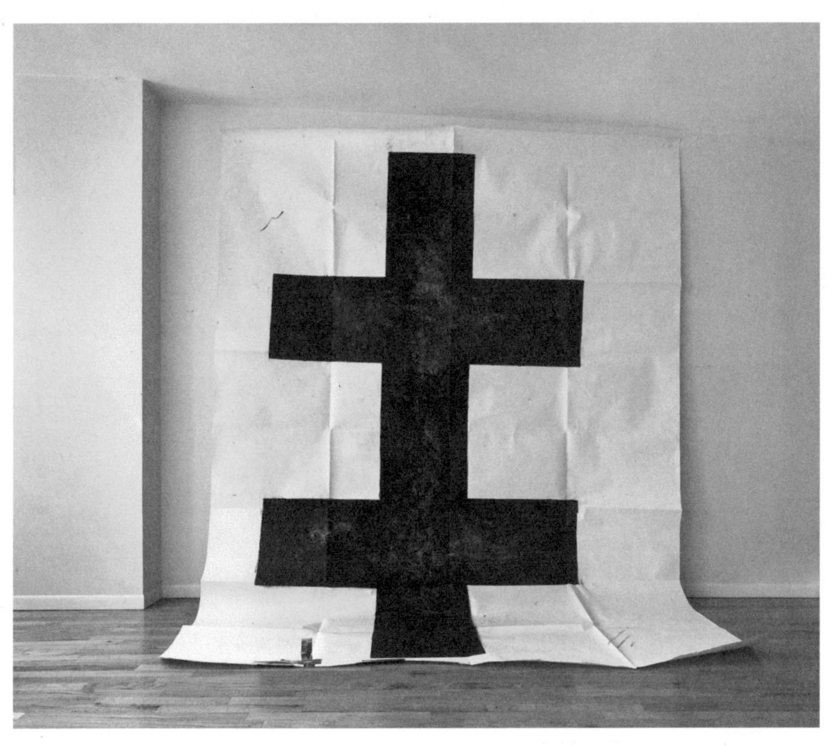

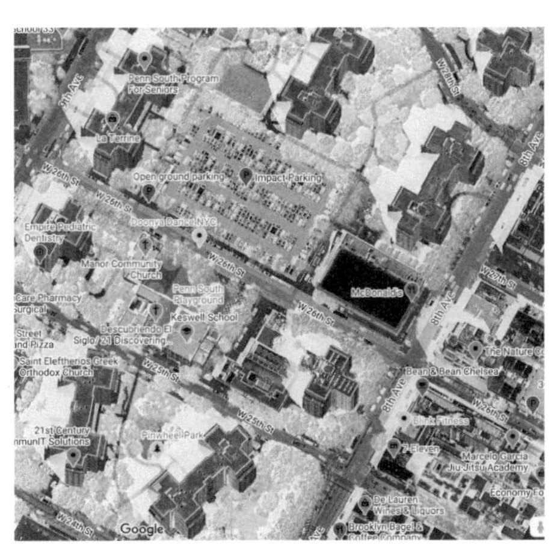

Penn South Program
For Seniors
9th Ave
La Terrine
W 28th St
8th Ave
W 26th St
Open ground parking
Impact Parking
W 26th St
Doonya Dance NYC
Empire Pediatric
Dentistry
Manor Community
Church
W 26th St
McDonald's
W 27th St
Penn South
Playground
Care Pharmacy
Surgical
Keswell School
W 26th St
8th Ave
Descubriendo El
Siglo 21 Discovering...
Street
and Pizza
Saint Eleftherios Greek
Orthodox Church
W 25th St
Bean & Bean Chelsea
8th Ave
W 26th St
W 25th St
21st Century
CommunIT Solutions
Pinwheel Park
7-Eleven
Marcelo Garcia
Jiu-Jitsu Academy
De Lauren
Wines & Liquors
W 24th St
Google
Brooklyn Bagel &
Coffee Company

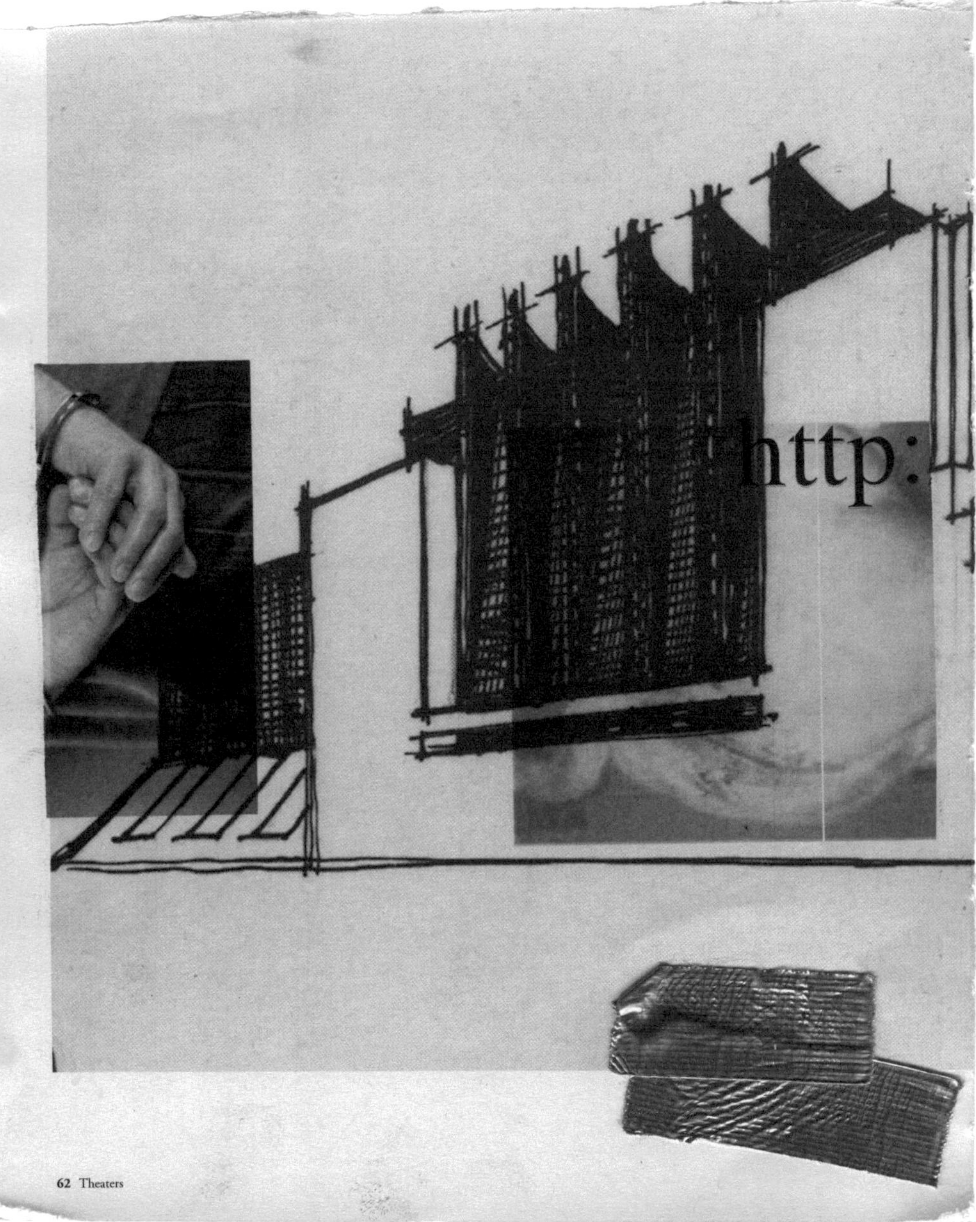
http:

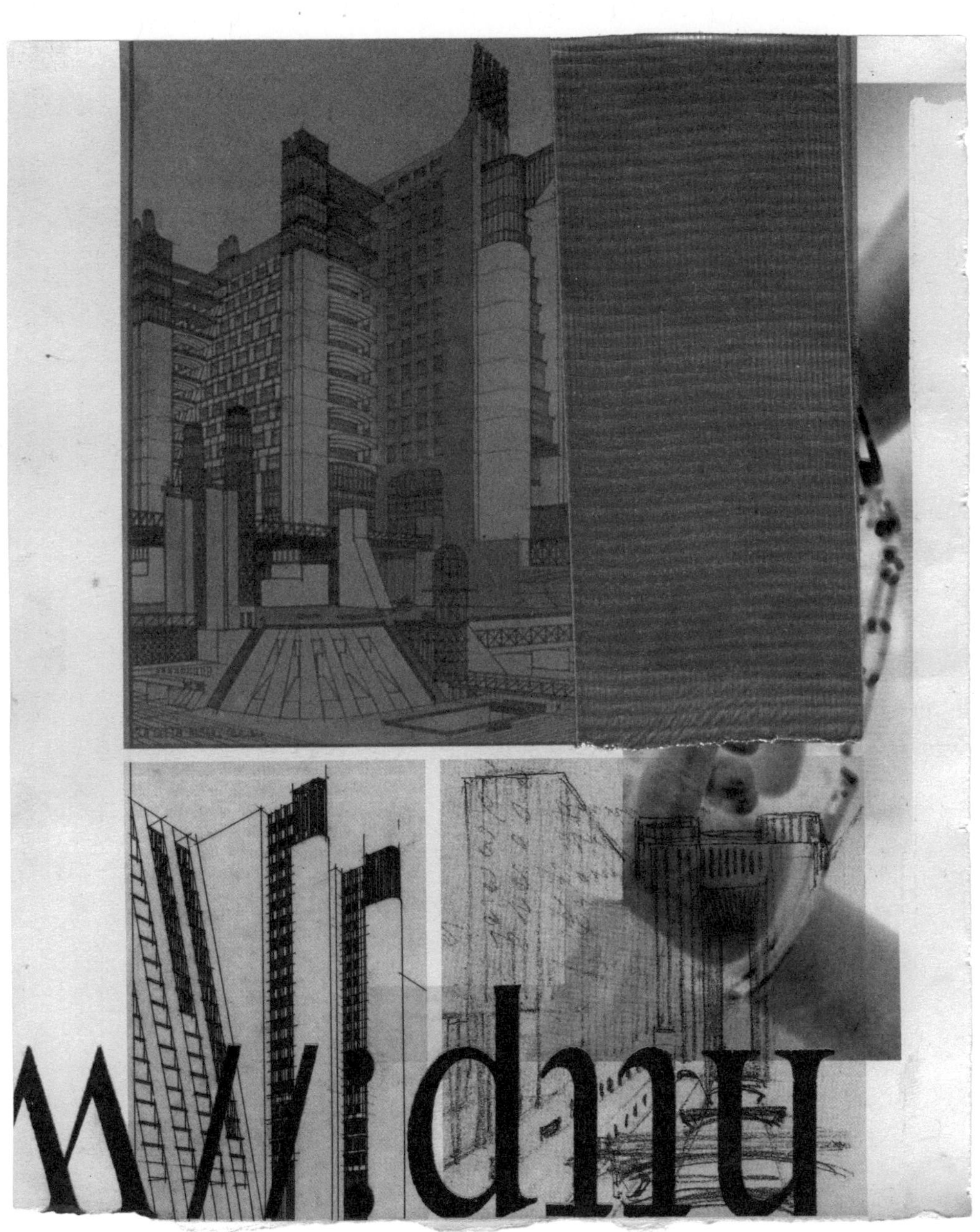

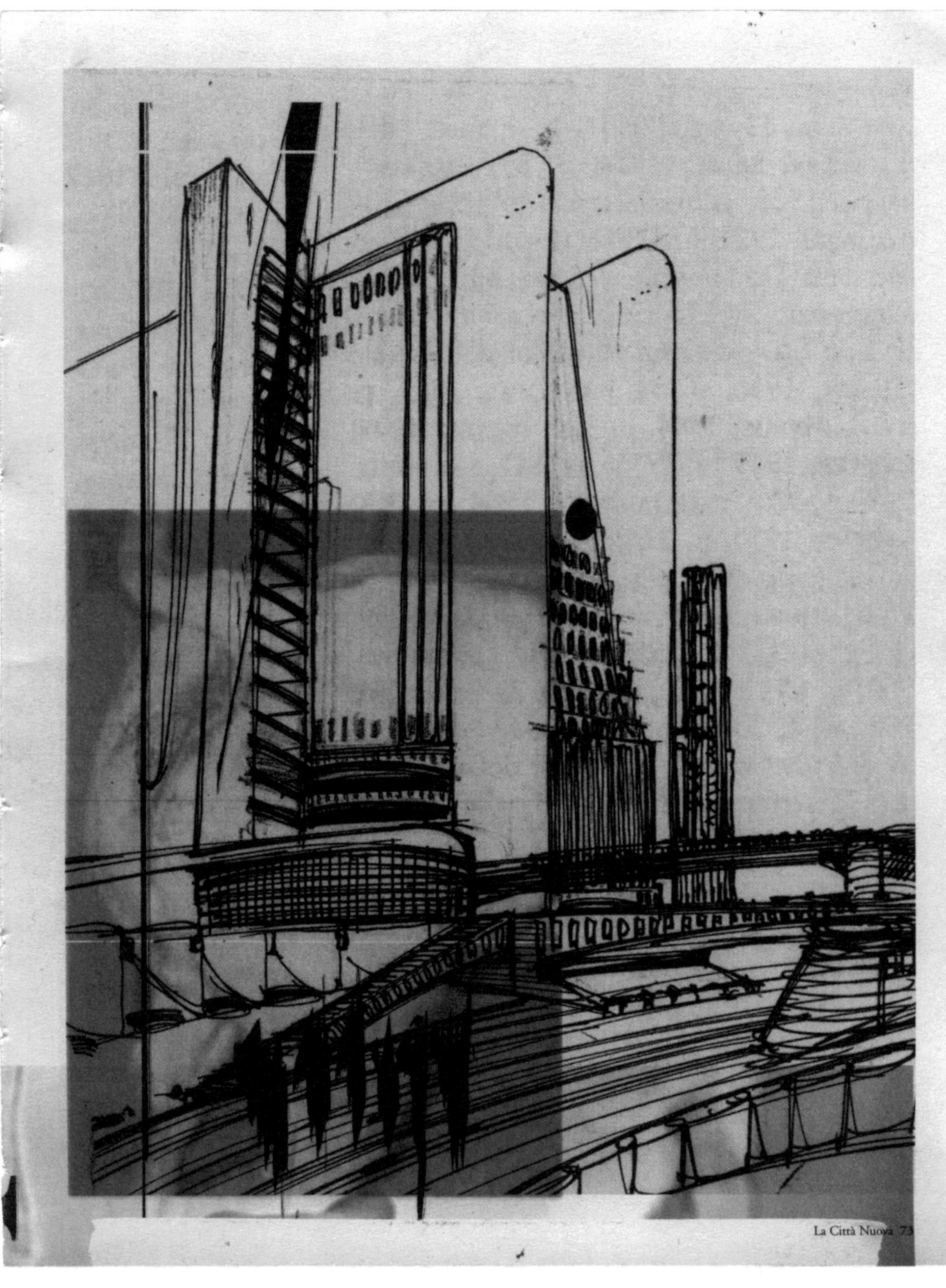

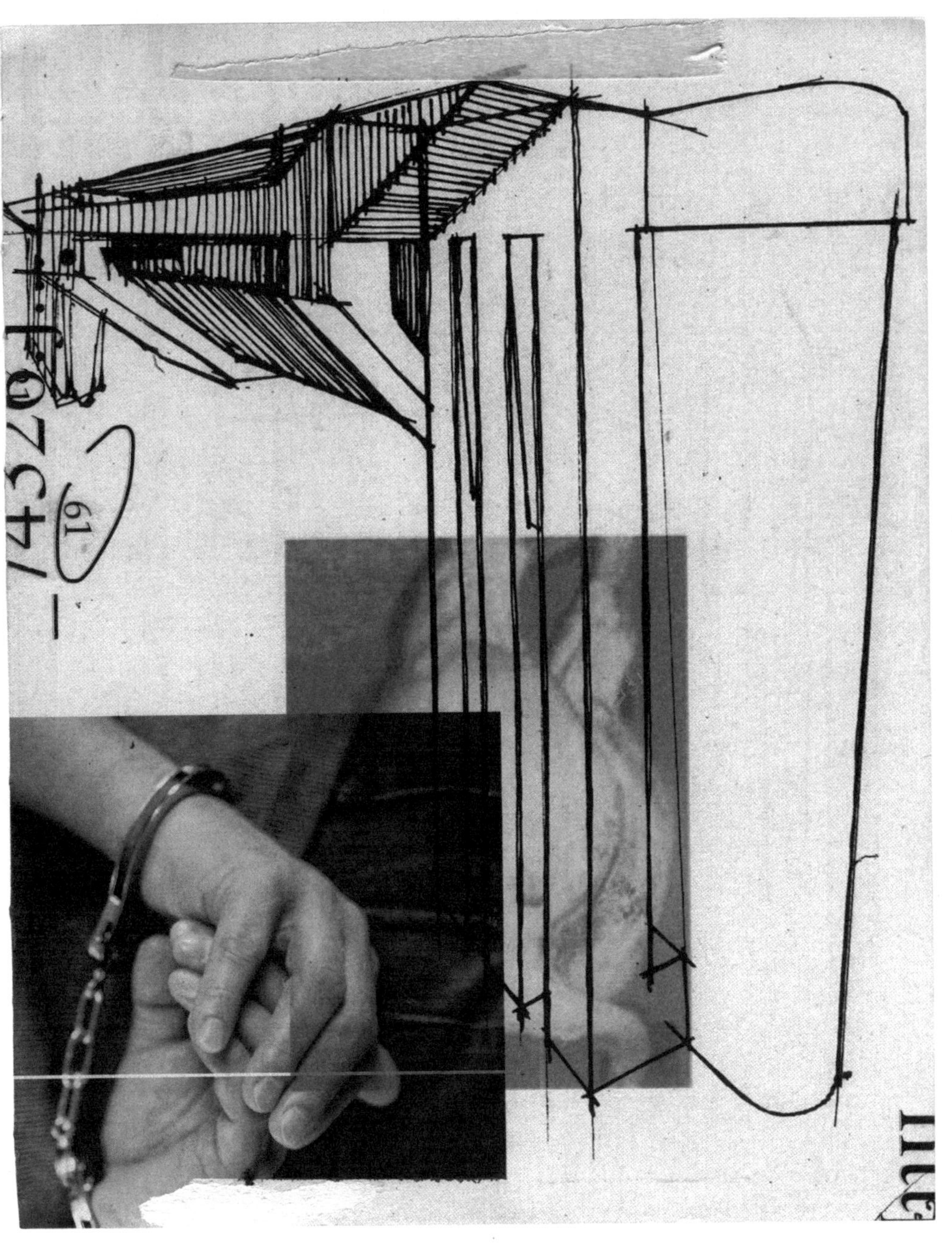

New York Times

Opinion

The two types of violence

By JAMES CARROLL APRIL 26, 2007

BOSTON — The two types of violence

Thirty-three people in Blacksburg, 230 in one day in Baghdad. Though residents United States and Iraq measure hurt on different scales, last week seemed off the char places.

There is neither physical nor moral equivalence between the carnage at Virginia T the latest explosions in the U.S.-sparked Sunni-Shiite civil war, yet such outbreaks dra attention to an underlying force that has taken both nations hostage: violence. At a tin this, it is necessary to step back from politics and grief to think about violence as such

"Violence is by nature instrumental," the political phil[illegible]her Hannah Arendt wr "Like all means, it always stands in need of guidance [illegible]stification through the end pursues." By "instrumental," Arendt essentially mean[illegible] aimed at accomplishing somet Clausewitz had taken such purposefulness for granted when he defined war as "an act violence to compel the opponent to do as we wish." Such violence, however much to be regretted, or even opposed, can claim to be both rational and right.

But Arendt's assumption about violence as "by nature instrumental" seems under the violence that, however differently, shook both America and Iraq last week. It was v that Seung-Hui Cho was not engaged in "instrumental" violence. He committed grotes for the sake not of power or dominance, but of their grotesquery. His was violence for sake, period. In destroying innocent lives, Cho was concerned not with those lives or w others, but only with himself.

As the video package he sent [illegible]wed, Cho's was an act of what might be c "expressive" violence. Cho's murders, that is, were a form of communication, and their perversity adhered in the way in which he succeeded in conscripting the contemporary communications industry, centered on television news. He killed, and by the world's st and taking note of his having killed, the purest form of expressive violence was achieve making accomplices not only of the broadcast media, but of all who viewed it. Cho got nakes no difference whether that expression is a scream of rage or a cry for help. Such e for its own sake lands on the vulnerable like typewriter keys on paper, but persons ar e used as ciphers in someone else's message. That conviction explains the universal ance felt at Cho's actions, even if repugnance comes tinged with a broad feeling of :ity. A moral principle suggests itself: Expressive violence is always wrong. A corollary : Responsible media should censor it.

t instrumental violence is different, and may or may not be wrong, depending on how and ends are measured. The move to this level of abstraction prepares for the more : moral and political question: What about the American war in Iraq? Even those of us posed the war from the start must acknowledge that, in the beginning, the Bush stration's violence toward the Iraq of Saddam Hussein was instrumental. Regime was the purpose, and whether one opposed or supported it, the war's violence could be :d as aimed at something beyond itself.

t where is the purpose now? If war is violence "to compel the opponent do as we wish," ctually, do we wish at this point?

viously, everyone wishes the killing to stop, the Sunnis wish to regain some measure ver Iraq and its resources, the Shiites wish to assert the control proper to their super s, and varied factions want the American occupiers out. But what, actually, does W. Bush want?

t week marked the dawning of a horrible American question: Has our once- ental violence become merely expressive? Since our purpose no longer has to do with regime change, no democracy, no connection to global terror, not even oil), does it do now only with ourselves (maintaining "credibility," avoiding catastrophic defeat, that more than 3,300 American soldiers died in vain)?

erican violence is the condition within which Iraqi violence explodes. The removal of in violence may or may not dampen Iraqi violence. But Iraqi violence of various stripes s for power, control, or, at minimum, revenge. Iraqi violence is purposeful. Last week hard question to Americans: What is the purpose of ours?

nes Carroll's column appears regularly in The Boston Globe.

of this article appears in print on April 26, 2007, in The International Herald Tribune.

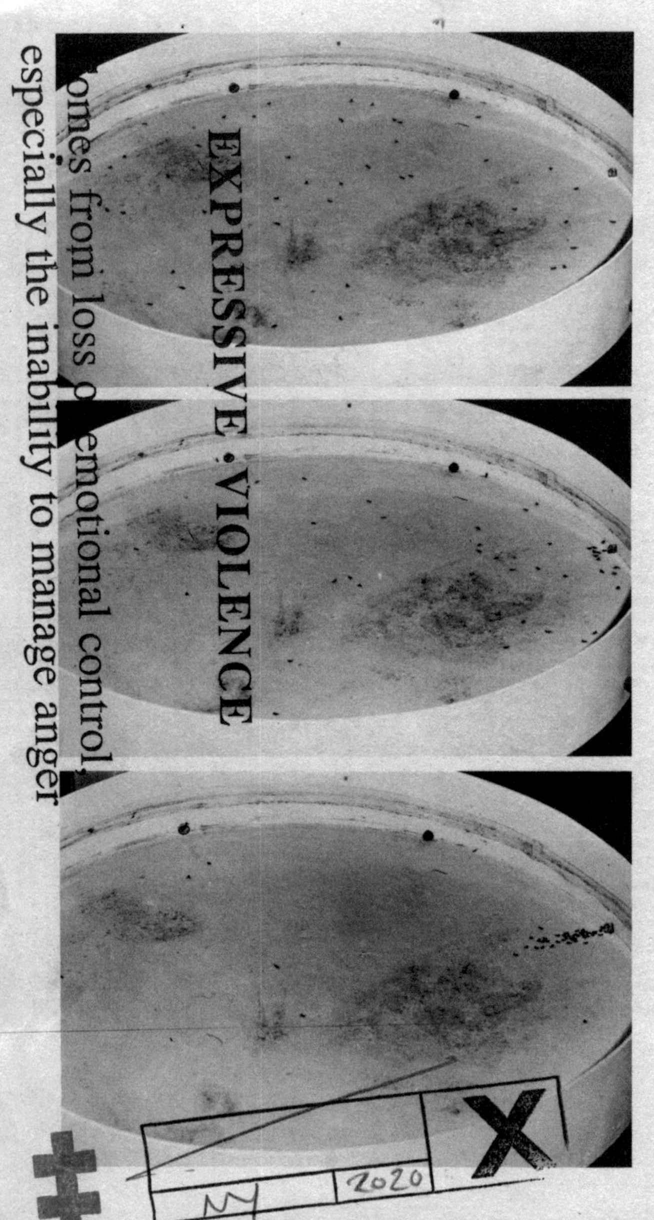

Figure 58 ROLE OF SCENT in directing the migration of *Atemeles* beetles from their initial residence in *Formica* nests to winter quarters in *Myrmica* nests is demonstrated in these laboratory photographs. At the start of the experiment (*top*) the beetles are distributed at random in a circular enclosure. Air scented with the odor of *Myrmica* ants is then blown into the enclosure through one of the eight holes around its rim (*center*). Ten minutes later (*bottom*) most of the beetles have collected in a cluster near the scent-emitting hole.

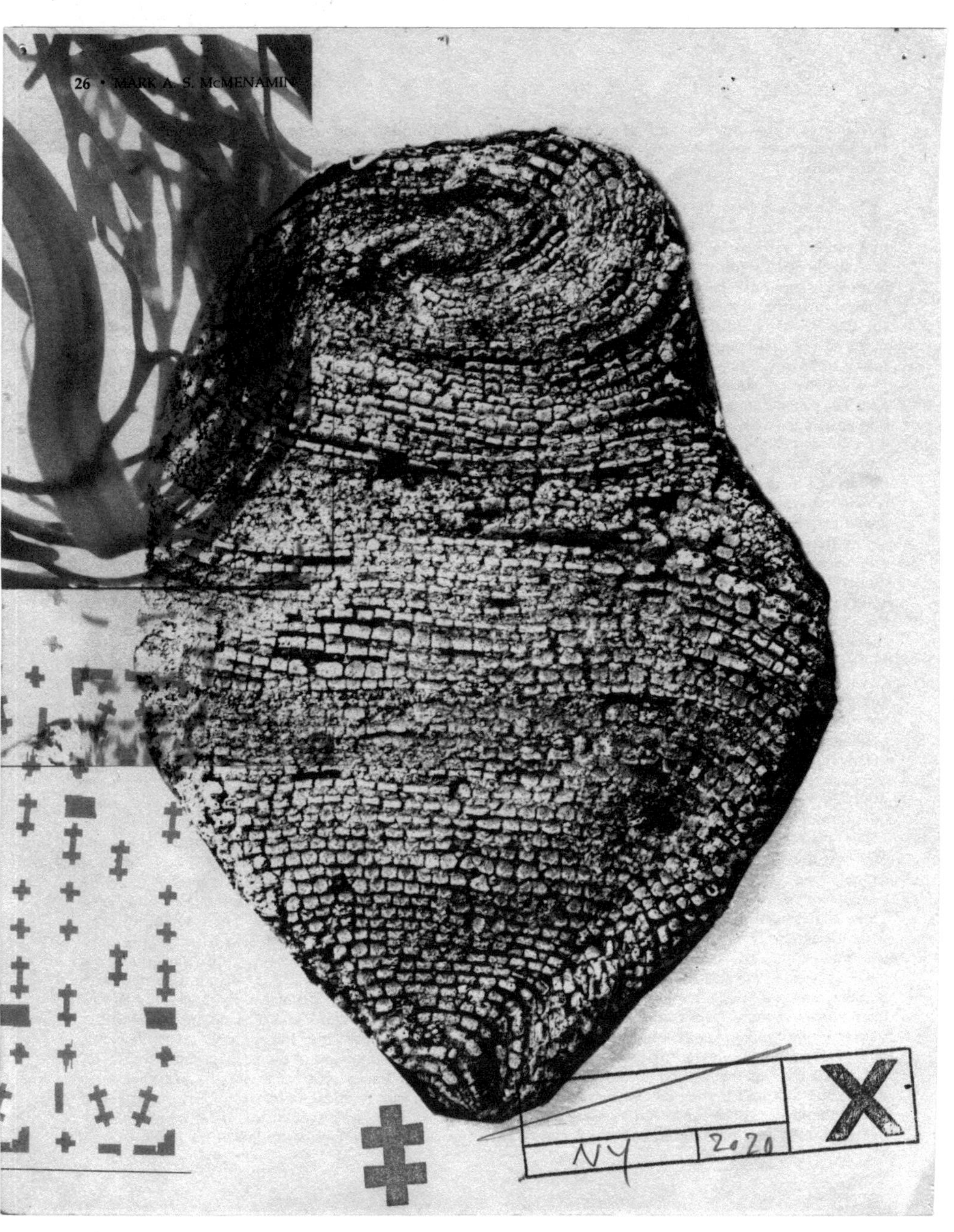
26 • MARK A. S. McMENAMIN
NY
2020
X

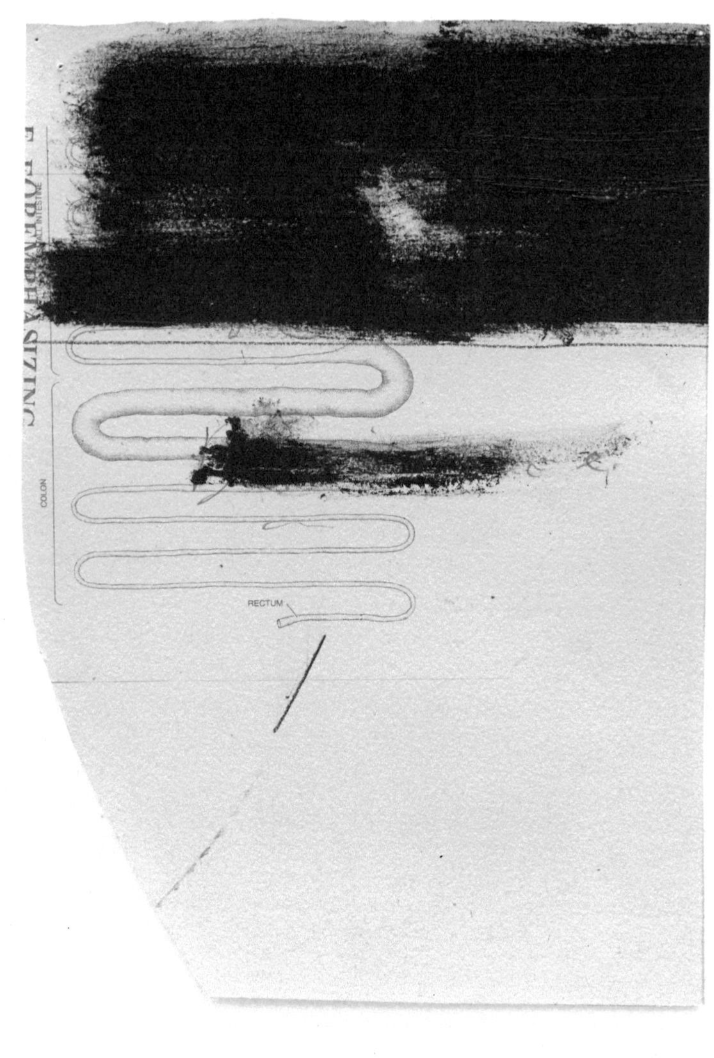
COLON
RECTUM

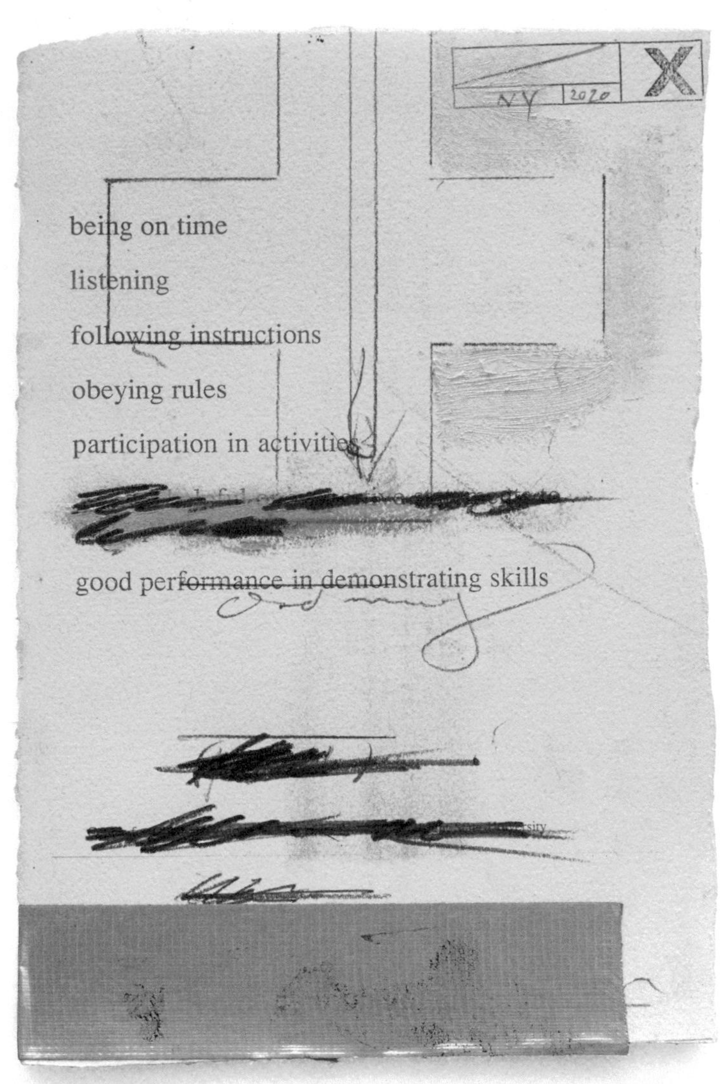
NY
2020
X
being on time
listening
following instructions
obeying rules
participation in activities
good performance in demonstrating skills

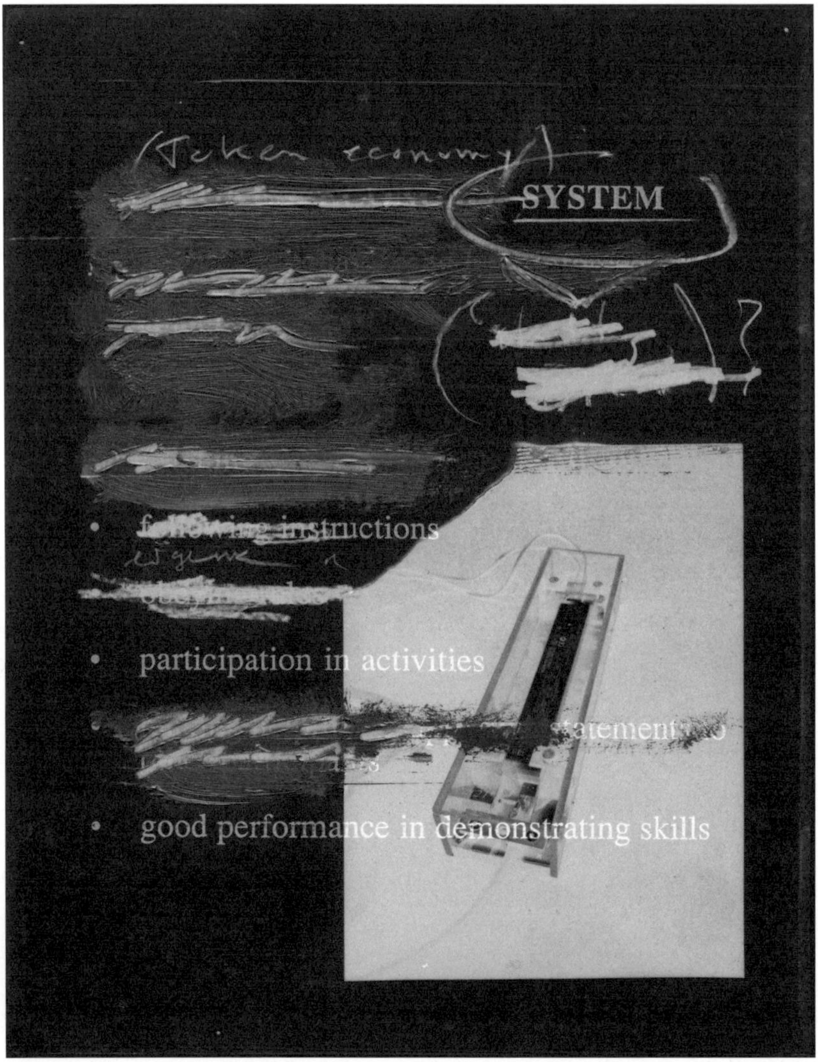

(Token economy)

SYSTEM

- following instructions
- participation in activities
- good performance in demonstrating skills

3

Dædalus Tower 3, 4 & 5 (Europe)

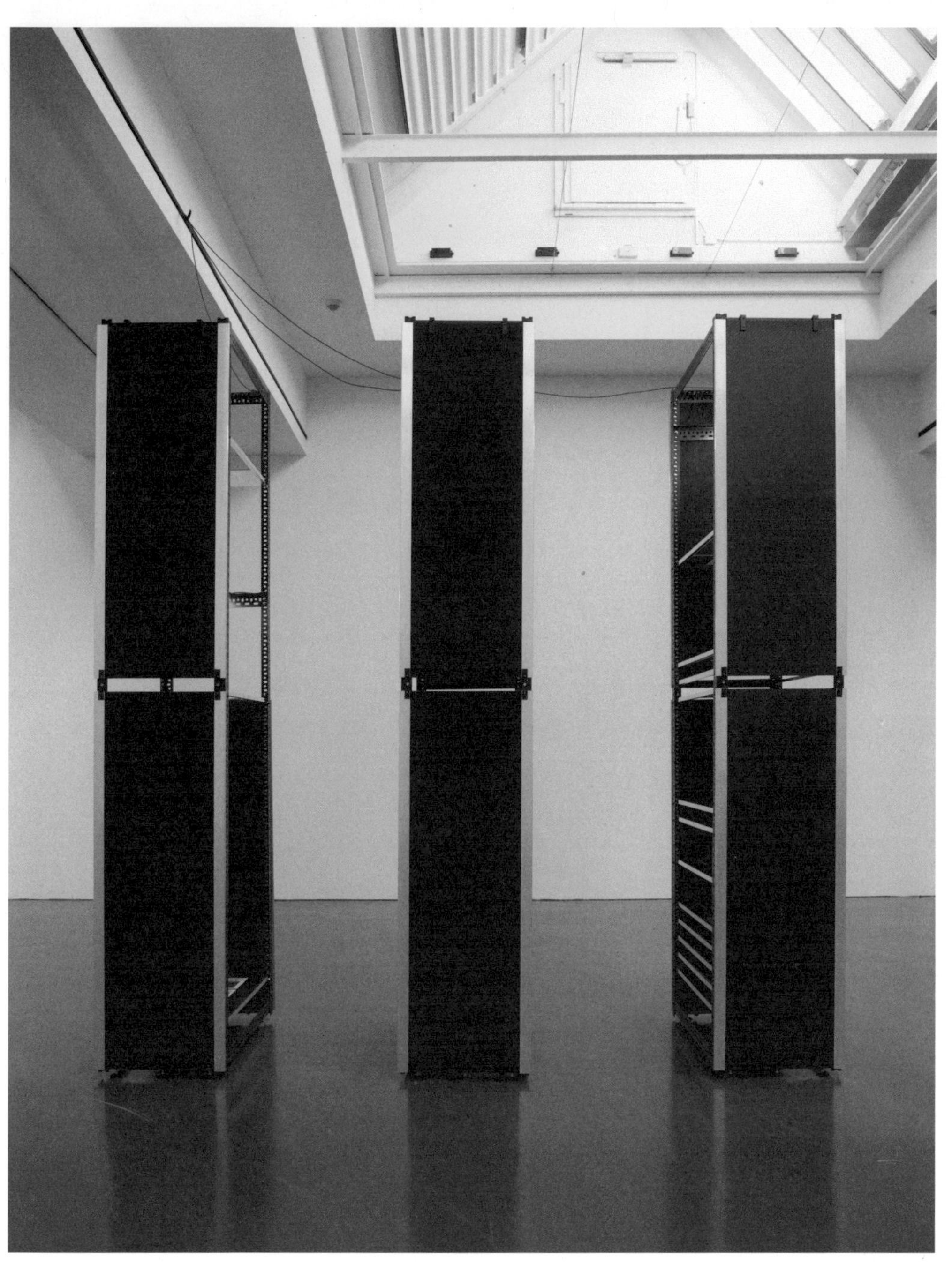

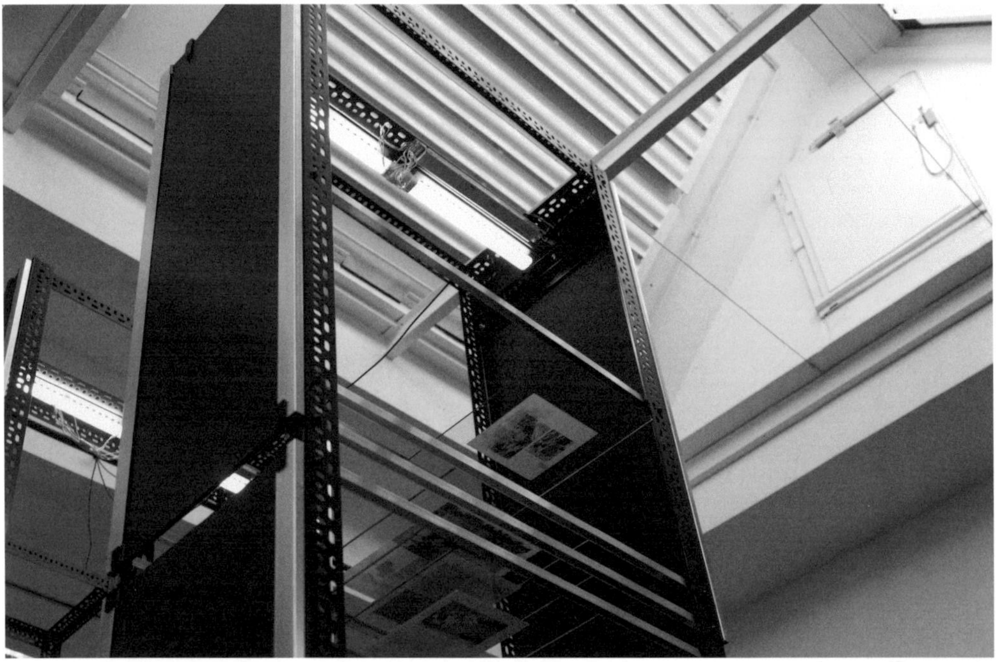

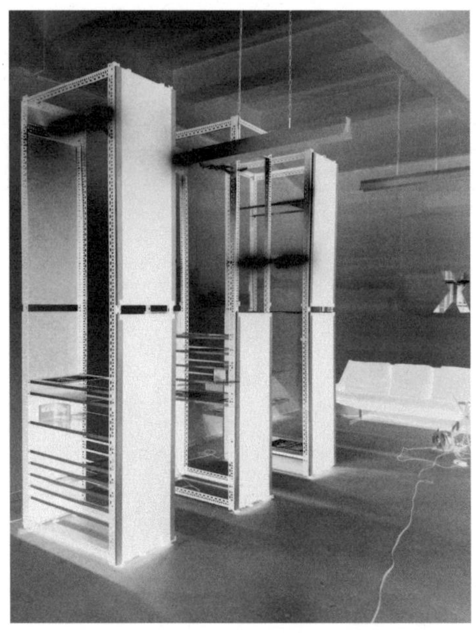

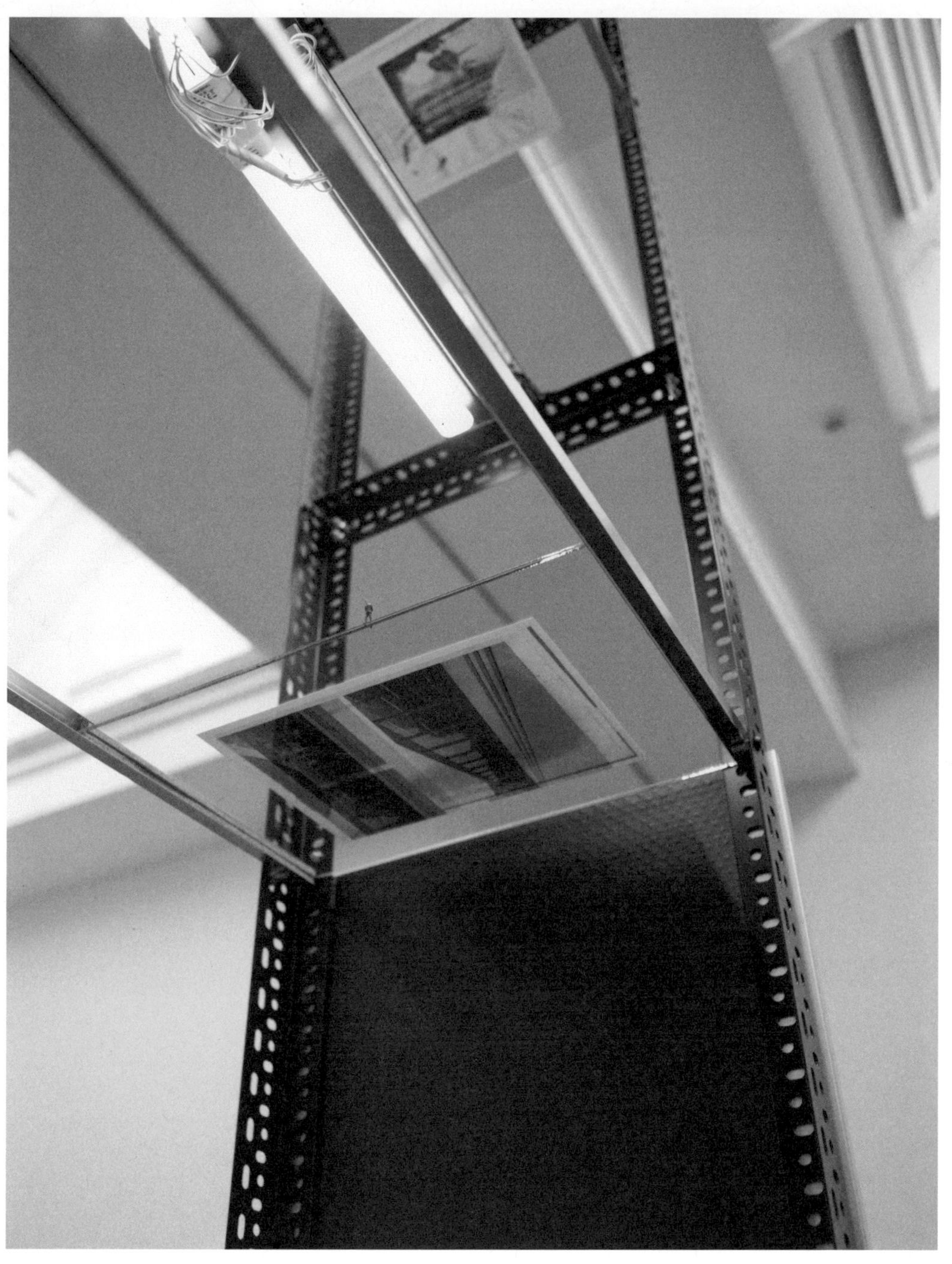

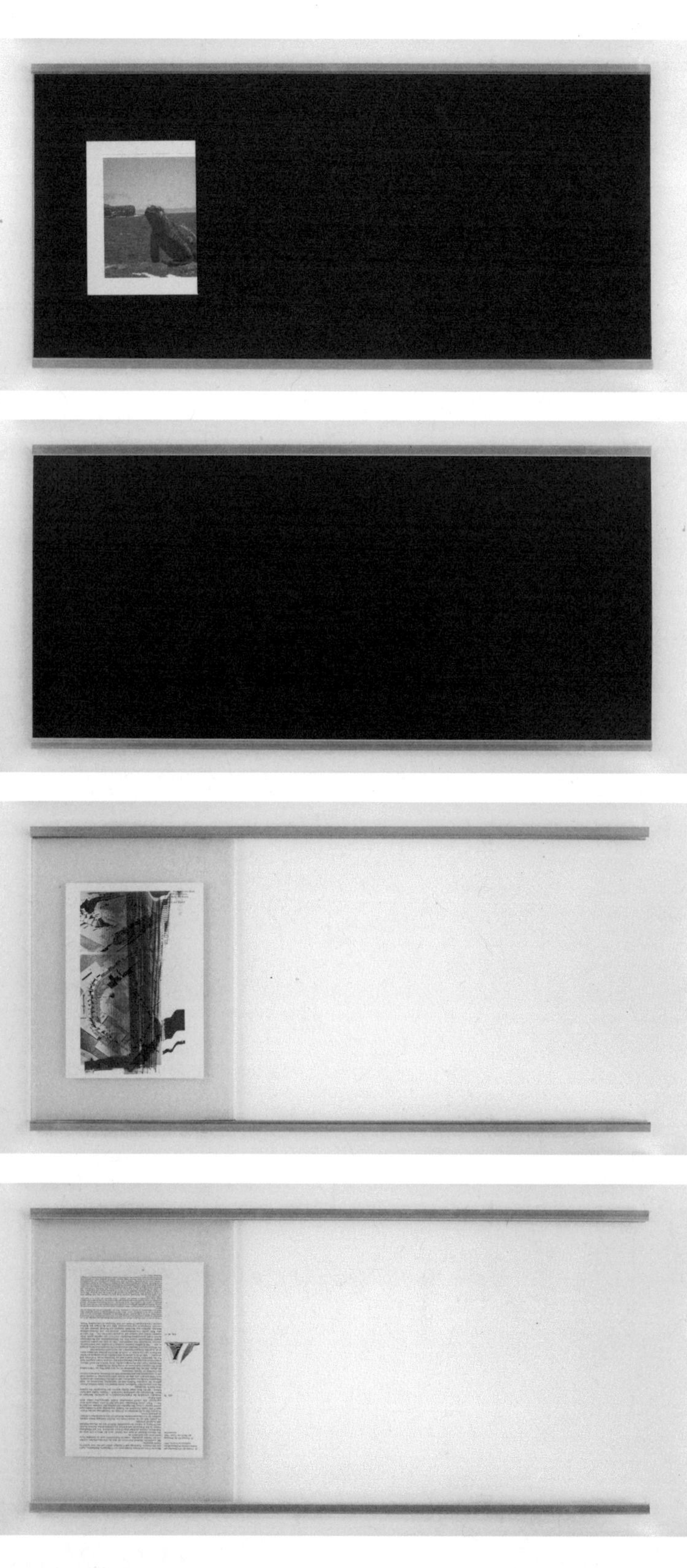

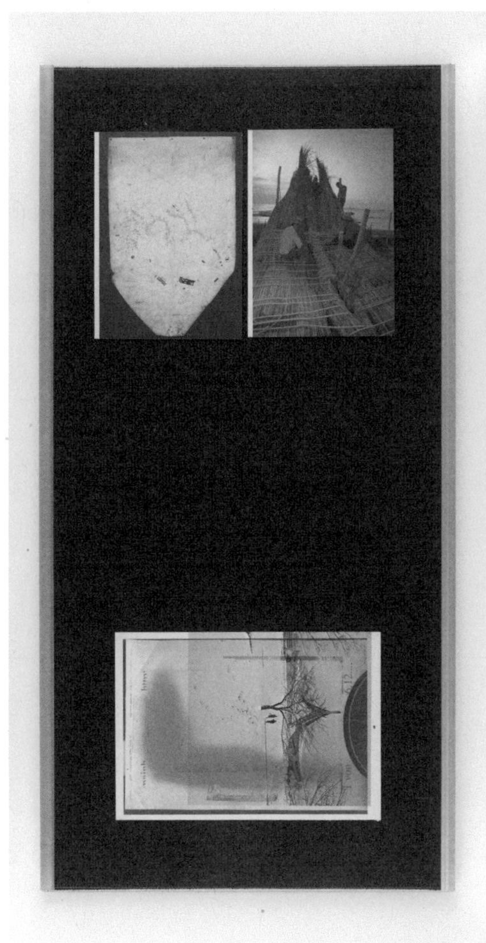

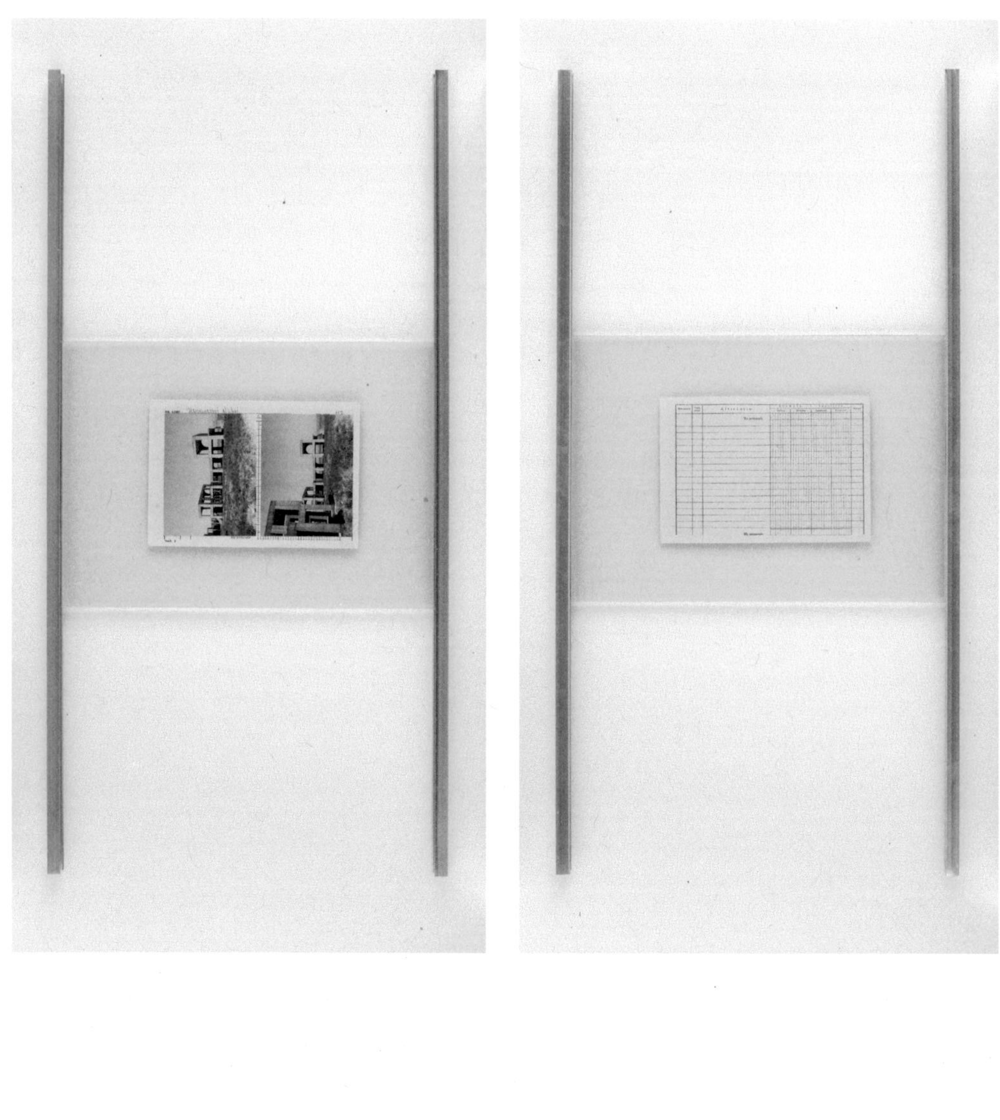

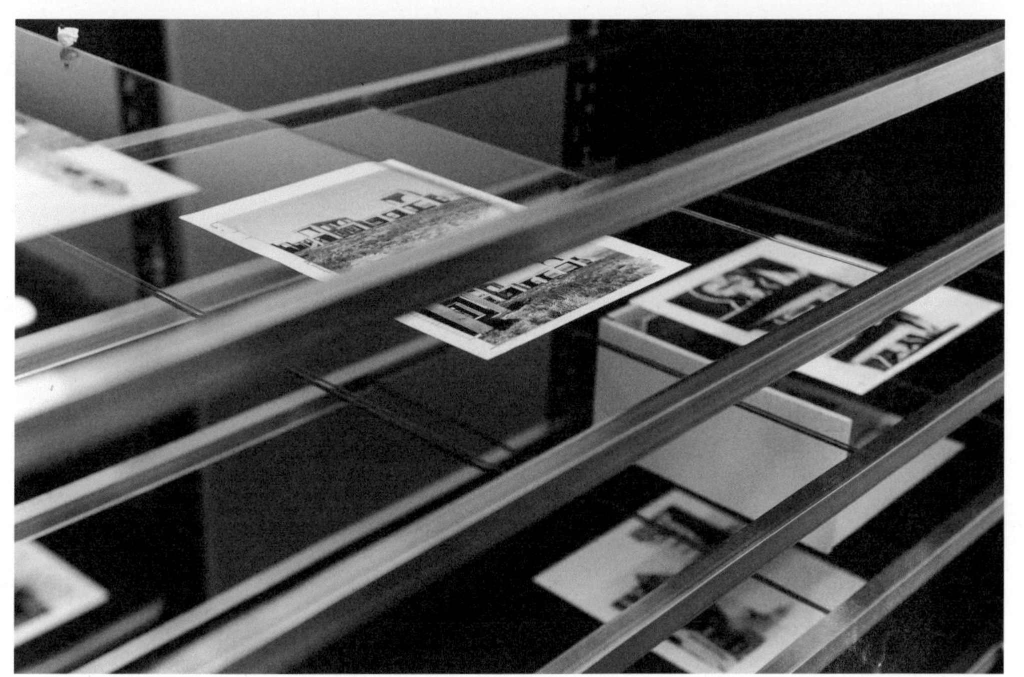

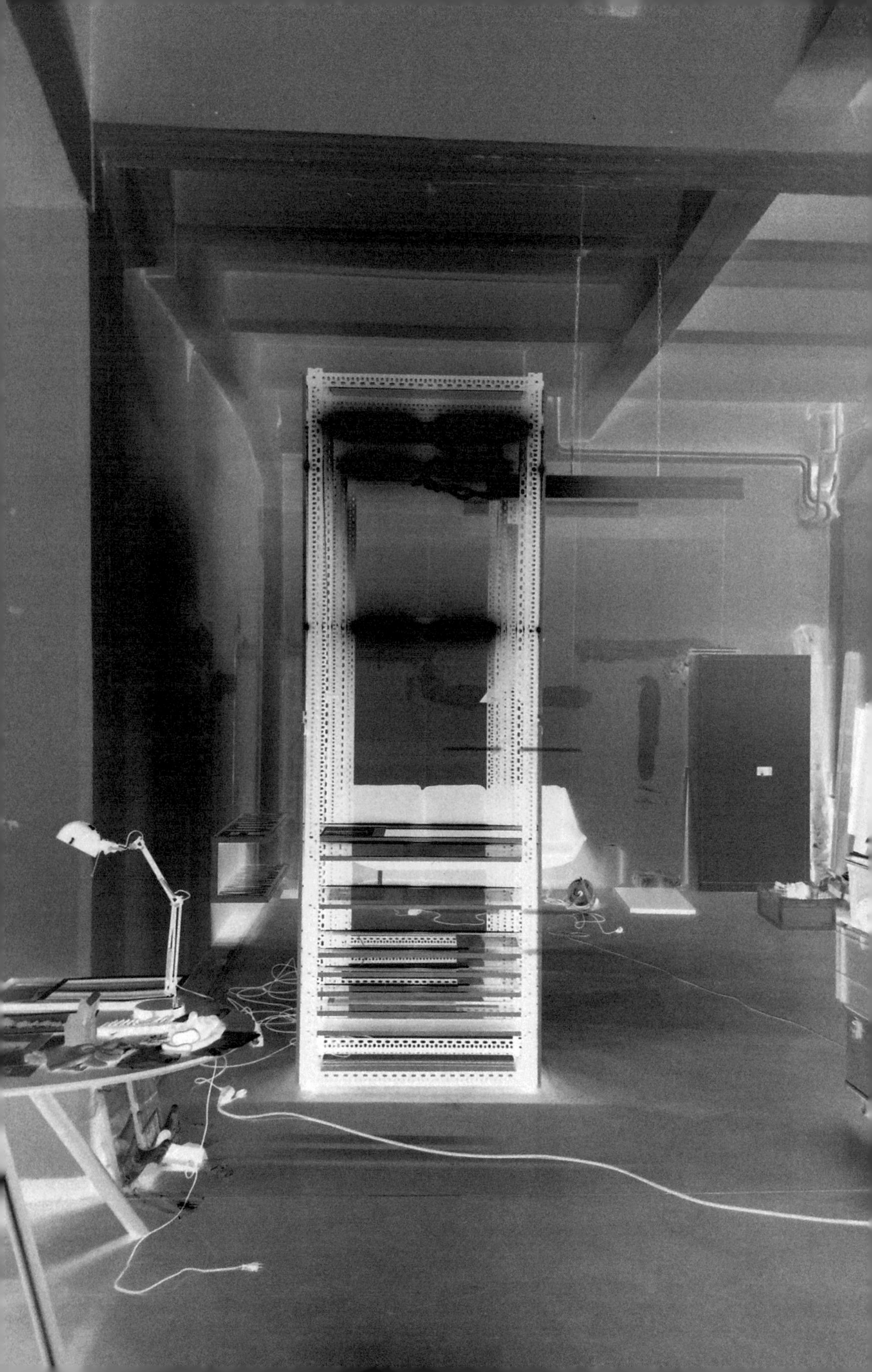

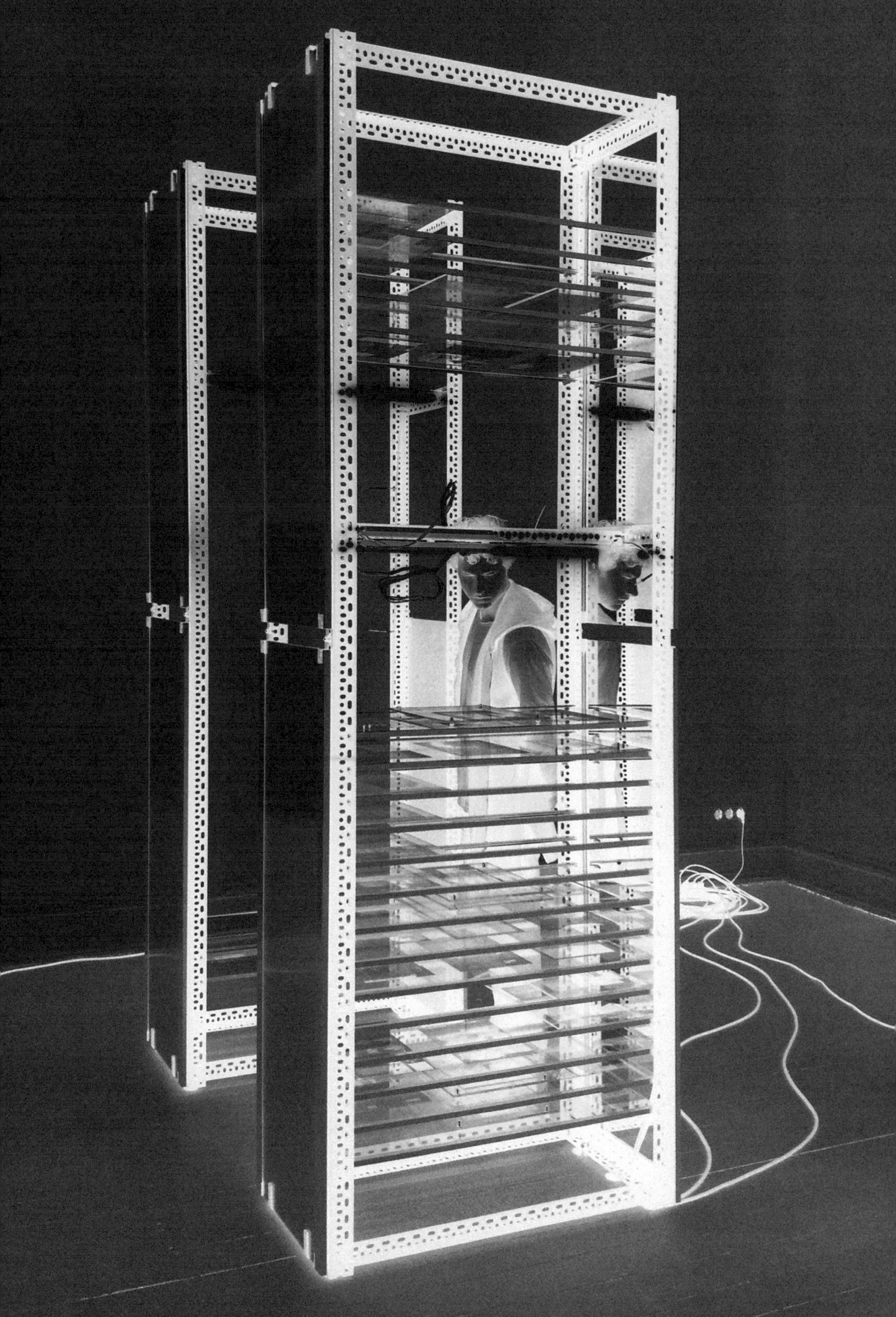

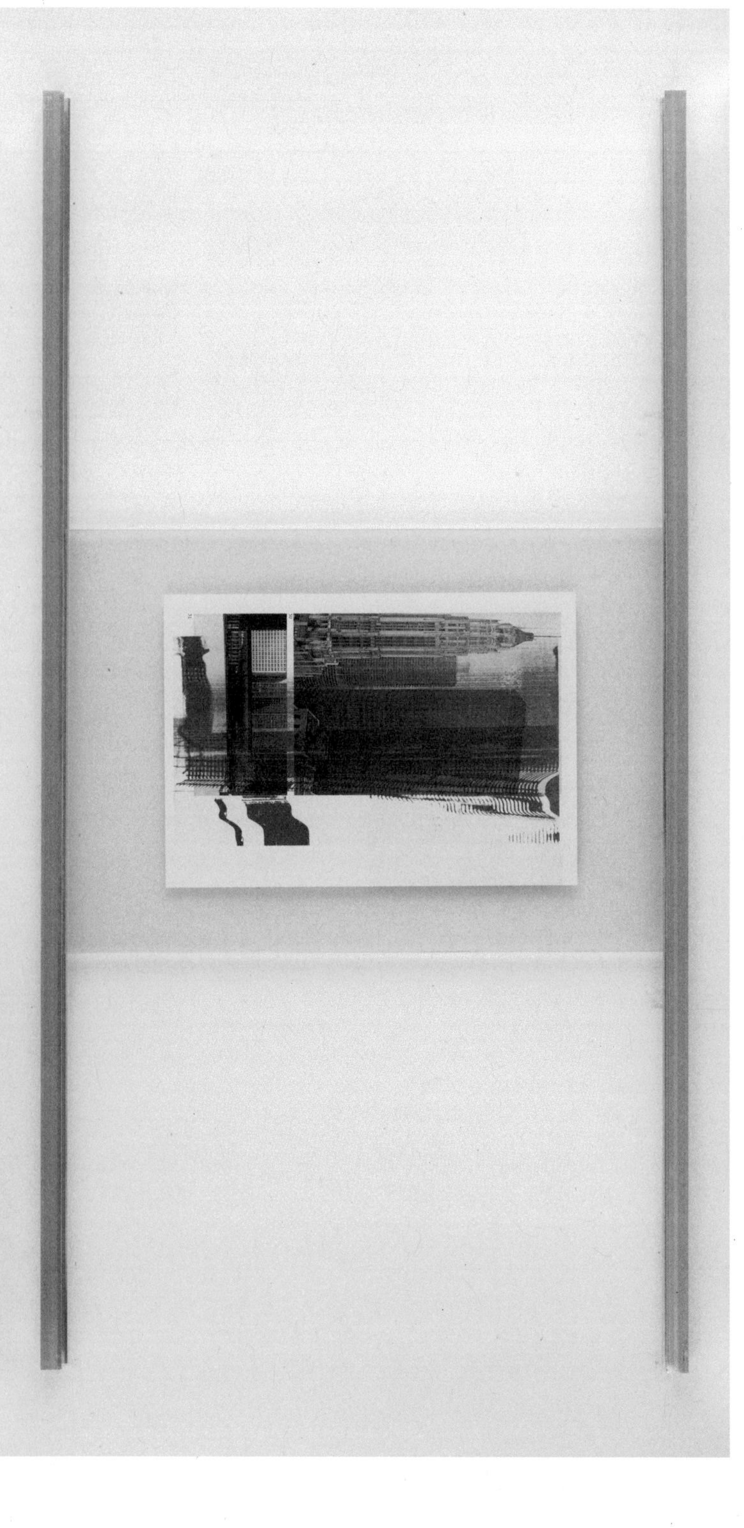

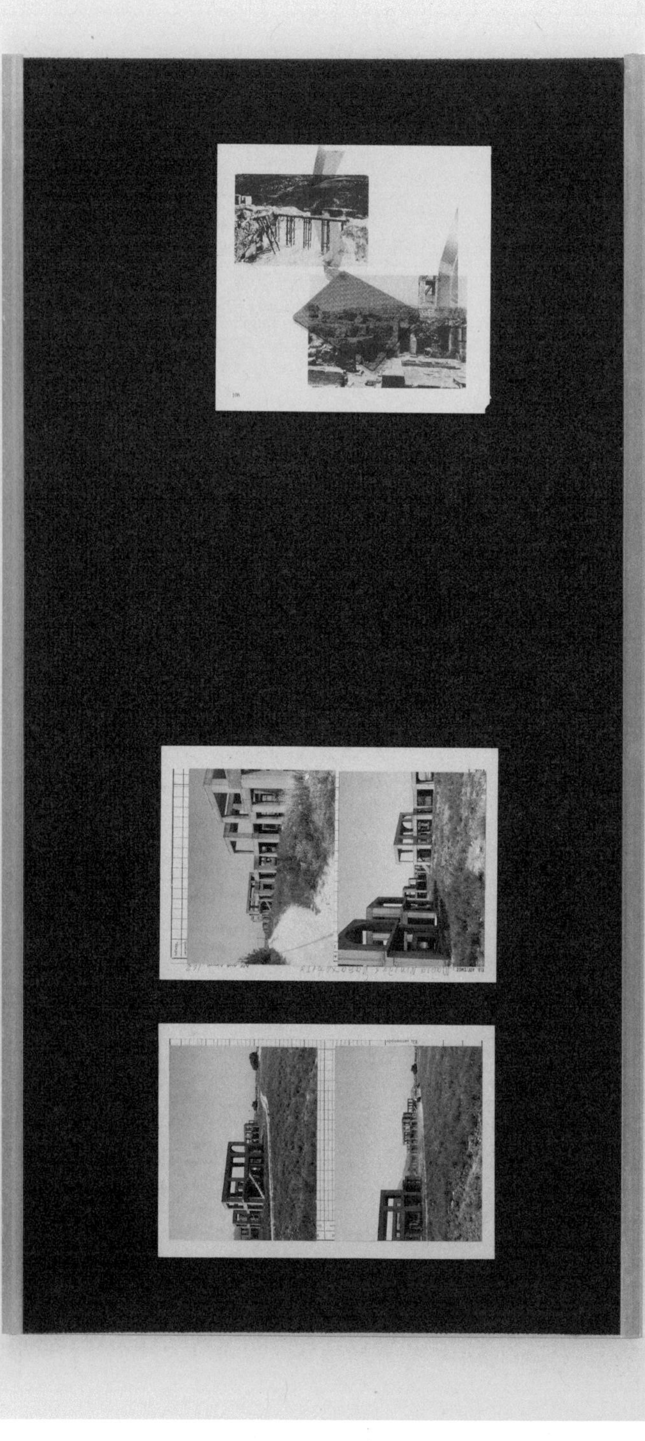

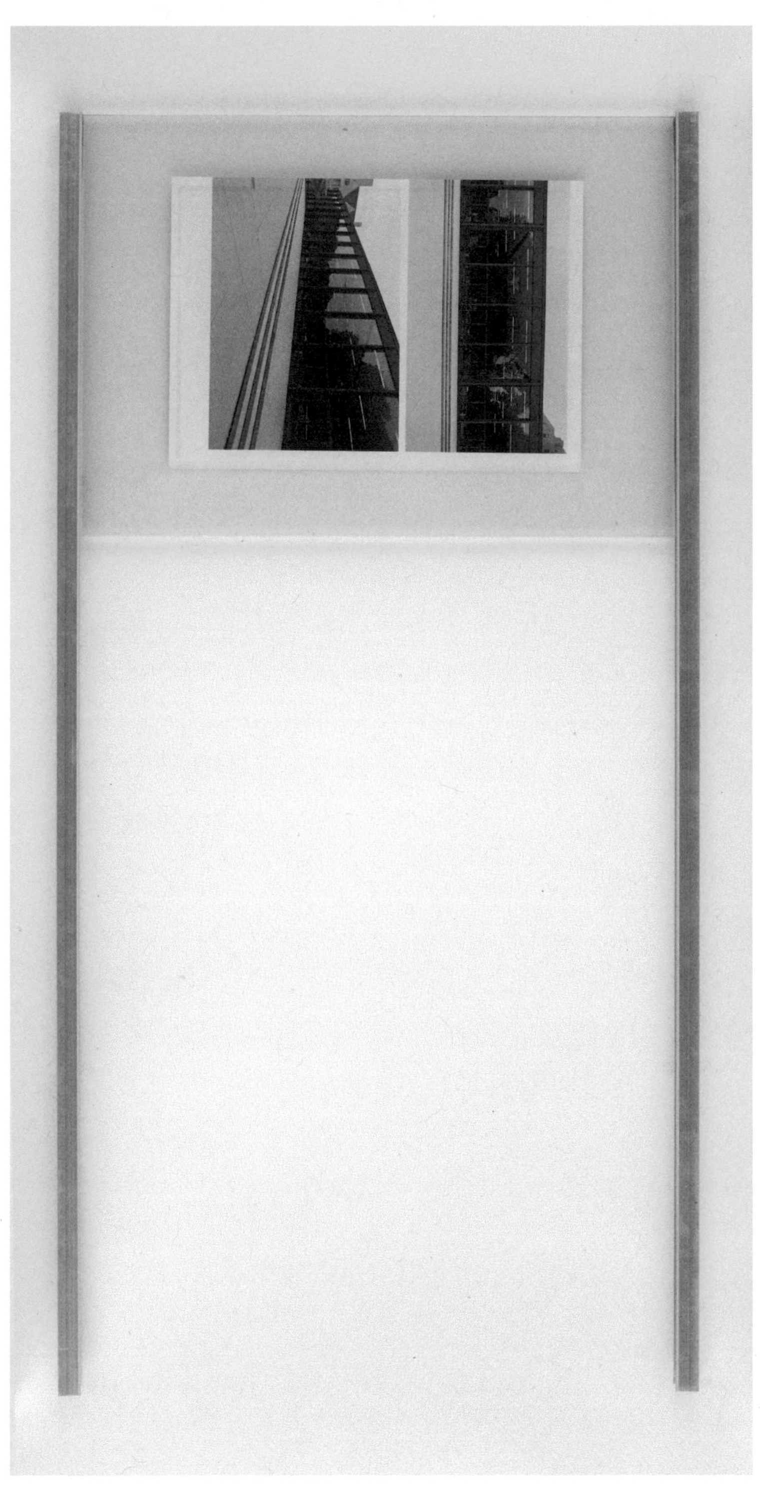

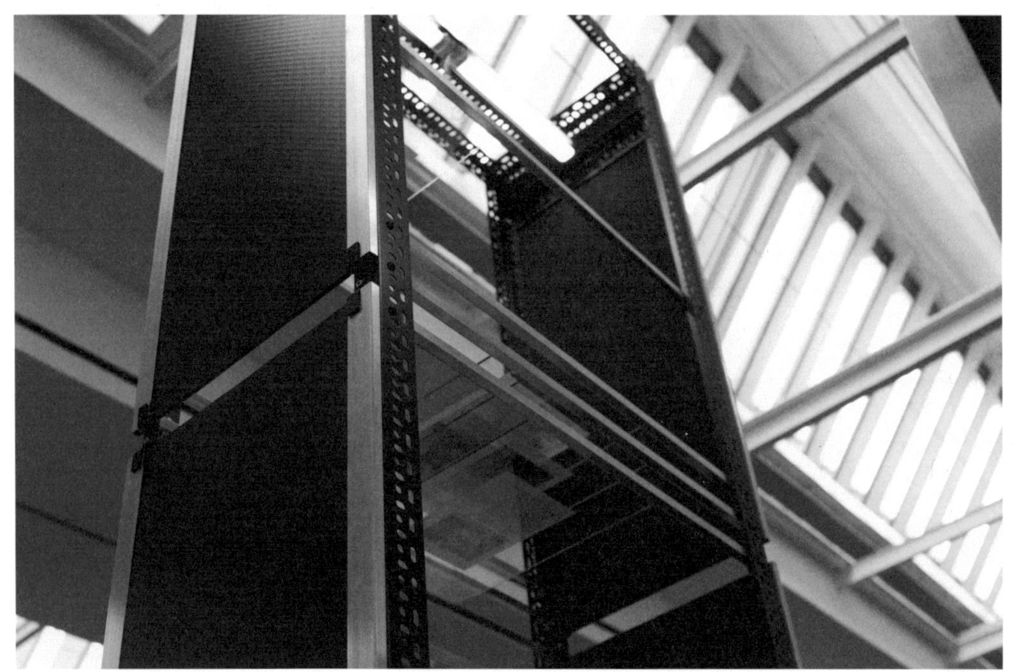

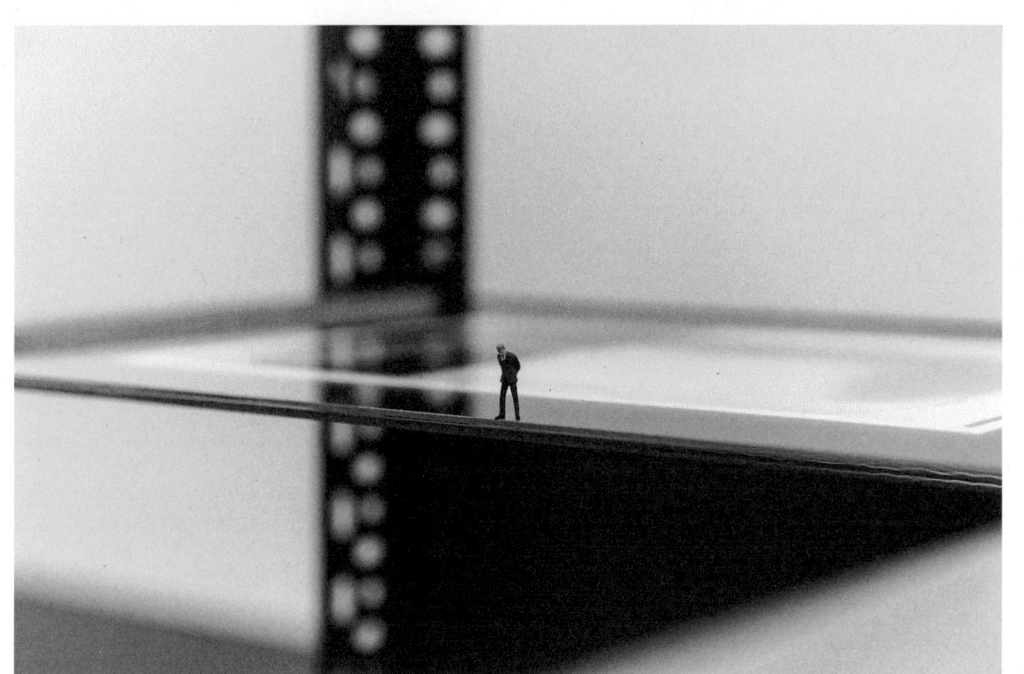

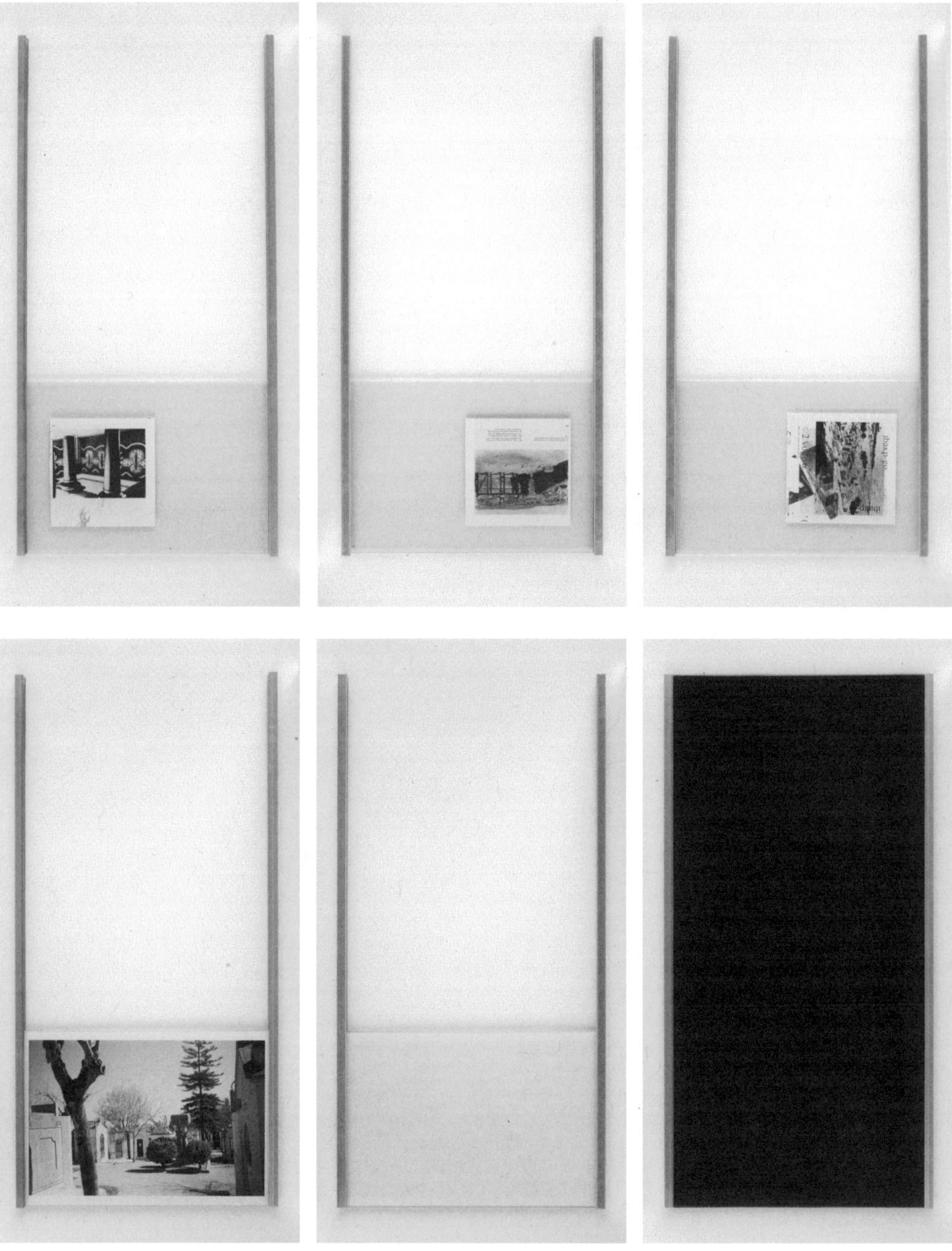

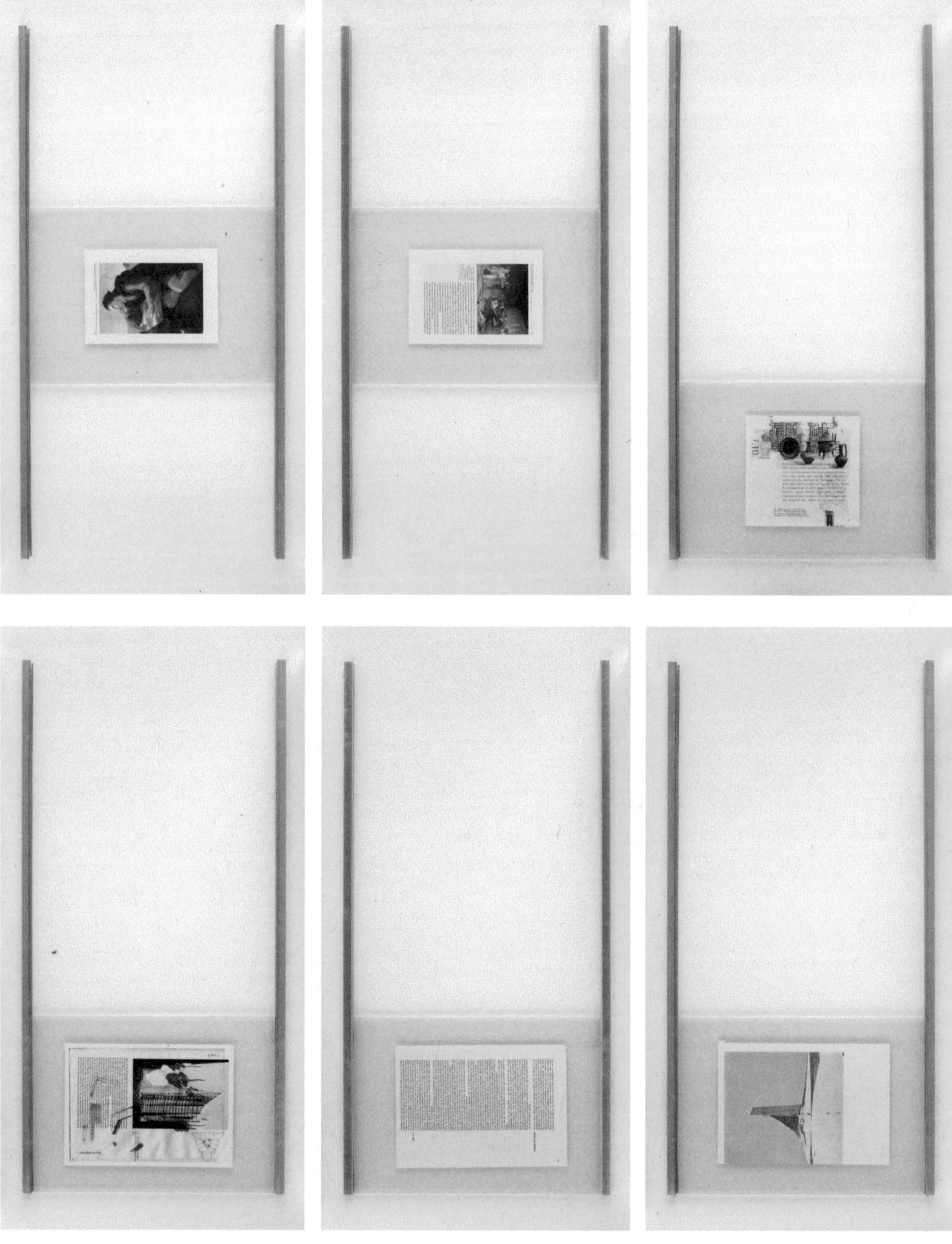

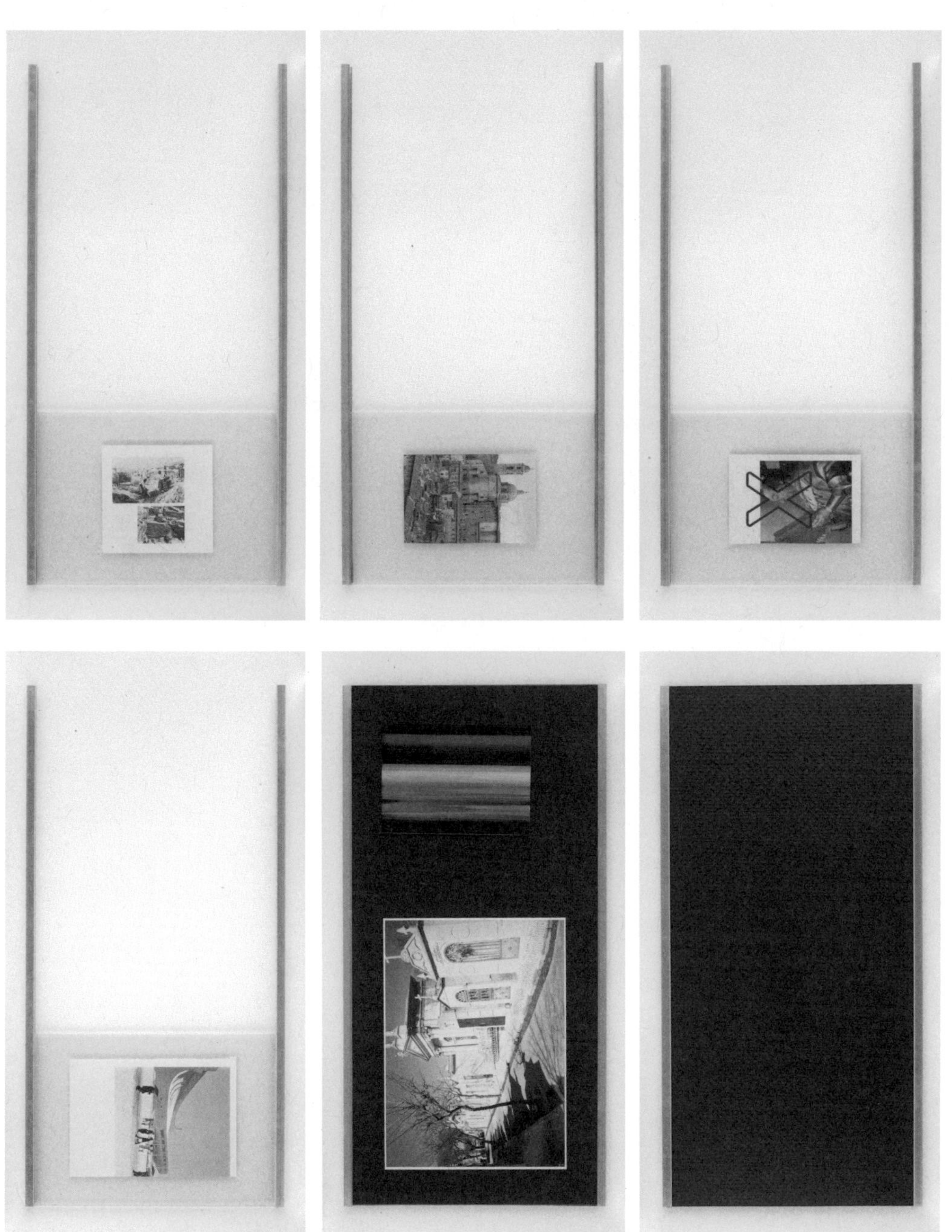

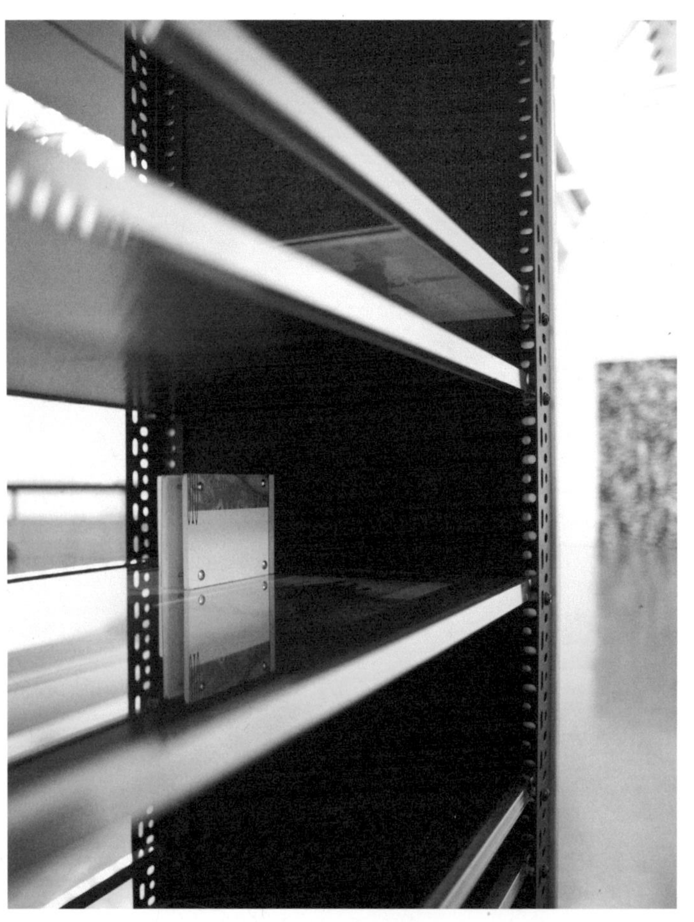

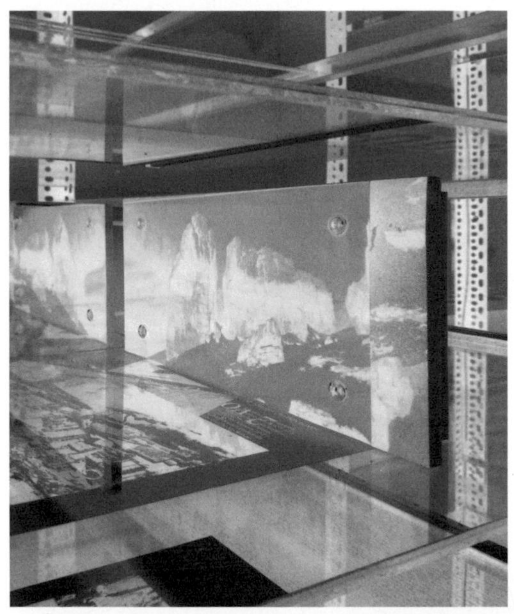

2

Dædalus Tower 1 & 2 (Europe)

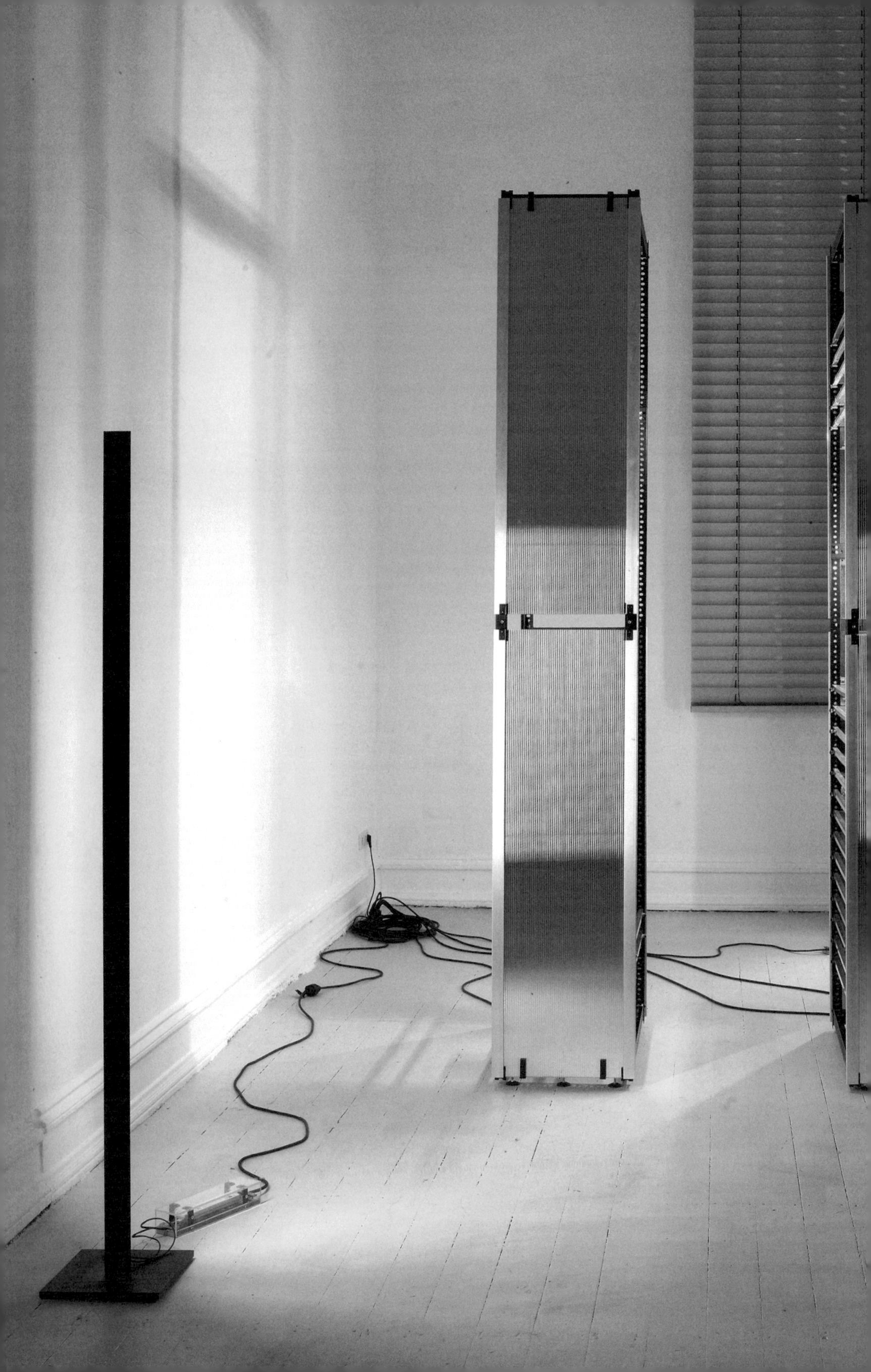

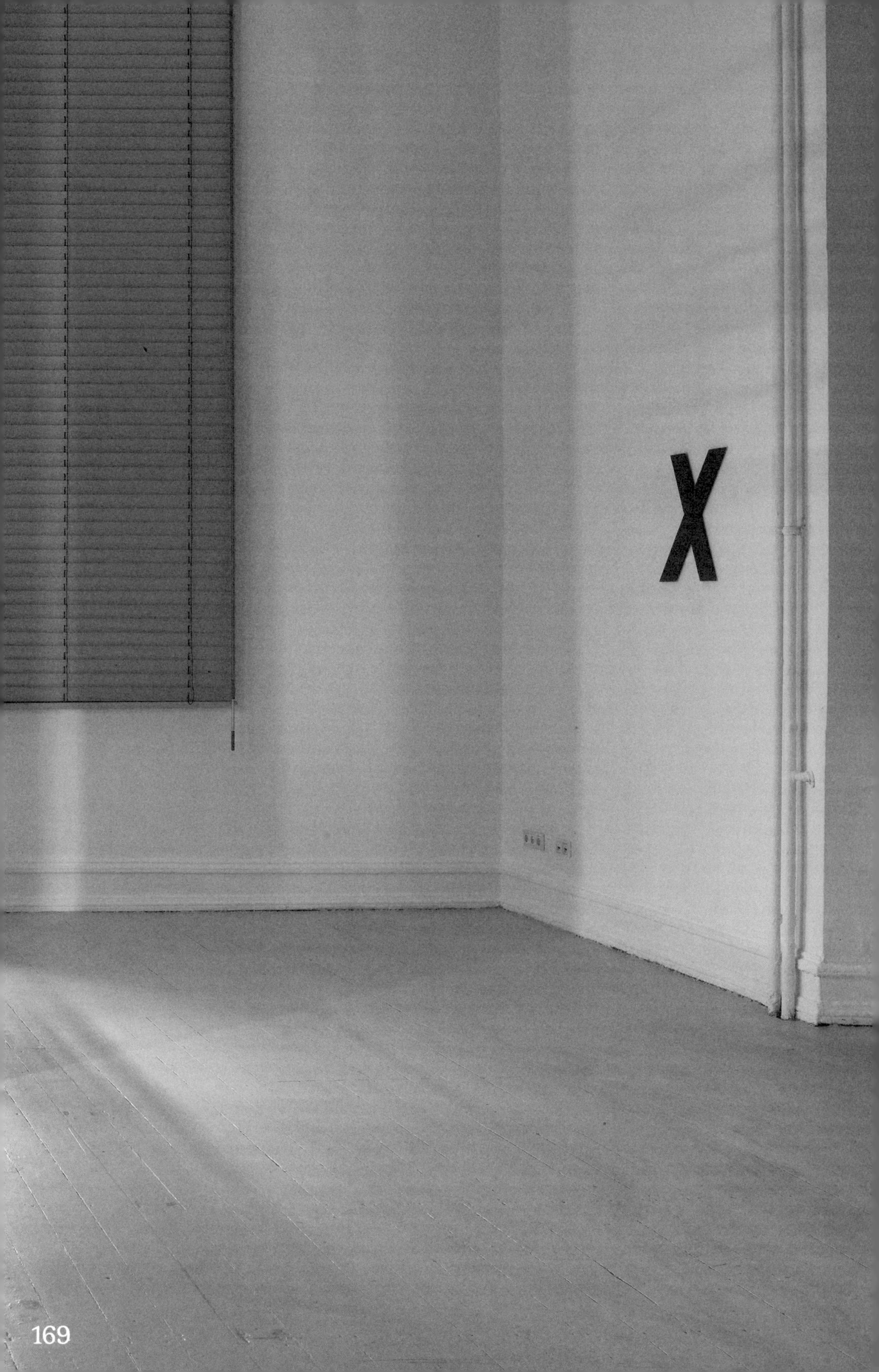
X

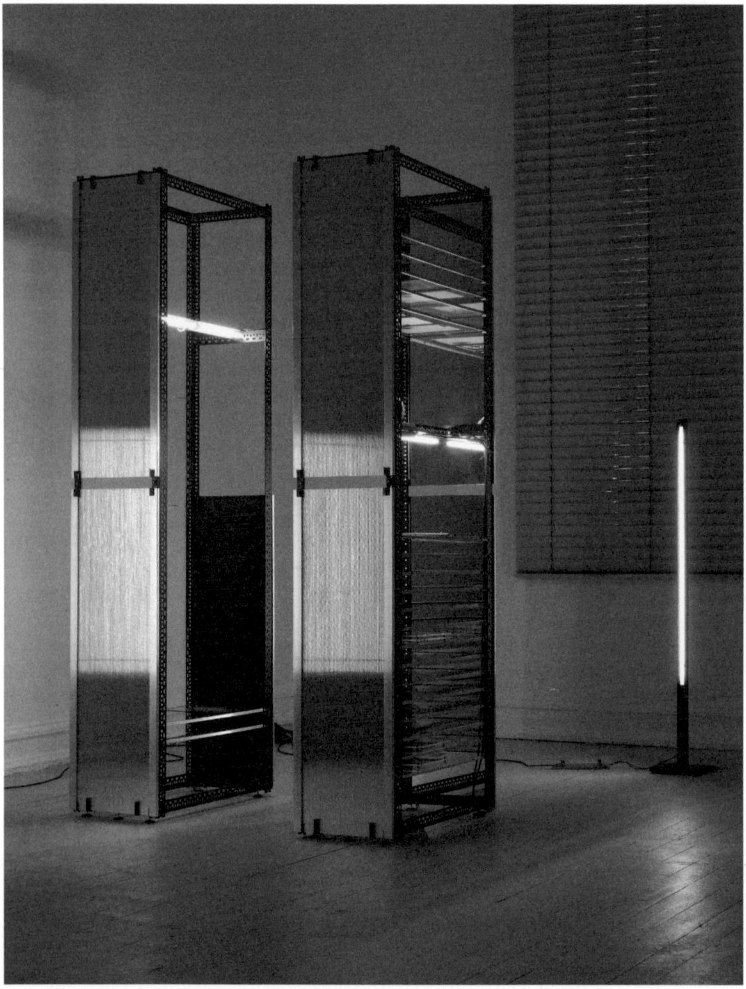

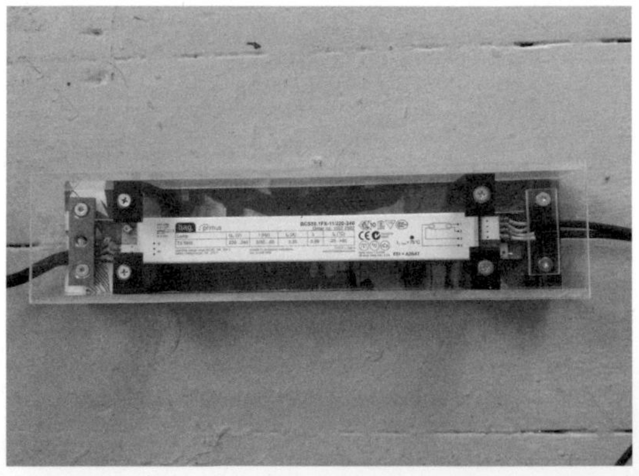

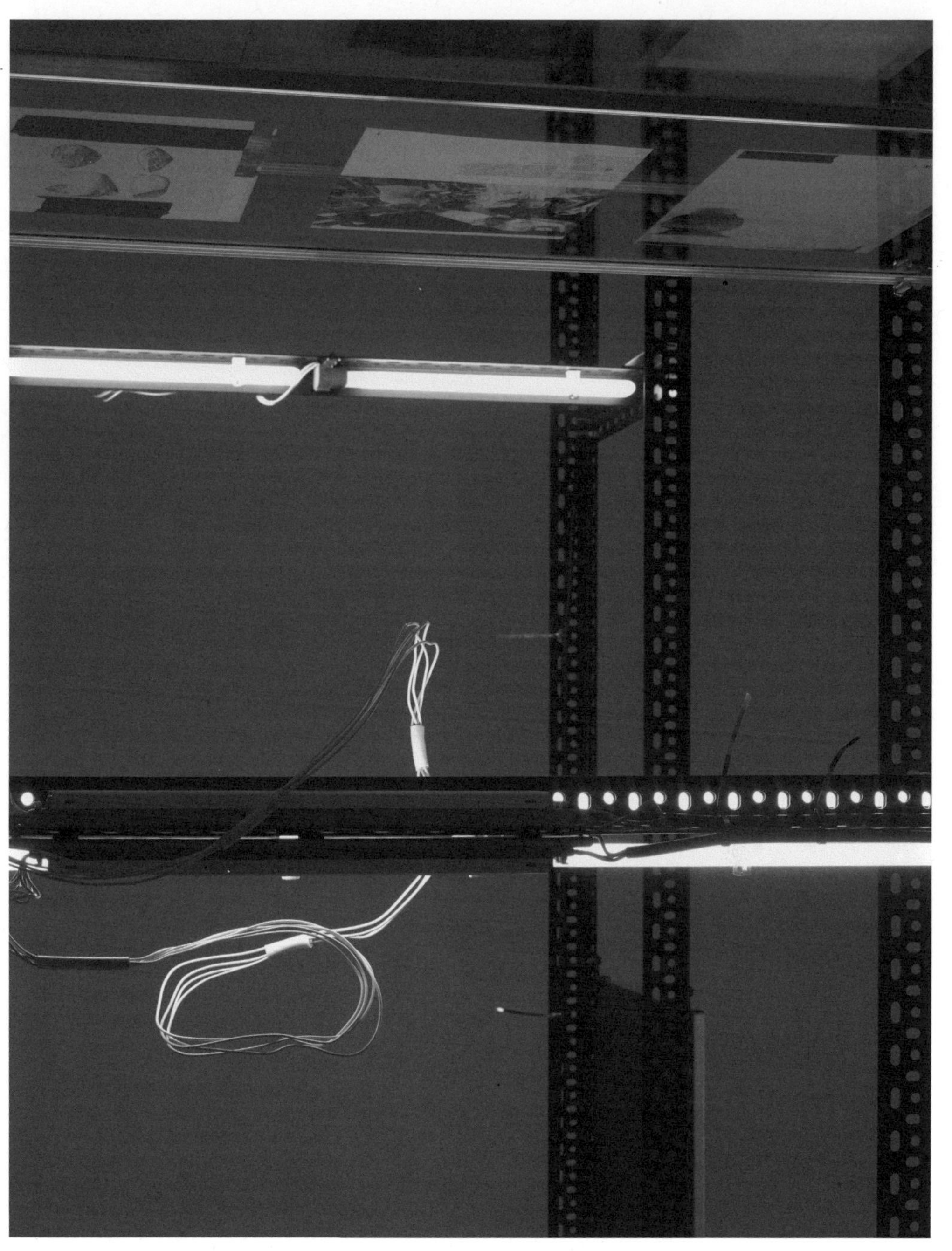

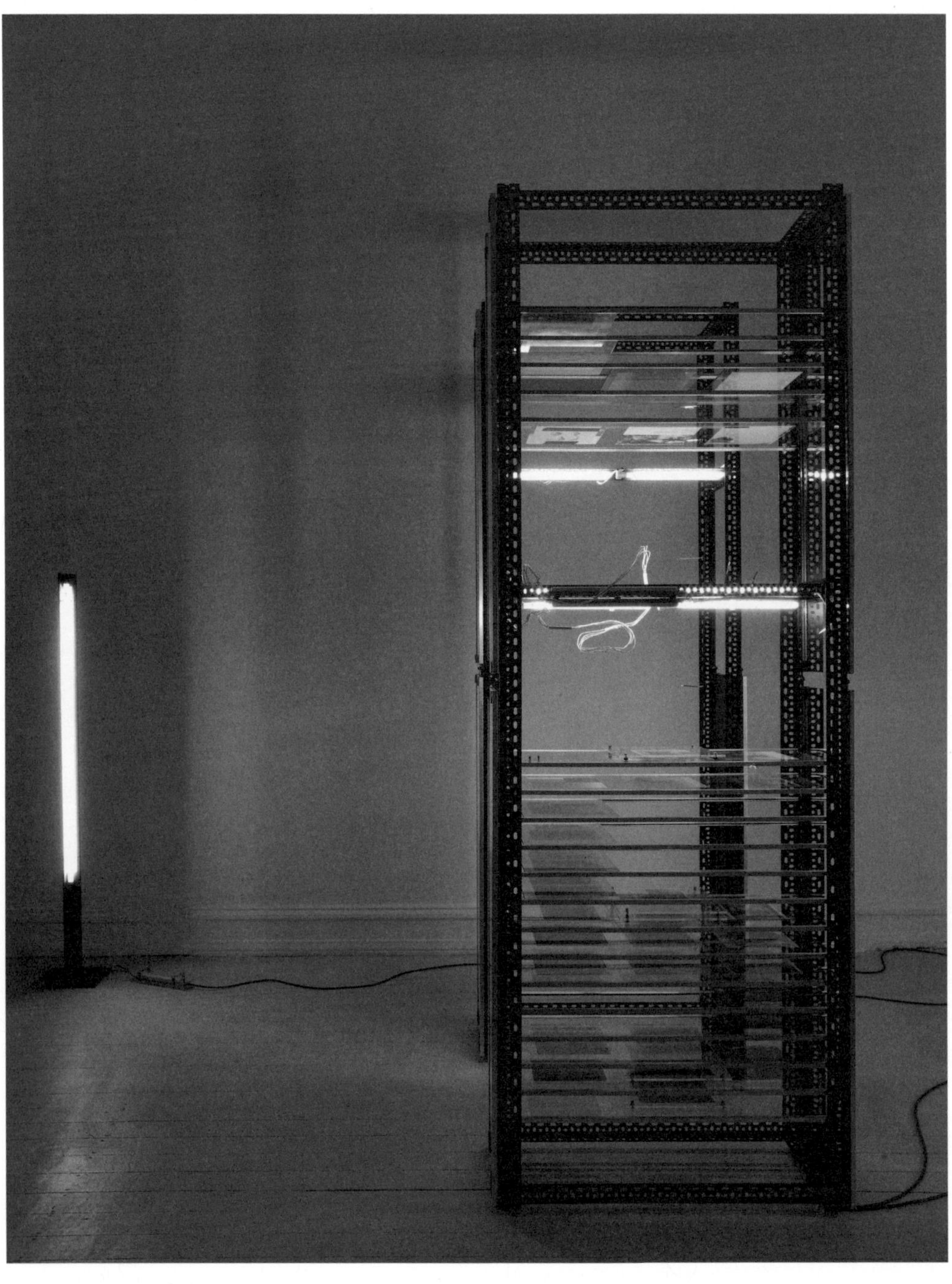

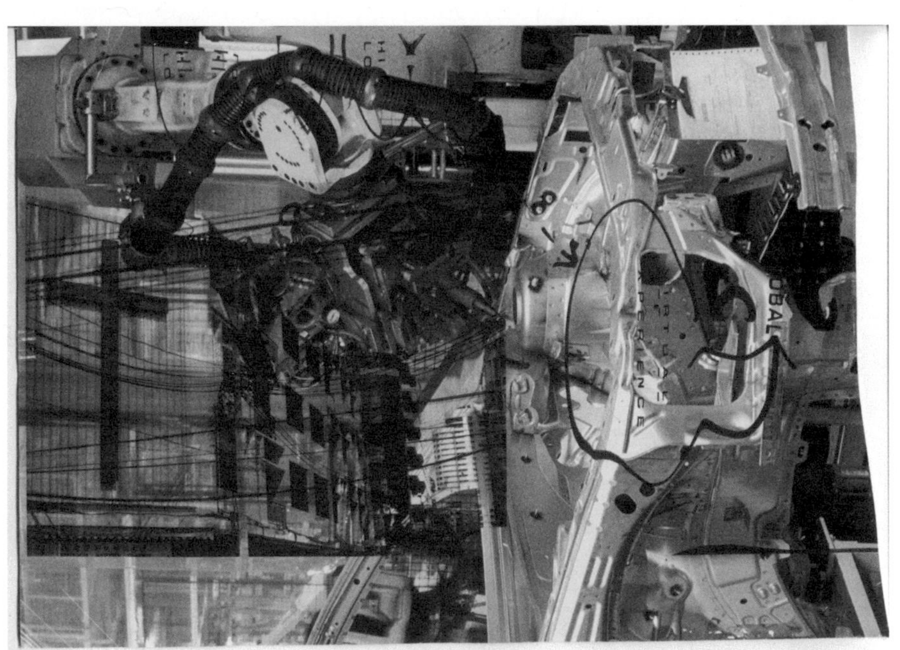

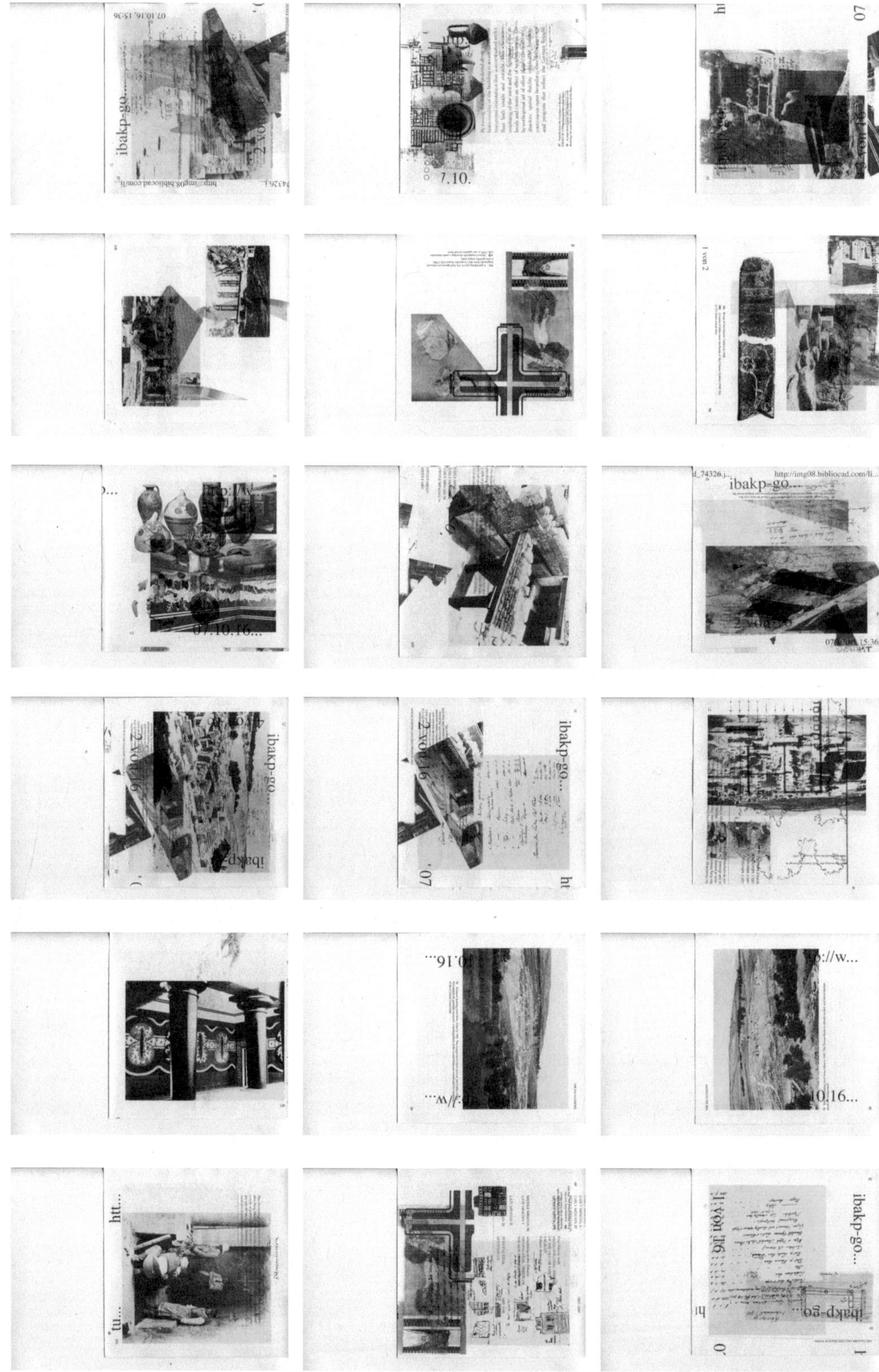

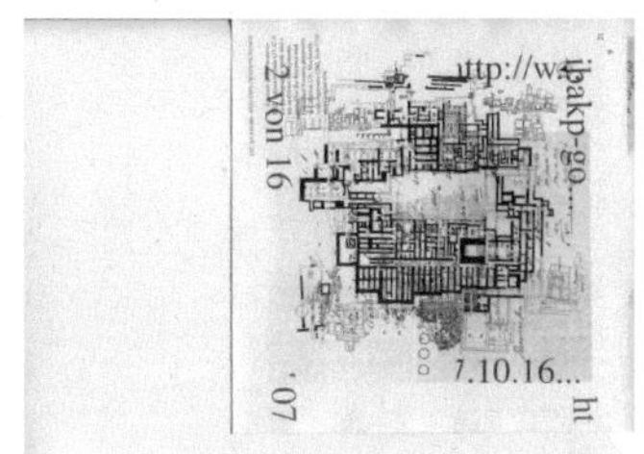
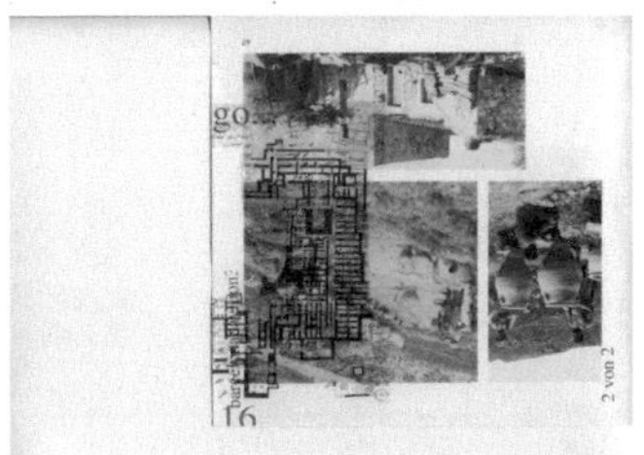
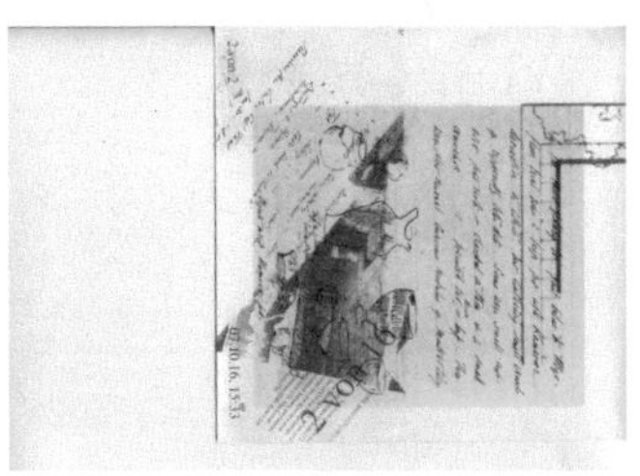
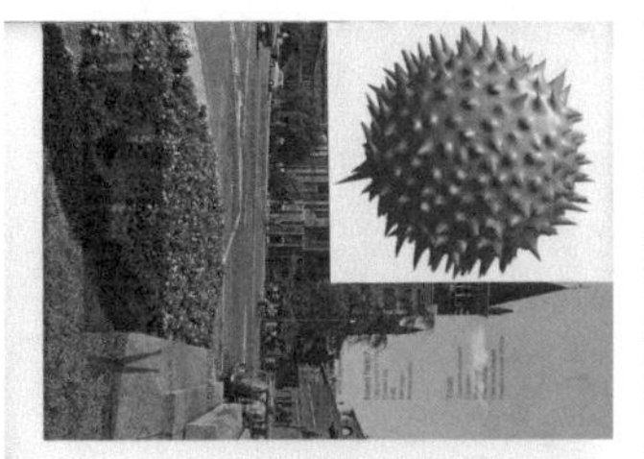
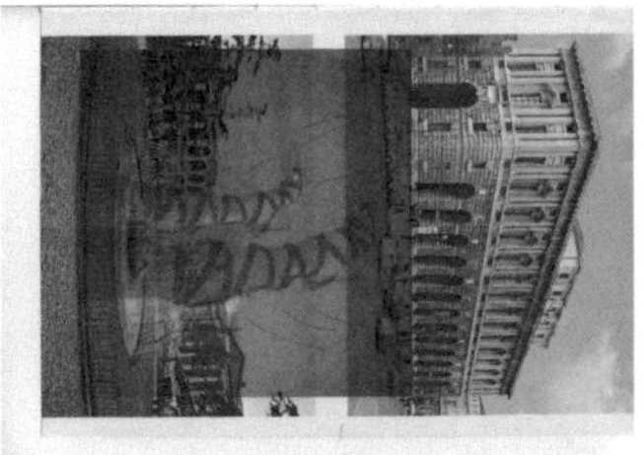
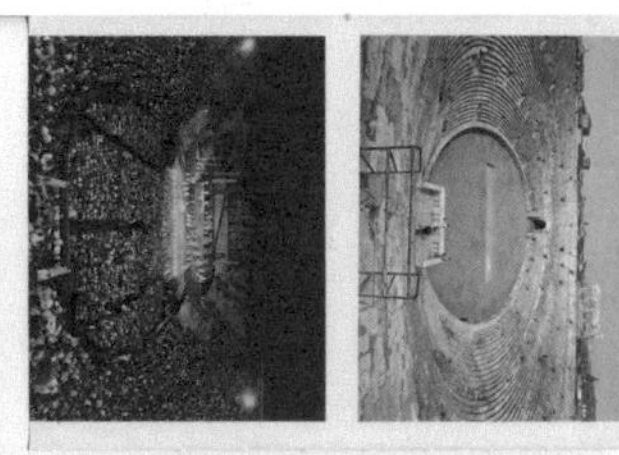
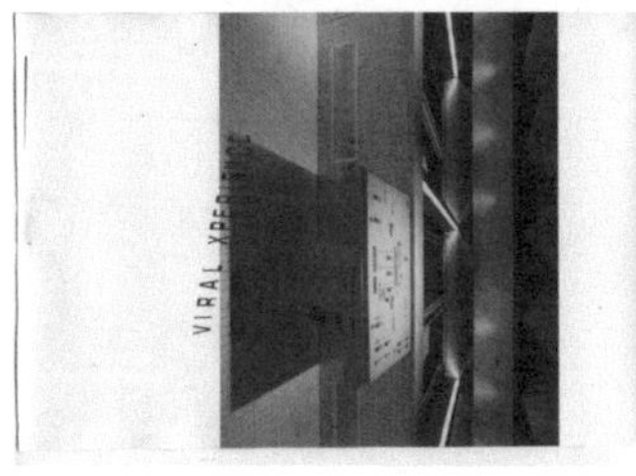
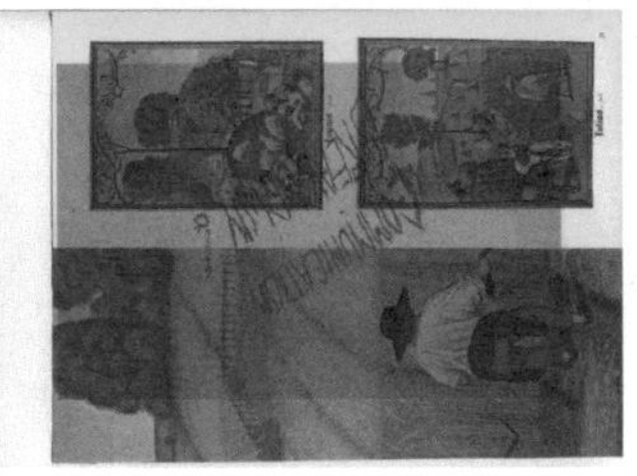
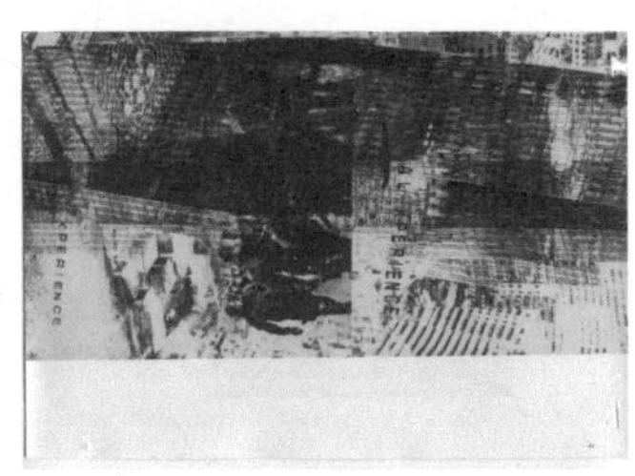
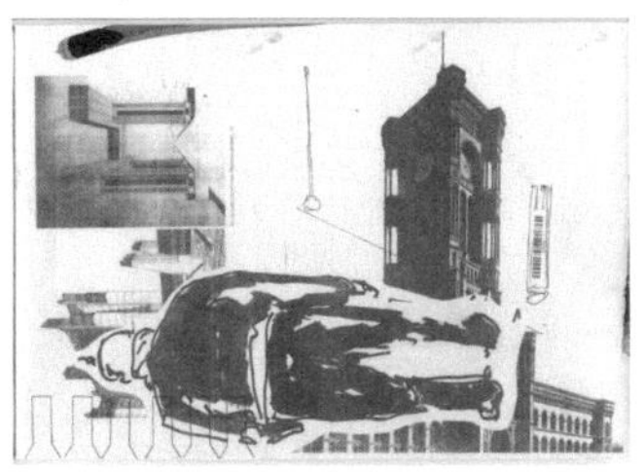
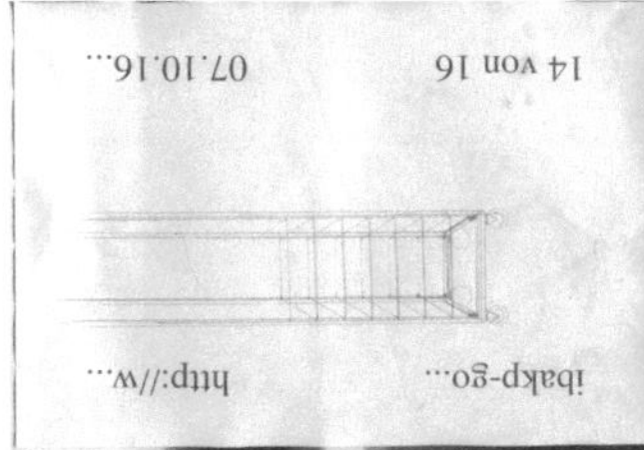
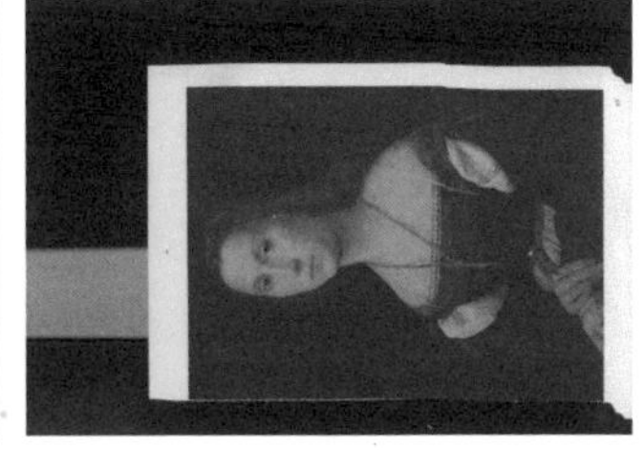
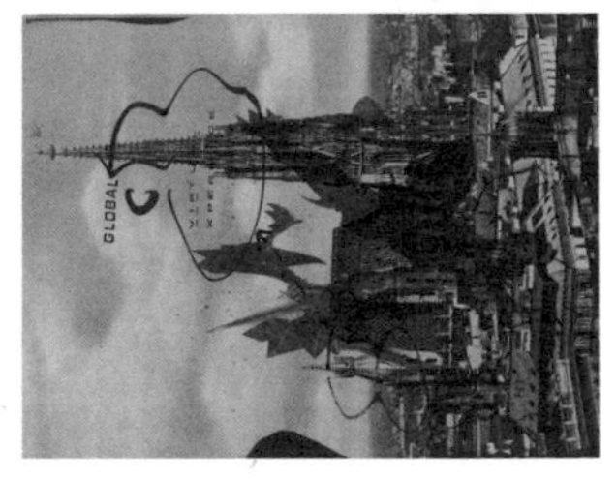
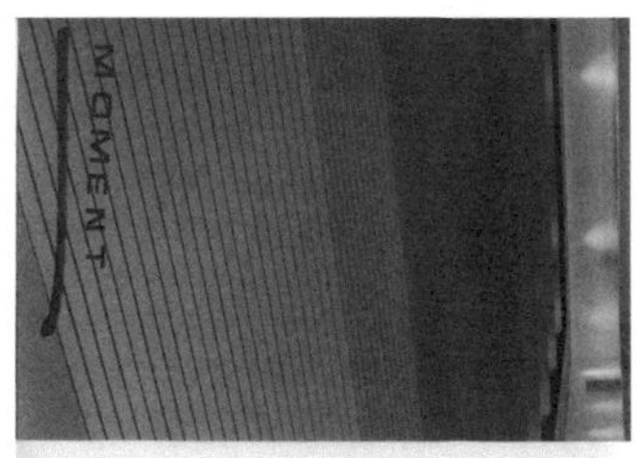

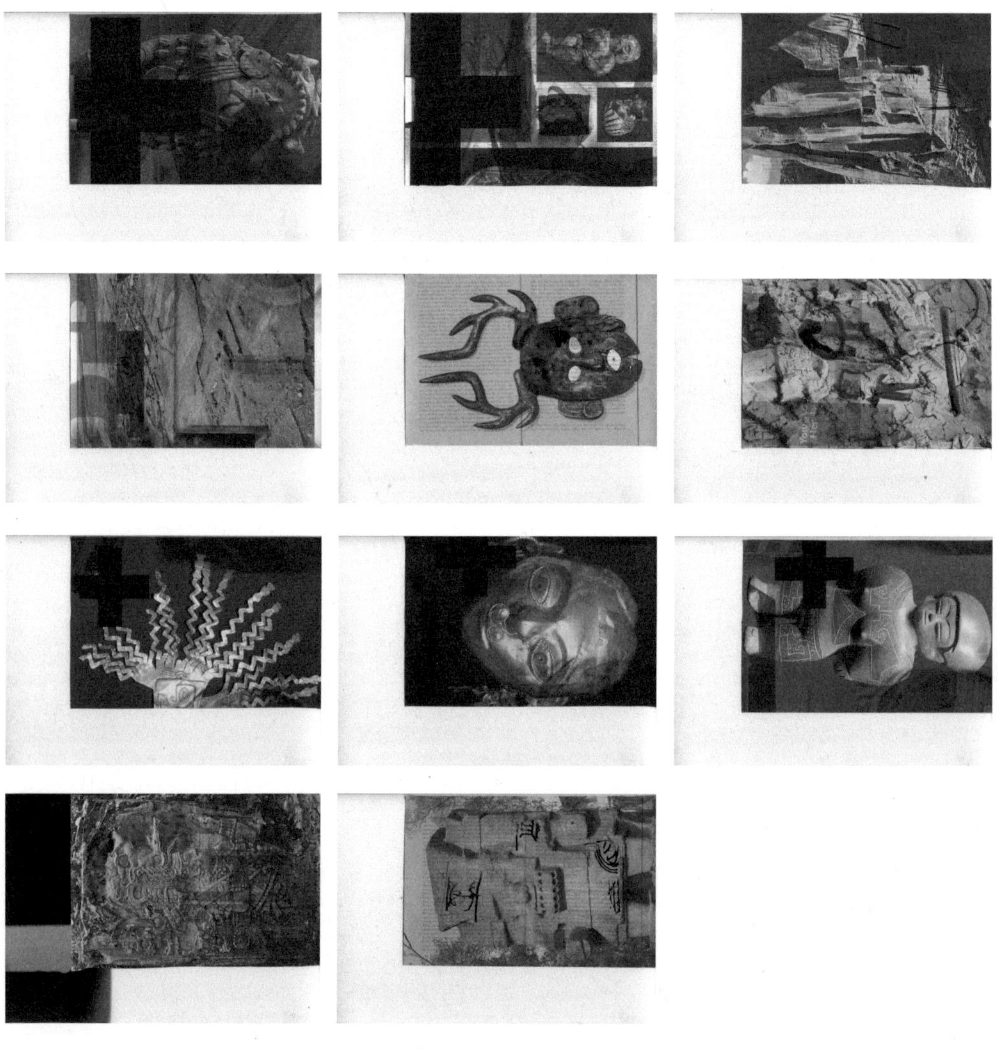

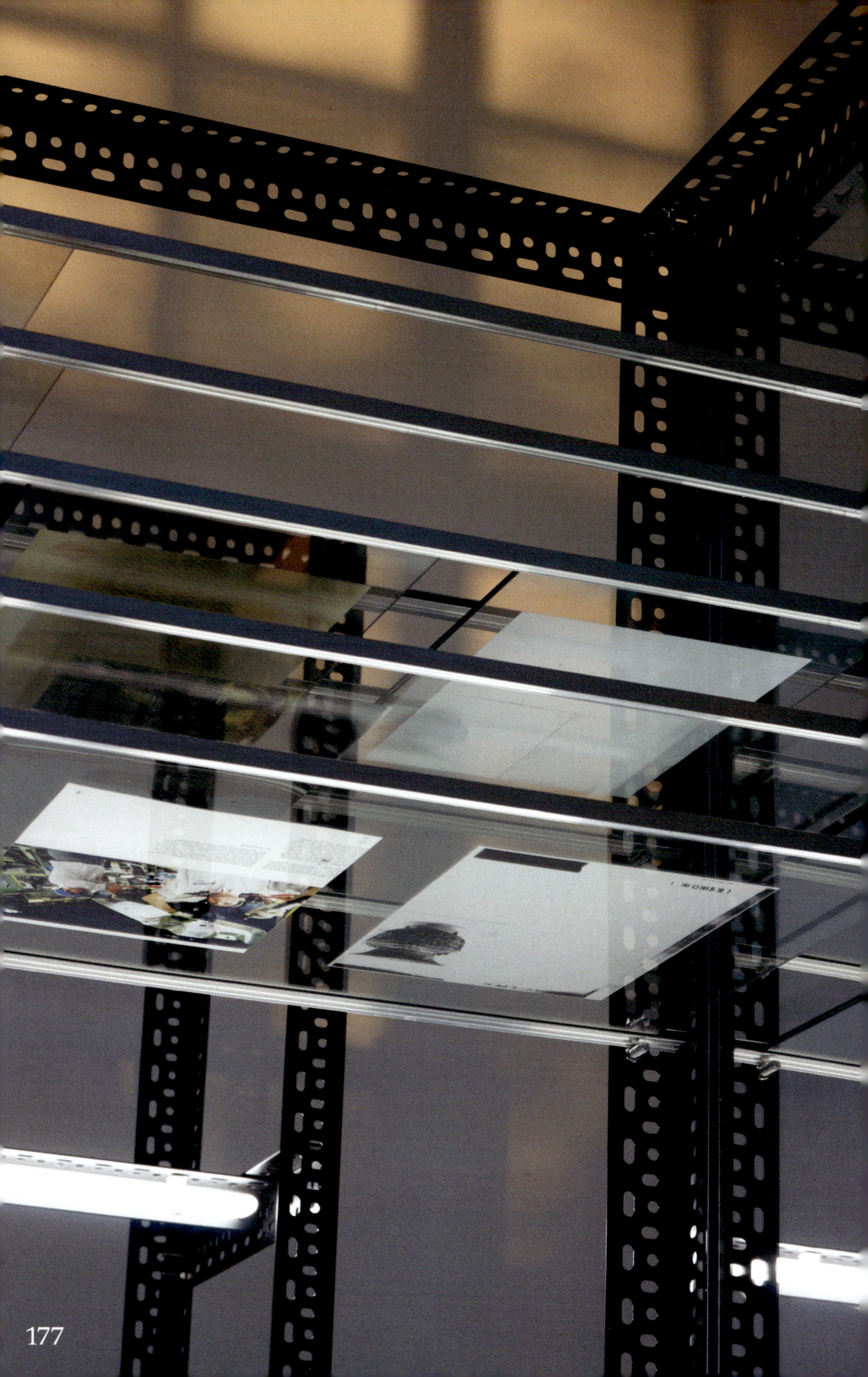

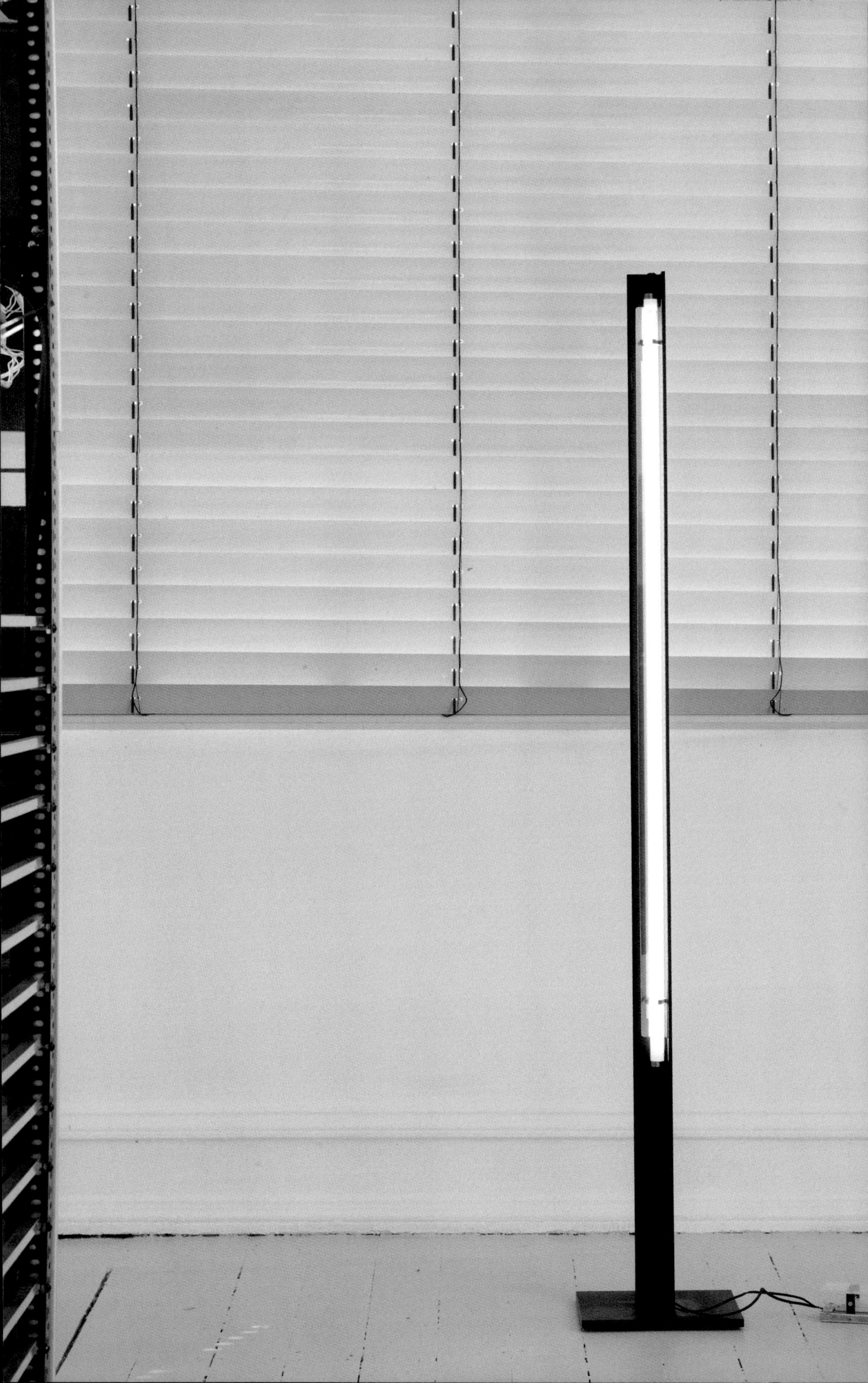

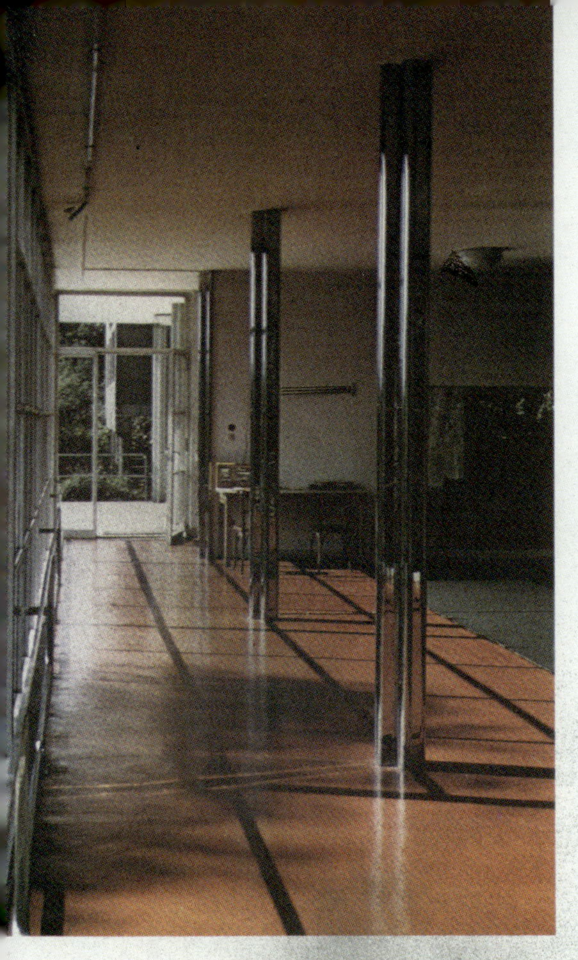

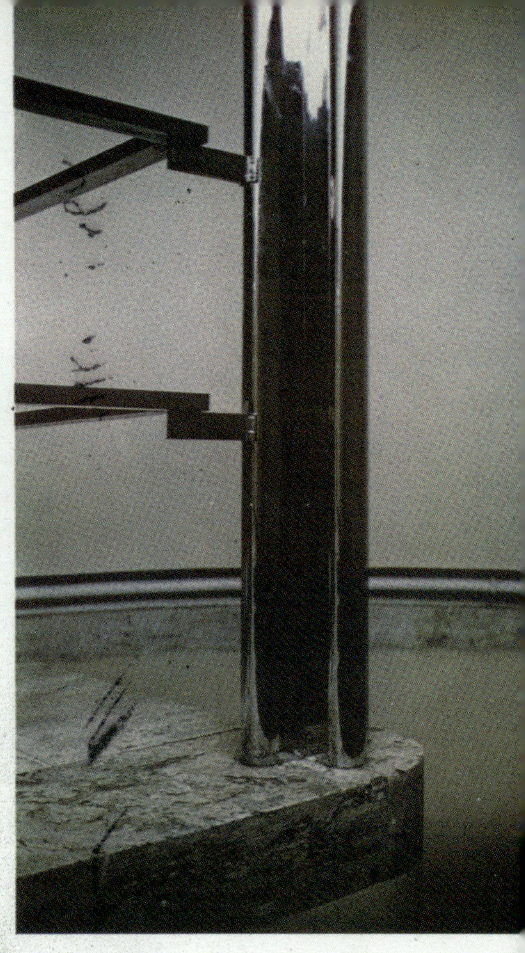

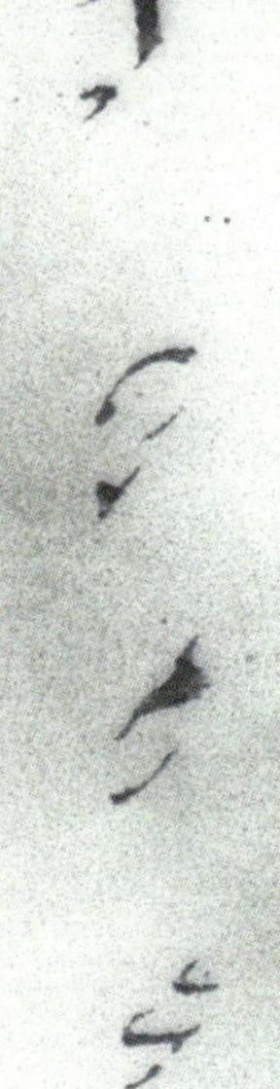

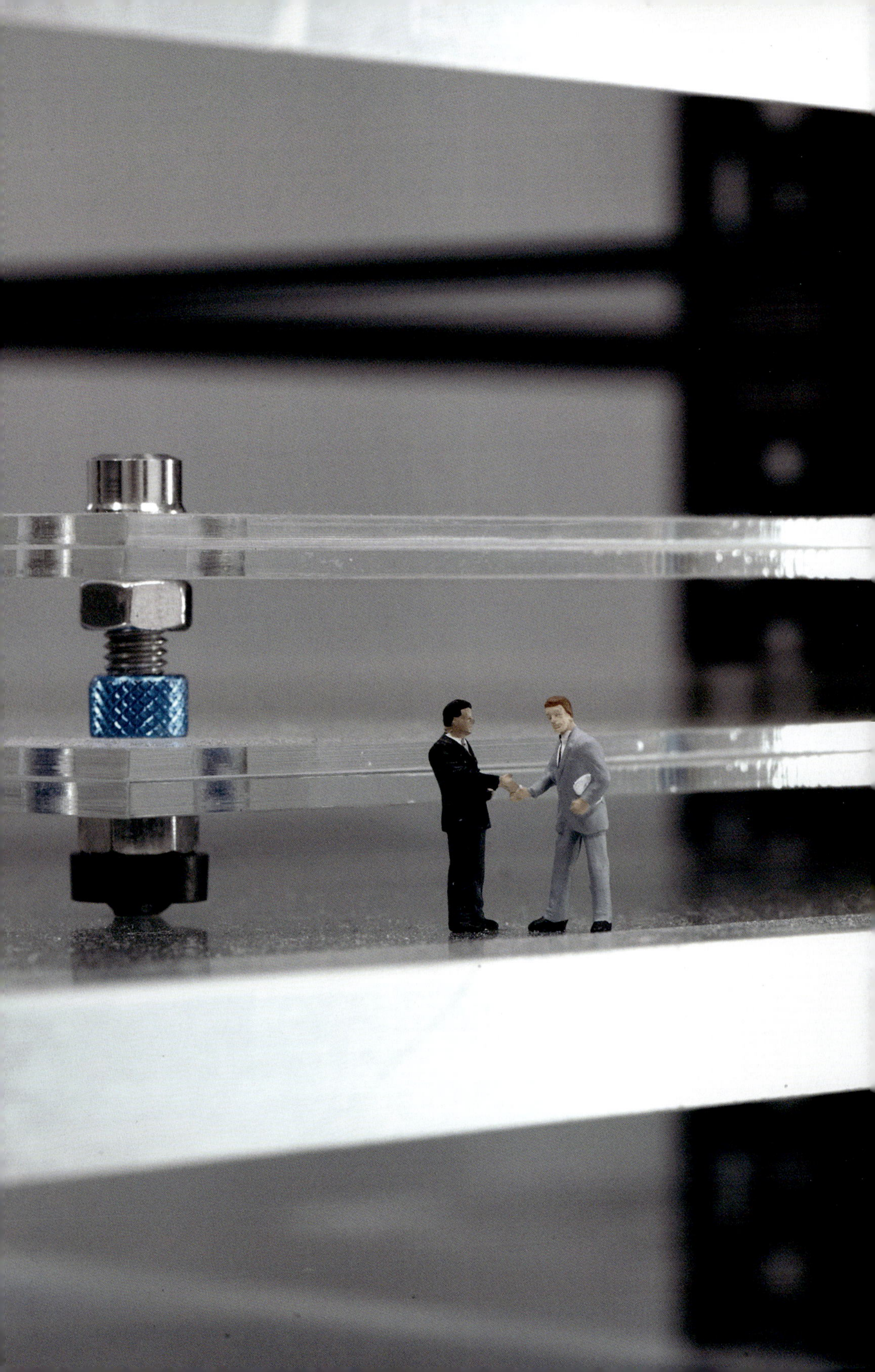

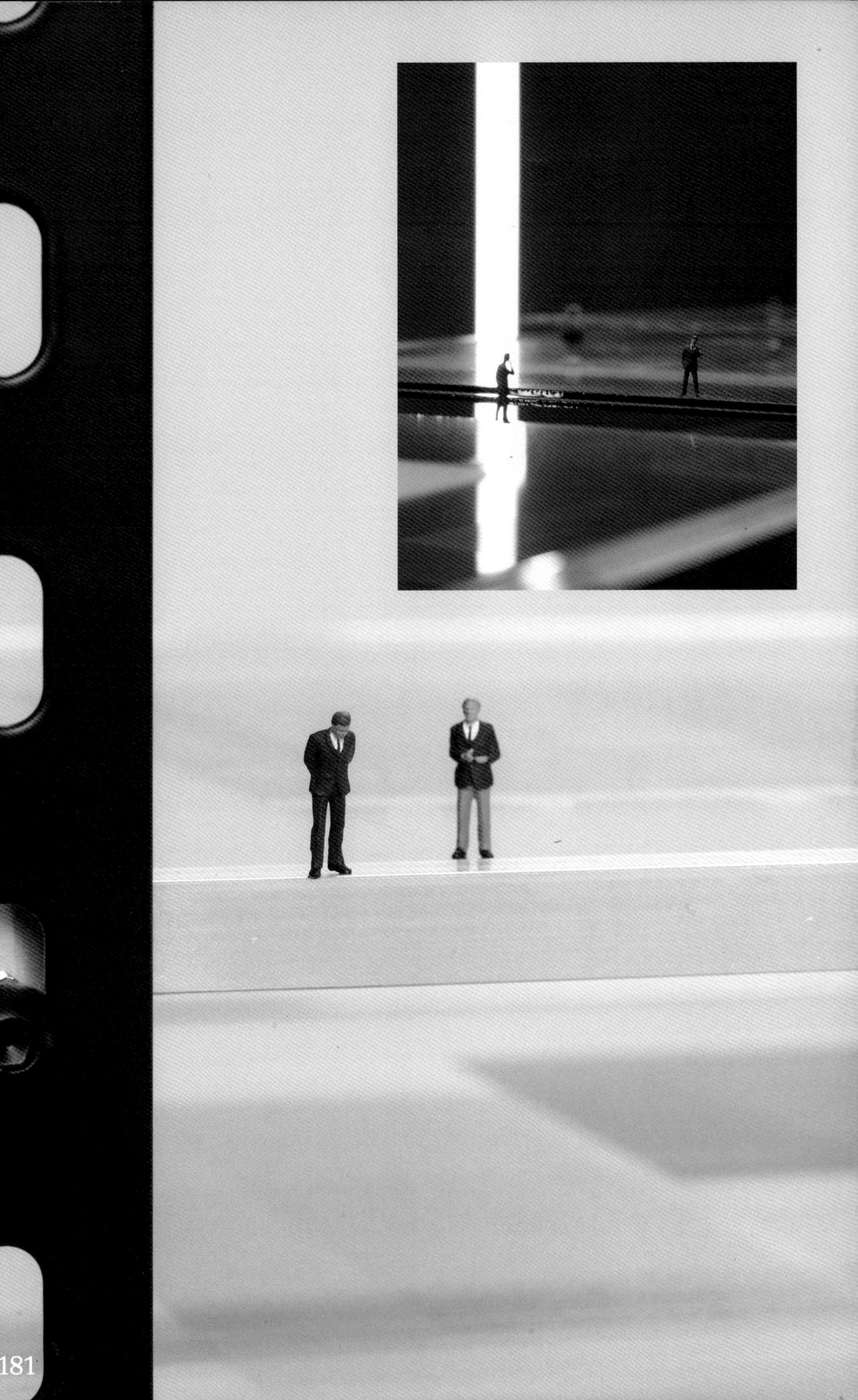

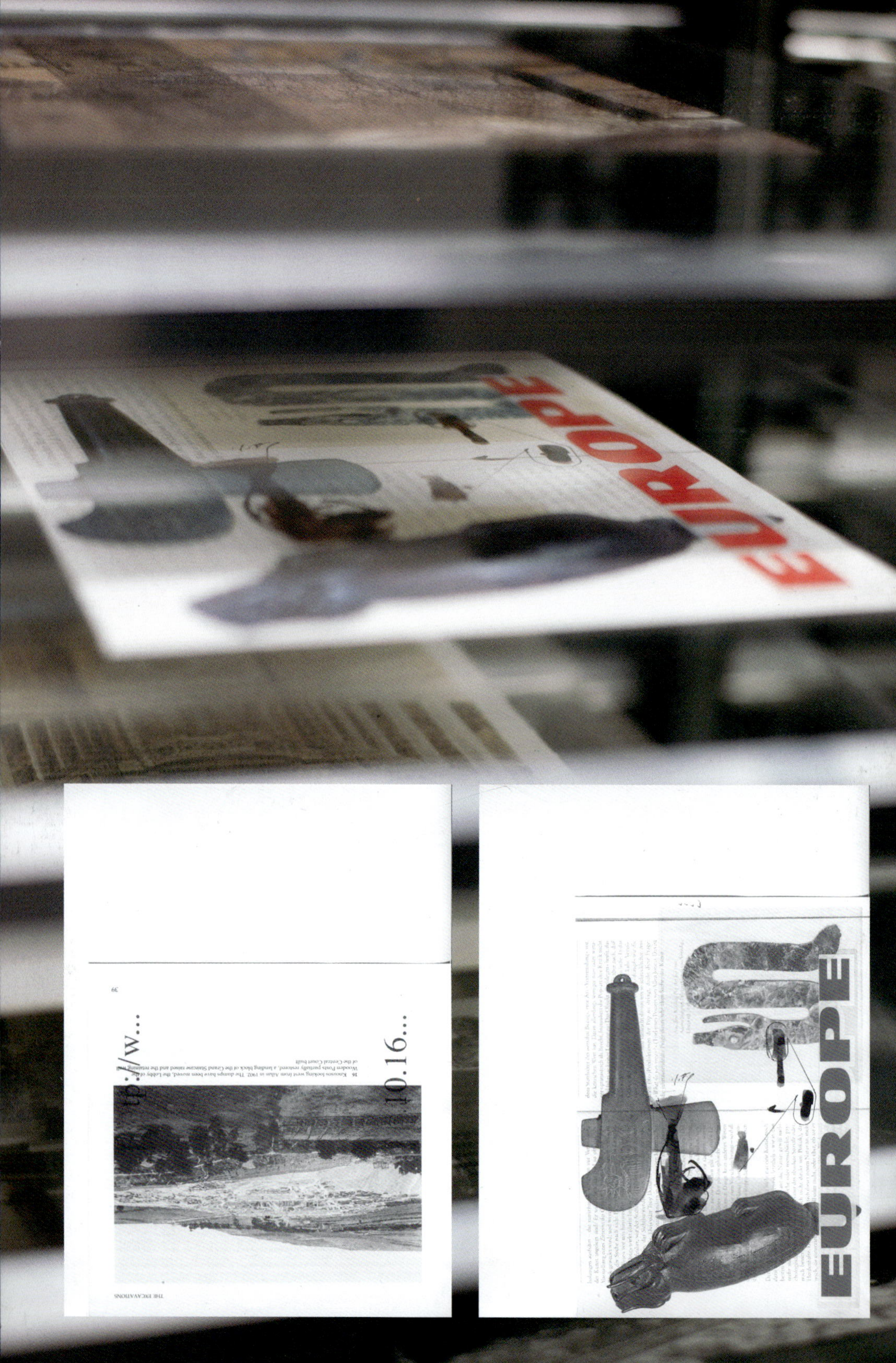

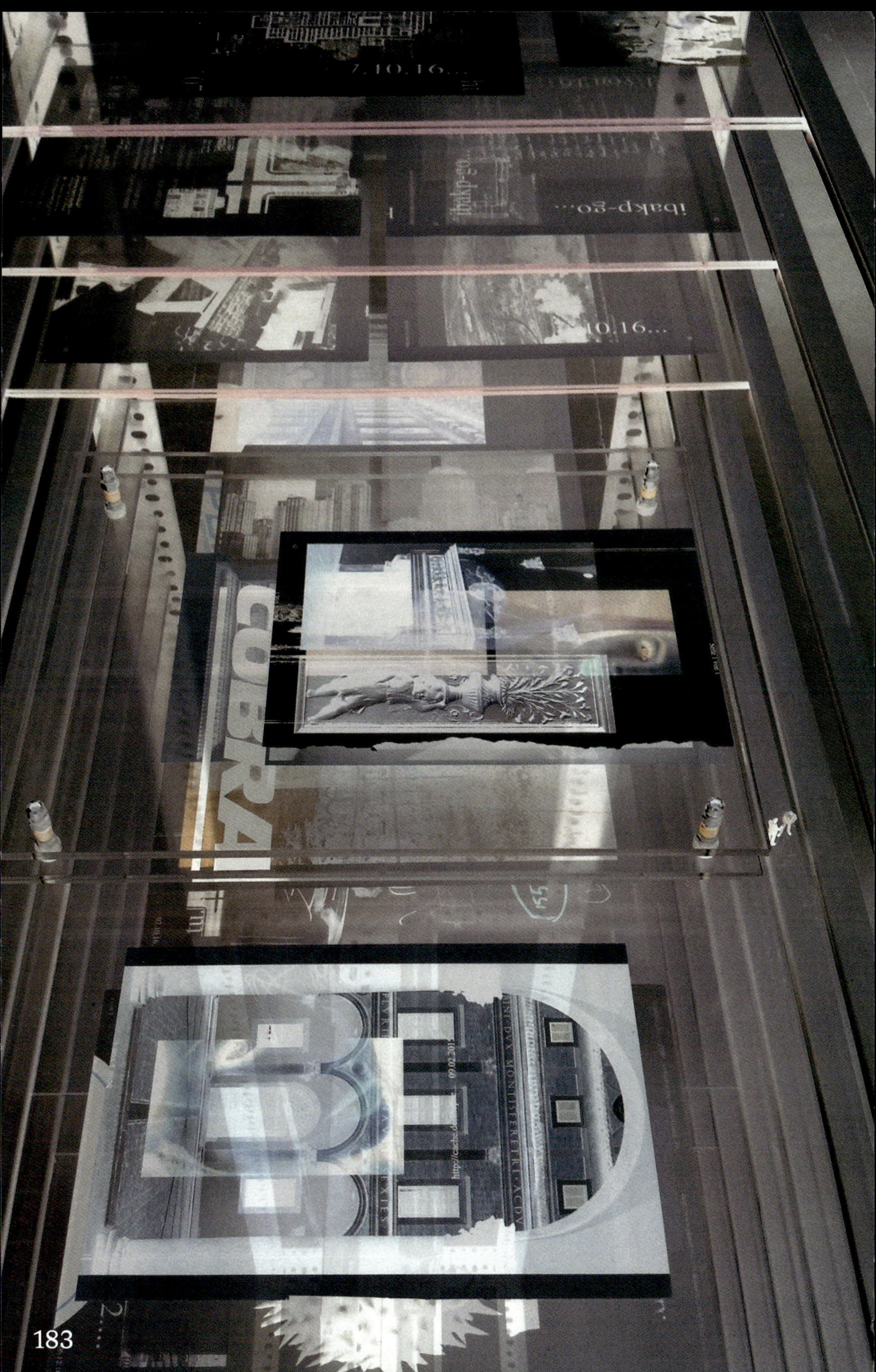

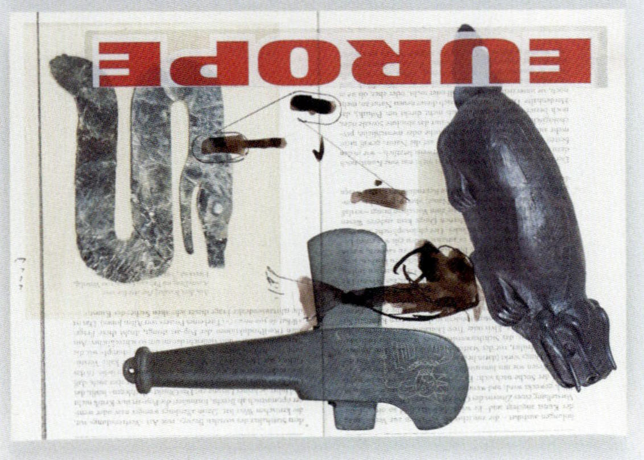
EUROPE

ibakp-go...
http://w...

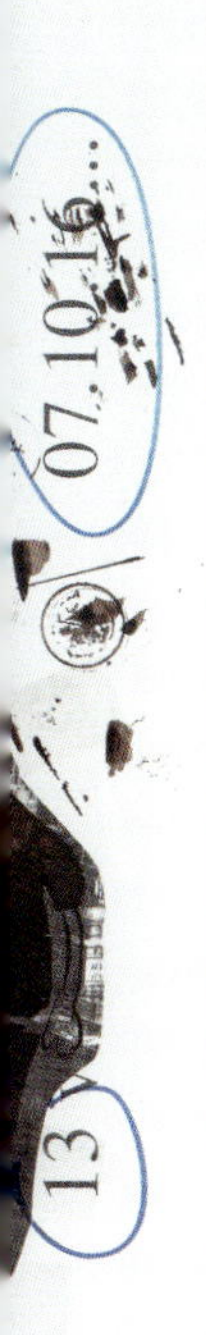

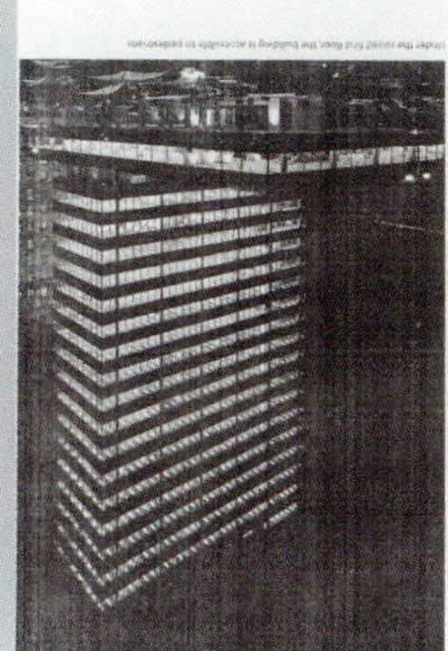

Under the raised first floor, the building is accessible to pedestrians

With Lever House, the headquarters of the detergent company Lever Brothers, one of the most influential design ideas in architectural history made its first appearance on Park Avenue in New York—the glass curtain wall facade. At the time of its construction, Lever House, viewed in the context of its surroundings (buildings still clad mainly in stone), seemed like a building from another civilization. The facade of alternating transparent green and opaque blue glass in an aluminum frame for the first time opened the view of the load-bearing structure of the interior to the outside. No longer is any tectonic articulation applied to the facade; it has been entirely dematerialized. Ludwig Mies van der Rohe's vision of the glass skyscraper of the 1920s had become a built reality. And Lever House also translated into reality another central lesson of architectural modernism: Le Corbusier's Piloti system. Standing entirely on supports above its own site, it creates new public space underneath, and allows the edge of the building experienced by pedestrians to disappear. The concepts of interior and exterior are thus radically called into question. In the center of the site's surface, where otherwise the elevator shafts and lobbies would have been, lies a garden, lit from above through an opening cut in a rectangular shape. This further underlines the building's aspect of bodilessness and the removal of borders.

The use of the surface of the site by Lever House was extravagant. The slender, rectangular office tower of only 18 stories is placed at an angle at the north edge of the site which itself floats above the one-story, panel-shaped distribution area on the first floor. However, this positioning enabled the adoption of a new zoning provision, according to which a building could be constructed without any set-backs, if it occupied only twenty-five percent of the surface of the site. This leaves a large part of the space available for construction unused, but the structure can be designed as a perfect cube. In this way Lever House anticipated by several years the idea of the nearby Seagram Building by Ludwig Mies van der Rohe (p. 66).

The detergent company Lever wanted this building, which was originally intended for Chicago but then for strategic reasons transferred to New York, to project an innovative and "clean" image. Gordon Bunshaft, as designer in the office of Skidmore, Owings & Merrill, realized this idea in exemplary fashion. Apart from the outwardly recognizable innovations, Lever House was also the first skyscraper to be fully air-conditioned; as a result, the windows could no longer be opened. To enable the facade to be cleaned, movable window-cleaning cabins running on tracks on the roof were invented, and these were later adopted throughout the world.

In Lever House, the modernist idea of the glass cube as an absolute, autonomous form without any formal reference to its urban context was realized in a totally logical manner. As such, it marks a decisive turning point in the history of high-rise construction: on the one hand, early utopias of modernism find a satisfying conclusion in this building; while on the other, it also points the way into the abyss of shallow plagiarism throughout the world.

302 feet
92 meters

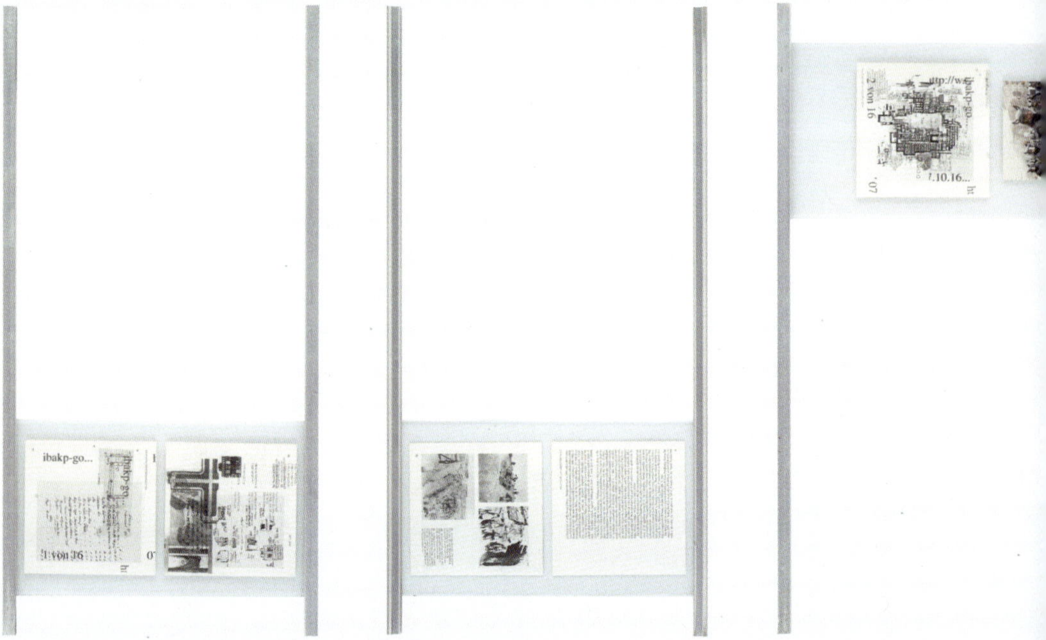

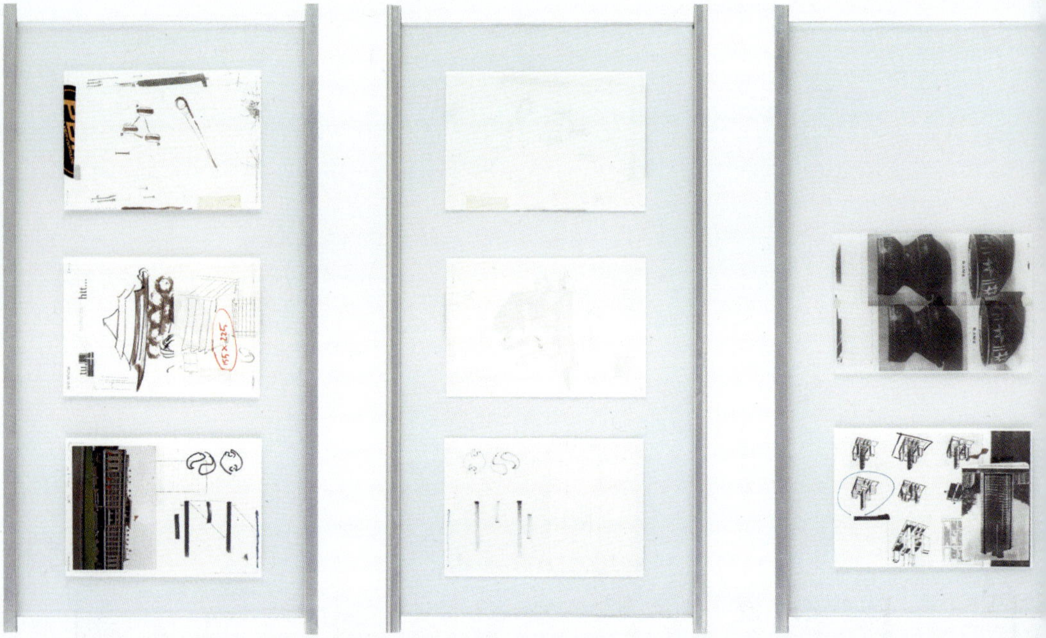

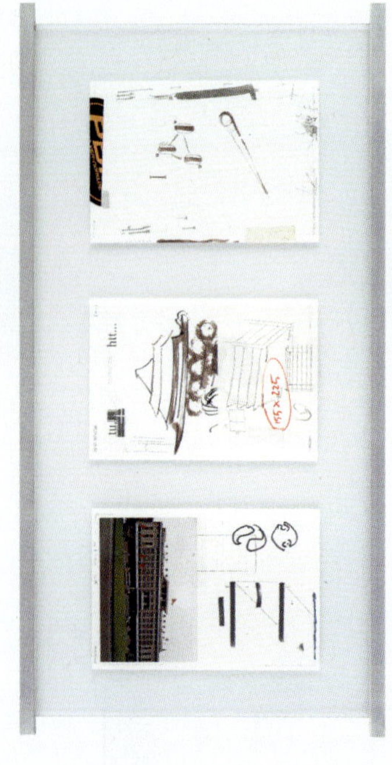

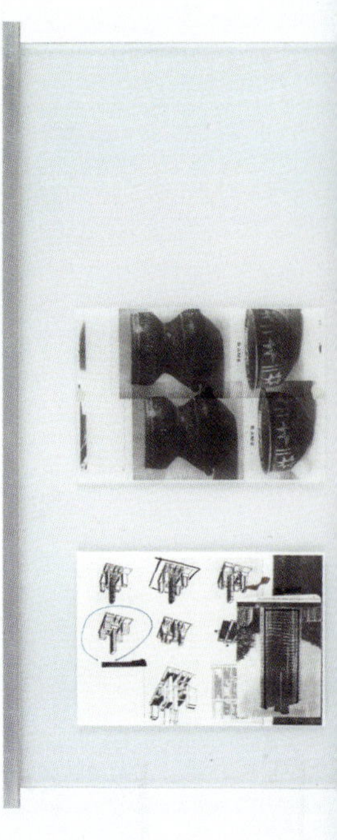

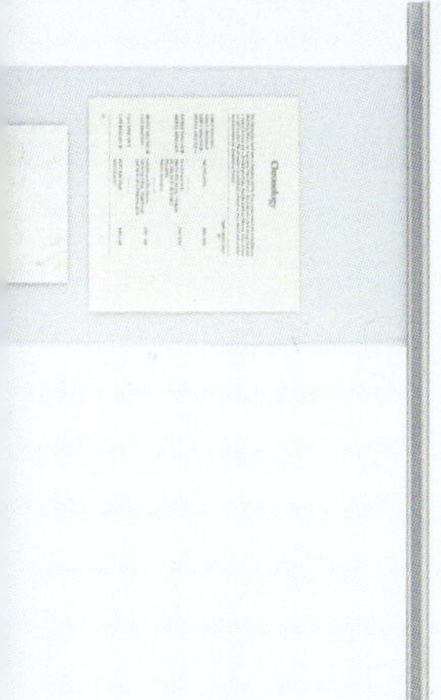
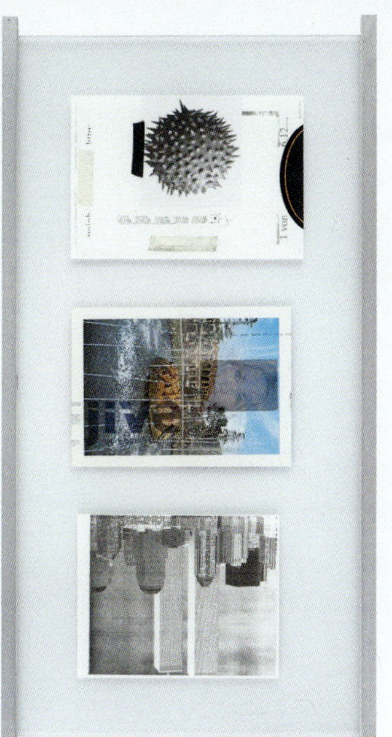
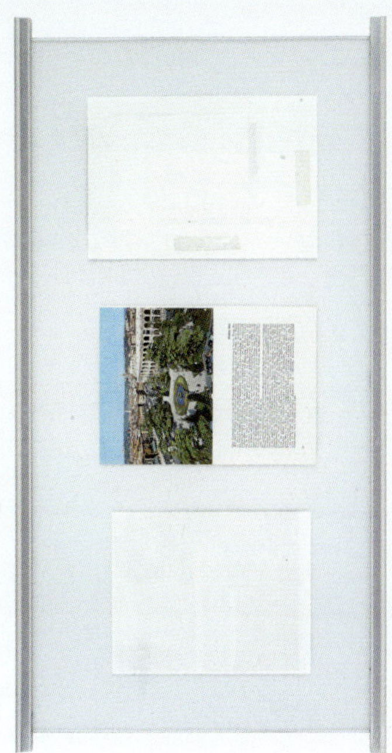
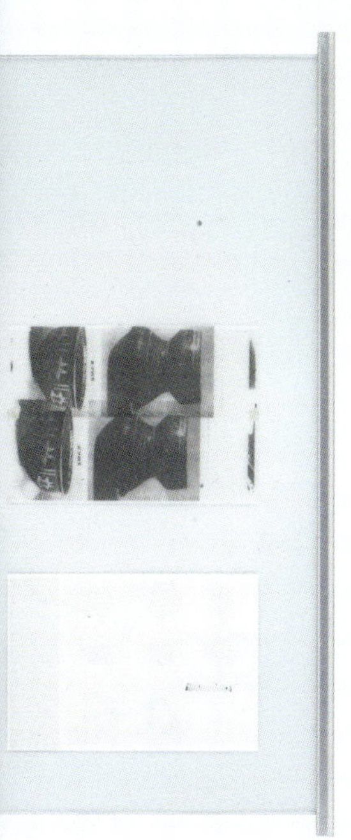
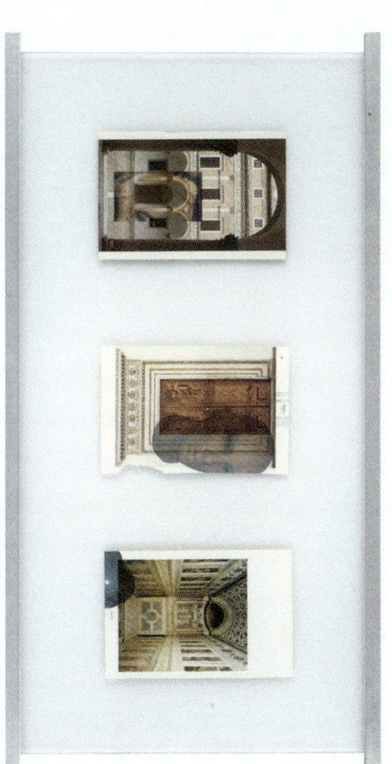
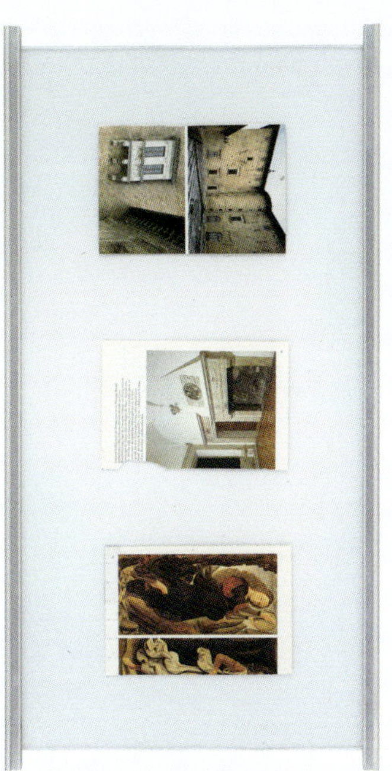

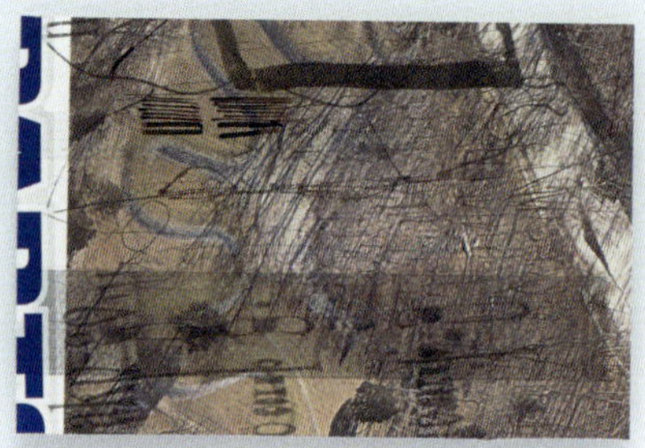

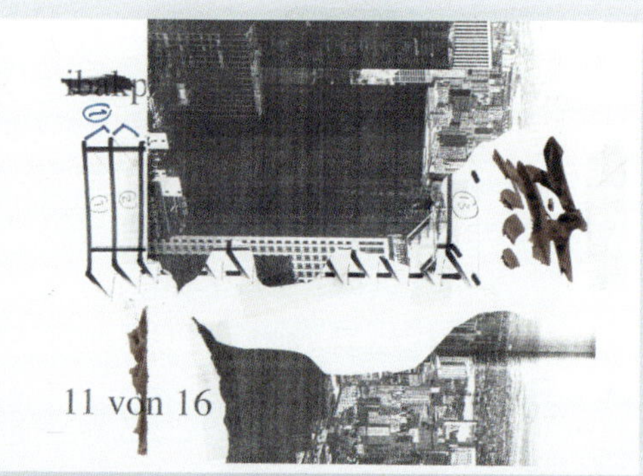

11 von 16

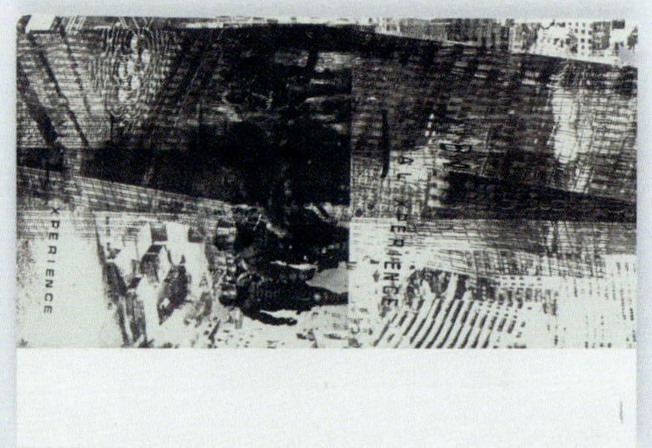

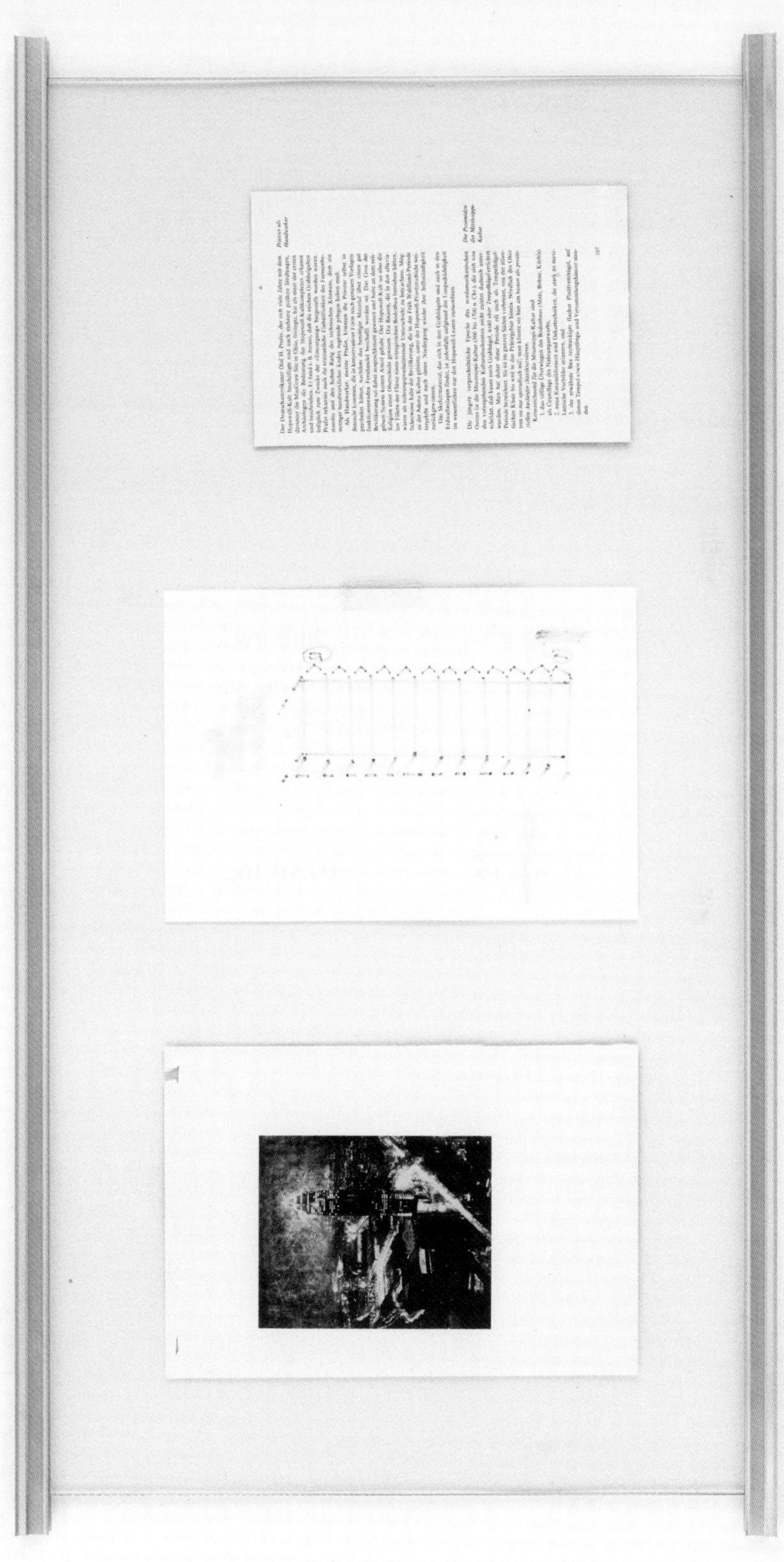

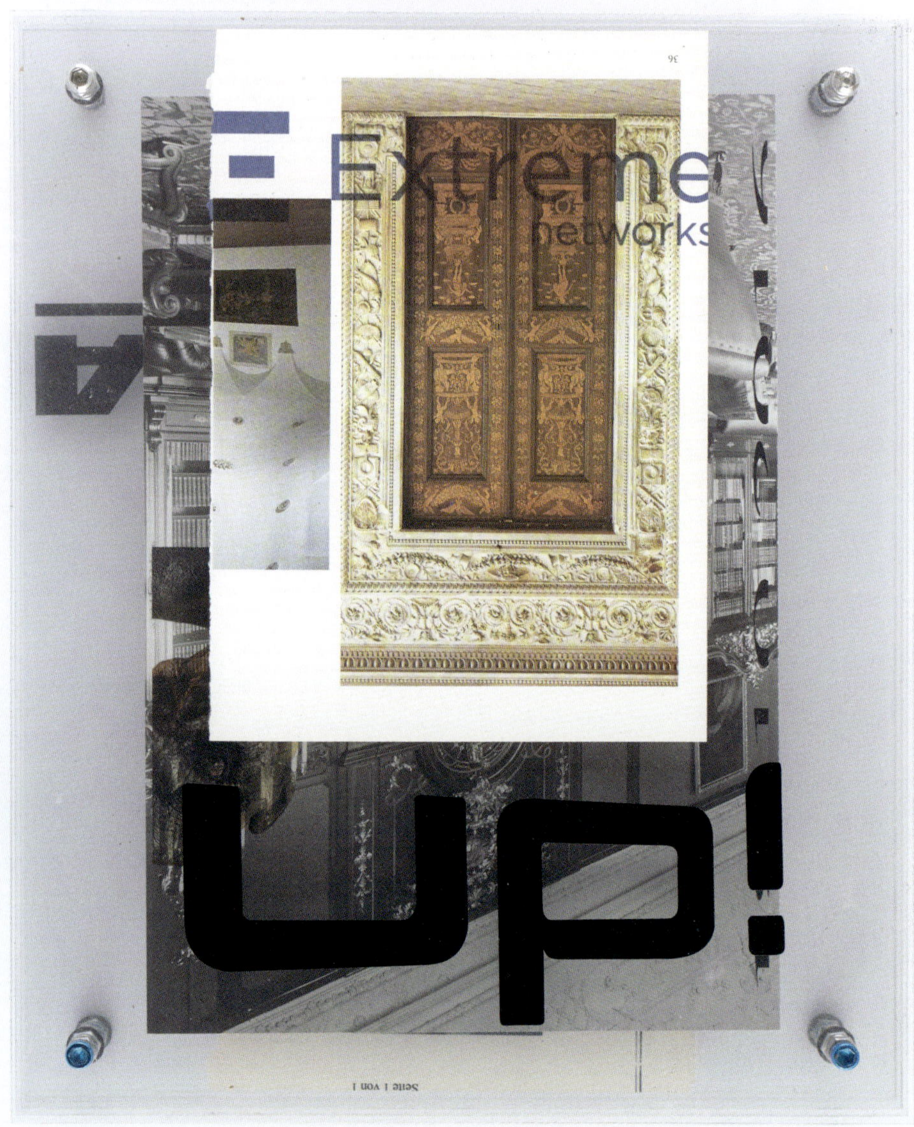
Extreme
networks
Up!

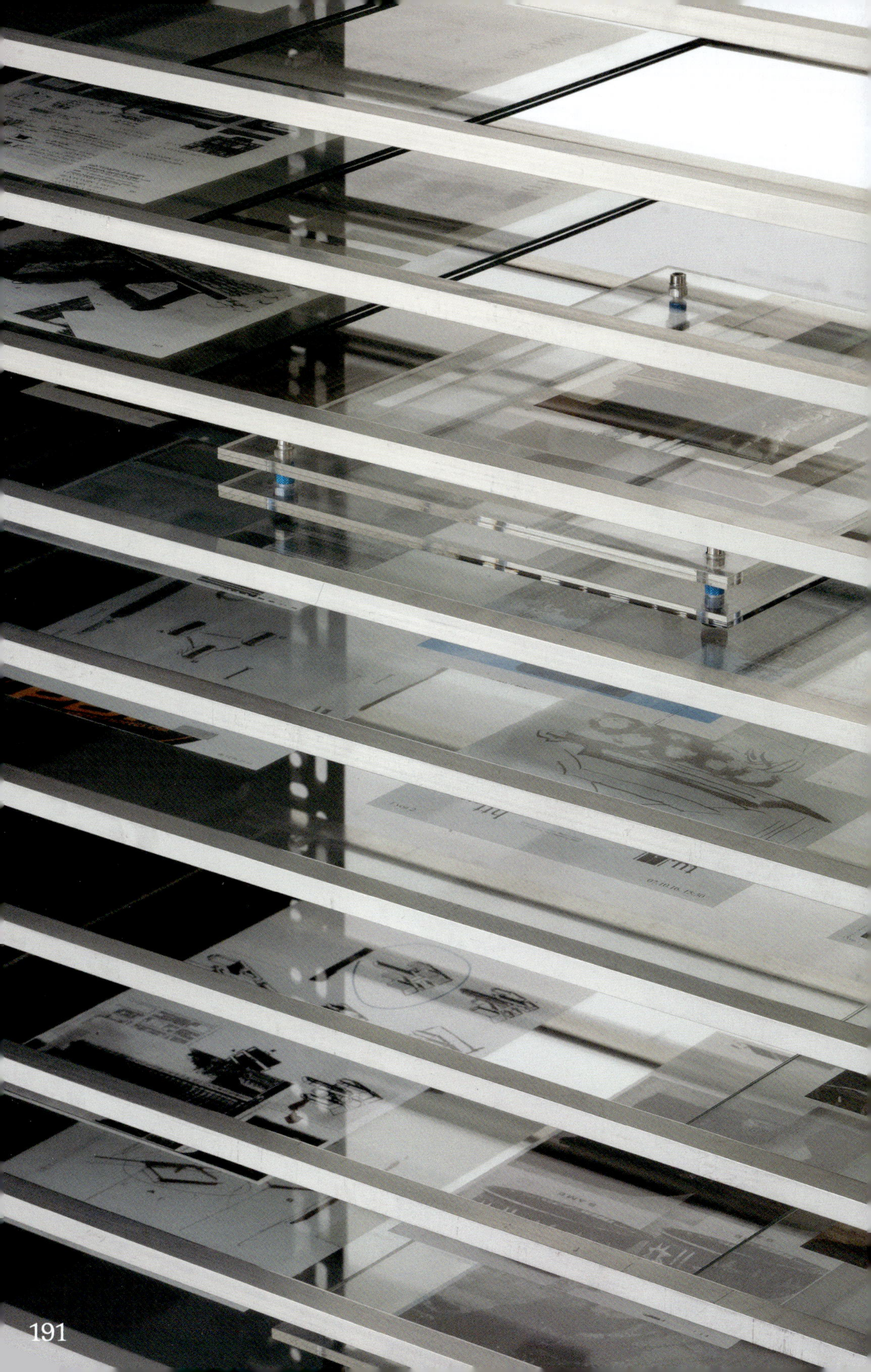

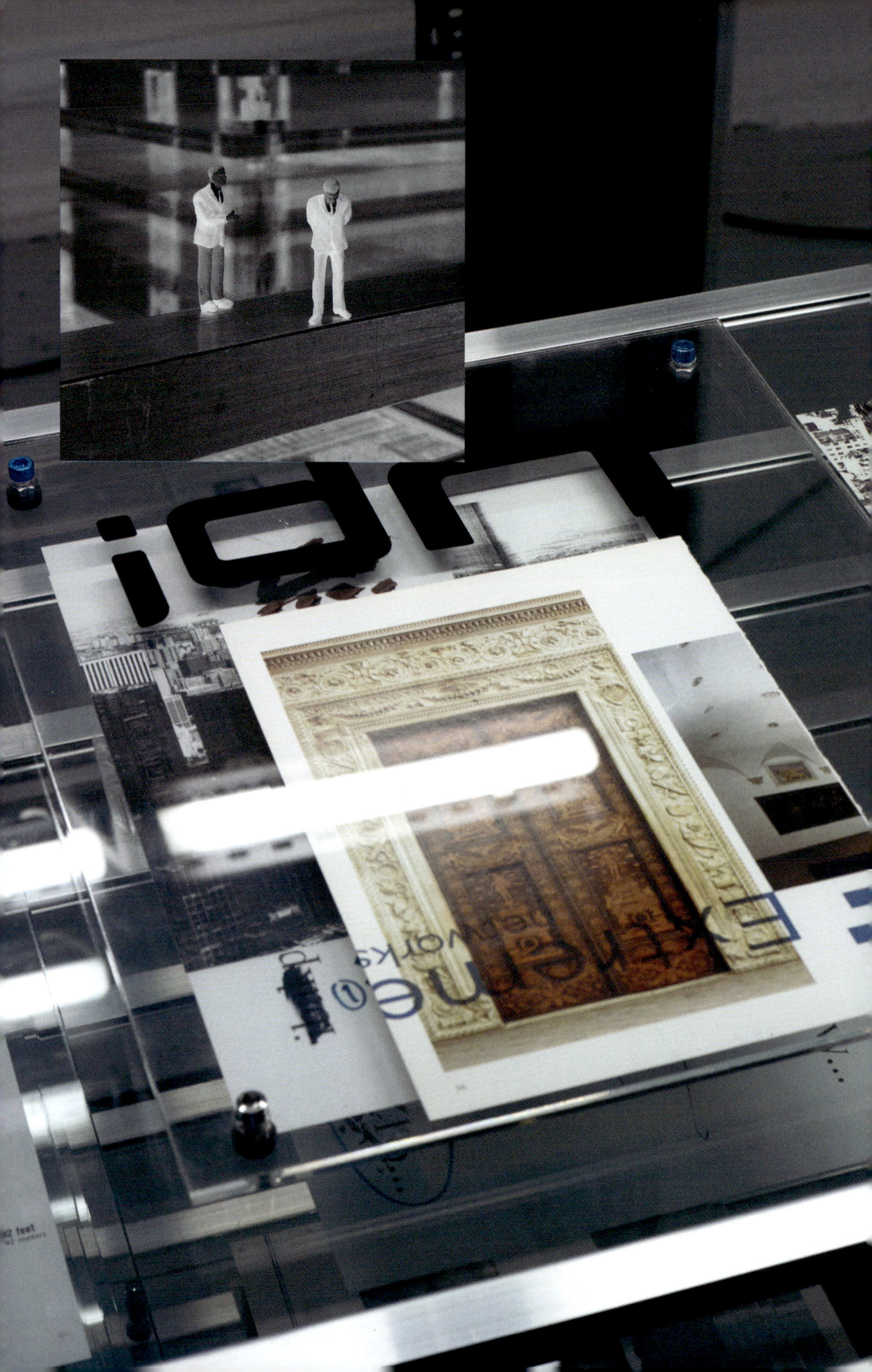

★L

The American Abyss
by Franco
"Bifo" Berardi

The Vertigo of
the Corporate Soul
by Pujan
Karambeigi

Falling
by Anna
Lena Seiser

THE AMERICAN ABYSS

by Franco "Bifo" Berardi

SURFING THE WAVES OF THE UNKNOWN

During the summer of 2016, I was writing the last chapters of a book titled *Futurability: The Age of Impotence and the Horizon of Possibility*, where I outlined the prospect of a bifurcation: either social solidarity and conscious subjectivity will be reconstituted, or the world will be drawn into a new form of global fascism. In that context, I was obliged to confront the impending American elections given that after Brexit in June of that year, the victory of Donald Trump became possible. Both of these events were symptoms of a widespread psychosis invading the scene of the global brain.

That book was not especially about America, nor about elections, nor about Trump. Nevertheless, a consideration of the American scenario was crucial to understanding trends in human evolution.

Now, in summer 2020, Trump seems to be drowning, but it's hard to say what will happen next. The man has many arrows in his quill, even if his victory becomes more unlikely. He is already sending signals of his unwillingness to accept the results of the election; he is already hinting at Democratic Party fraud; and, most dangerously, he has referred his followers several times to the Second Amendment, which, in plain words, is a threat to trigger a wave of armed violence.

I know that it is dangerous to write in simultaneity with events that nobody can precisely foresee, that can only be vaguely intuited. But the only way to imagine something about the becoming of the psycho-sphere is to run ahead of the dynamics of the disaster. My job is not fortune-telling, so I will not engage in predictions about the results of the American elections, but my point is that whatever happens in November, a conflagration has been sparked in the US that will bring increasing violence and that, in due time, will lead to the explosion of the federal state, with unimaginable geopolitical implications.

THE UNMAKING OF THE USA

I would say that the main historical thread of the last twenty years of world history is the not-so-slow disintegration of the US. Of course, the September 11 attacks are one starting point for this unbelievable process. This is by far the most powerful country in the history of the world, the most armed, the most aggressive, the least accessible, protected as it is by two oceans. The only way to destroy it is to turn the giant against itself.

This is exactly what bin Laden's strategy achieved. Under the unintelligent direction of Dick Cheney and George W. Bush, the giant entered into a process of self-destruction. First the quagmire of Afghanistan, and then the quagmire of Iraq, provoked a sort of self-destroying fury in the American brain.

Salman Rushdie recounted with some anticipation this self-destroying fury in a book published in 2001 titled *Fury*.

Then came the financial collapse of 2008, and the election of a black president. Barack Obama in the White House was a shock for the supremacist instinct, deeply rooted in American history and in the white American psyche.

The rise of Trump must be viewed as an effect of the white reaction to a long list of perceived humiliations: defeats in two wars, the impoverishment of the middle class in the wake of the 2008 financial crisis, and a sophisticated, elegant black person dancing in the rooms of the White House.

Four years of Trump have almost finalized the disintegration process of the structures of the US state. In 2020, this process was almost complete when the pandemic erupted and swept the country.

What's next? Obviously, I do not know, but I have noticed that, after a series of political setbacks, Trump has turned into the leader of the people of the Second Amendment. When the most recent Black Lives Matter protests spread across the country, and earlier when a group of Trumpists entered the Michigan state capitol building with their weapons drawn, the likely backdrop of the next five years was exposed.

Trump called for the army to crush the riots, and the army said no, defying the word of the president. Then he sent federal troops to Portland, fuelling rage and escalating the riots. Is he pointing to a fully-fledged fight just before the elections?

"The Masked Versus the Unmasked" is the title of a May 2020 article published in the *New York Times* by a liberal, moderately progressive, highly educated journalist — actually, my favorite American journalist, Roger Cohen. The title promises something enigmatic, but the text is very clear, from the very first lines:

> A neighbor in Colorado would tell me it was time for liberals to "gun up." The other side was armed, he argued, and would stop at nothing. What would we tell our grandchildren when Ivanka Trump took office as the 46th president of the United States in 2025 and term limits were abolished? That we tried words, all manner of them, he scoffed, but they had the rifles.[1]

Unsurprisingly, Cohen immediately adds that he disagrees with his neighbor and that American democracy has nothing in common with Hungarian democracy. I'm not sure that his optimism is well founded.

Even if Viktor Orbán is a fascist and Hungarian democracy is in very bad shape, I'm sorry to say that American democracy is even worse because it is the expression of the American people, and they are the product of centuries of genocide, of deportations, of slavery, and of systematic violence.

American democracy has been a fake since the beginning, when slave owners who wrote the Declaration of Independence stopped for a moment to consider the possibility of writing something about the prob-

lem of slavery, but instead decided to postpone such discussions indefinitely.
We should not think that Trump is an aberration of the American spirit, or the exception in a country of sensible people: he is the perfect representation of the white unconscious, pestered by a devastating sense of guilt resulting from the genocide of the native population, the forcible importation of millions of Africans, the long-lasting oppression of black slaves, military aggression against countless populations, the nuclear annihilation of Hiroshima and Nagasaki, the killing of millions of Vietnamese people, the extermination of Chilean democracy, the killing of Salvador Allende and of thirty thousand people after September 11, 1973. Not to mention the phosphorus bombing of Fallujah and the uncountable victims of the catastrophic wars in Afghanistan and Iraq.
Thanks to his ignorance and moral abjection, Donald Trump represents the true soul of America, the unmovable soul of a population formed by a never-ending sequence of exploitation, oppression, bullying, invasions, and abominable crimes. Nothing but this. There isn't an alternative America, as many thought in the 1960s and '70s. There are millions of women and men, mostly nonwhite, who have suffered from American violence, and especially at a certain point in the '60s and '70s, fought to reform America to become more human. They failed, because there is no way to reform a nation of bigots and killers.
Now more than ever, it is possible to envision the opportunity to destroy America, not to reform it. And this is possible because America is destroying itself. Osama bin Laden succeeded in his attempt to turn the greatest military power against itself. The 9/11 provocation succeeded in drawing the giant into a war against chaos. Those who wage war against chaos are doomed, because chaos feeds upon war.
In 1992, when George Bush Sr. said at the first summit on climate change in Rio de Janeiro that the lifestyle of the American people was not subject to negotiation, we learned that the planet faces a dilemma regarding its future: unless America is broken, humankind will not survive.
In the American literary consciousness, we can find countless footprints of this horrible manifest destiny, and in the following paragraphs I want to retrace some of them. At first I considered writing about the books of Joyce Carol Oates, particularly *American Martyrs*, or of Octavia Butler, especially the dystopian premonition of *The Parable of the Sower*. Instead I decided to speak only of white males, so that the abyss may be described from the inside: Cormac McCarthy, John Steinbeck, Philip Roth, and Jonathan Franzen. I know that this is a debatable choice, and some may reproach me for it. I am reproaching myself for this choice, but I excuse myself for a very personal reason: I am male, I am white, I am old.
I know what I'm talking about.

INNER DARK

Cormac McCarthy's second novel, *Outer Dark*, published in 1968, may be read as a metaphorical journey back to the original soul of white America. The time and the place of the story are nebulous: wilderness, the absence of historical references, and a pervasive sense of obfuscation.
Somewhere in Appalachia, sometime around the turn of the twentieth century, a woman whose name is Rinthy gives birth to her brother's baby. The brother, Culla, leaves the nameless infant in the woods to die, and eventually tells the sister that the baby died of natural causes. The woman does not trust him, and goes away, into the darkness looking for the child.
"The children of the kingdom shall be cast out into outer darkness: there shall be weeping and gnashing of teeth," reads the Gospel of Matthew. The oppressive presence of the Biblical God is in the background of the book: the shadows of guilt obsessively haunt the characters of the novel, but no consciousness emerges from their actions, nor from their words.
After abandoning the child, Culla goes wandering and looking for a job (what else?), finds a job and weapons, kills a squire, then finds a new job, then flees from the police.
Nothing makes sense. Culla's actions are like fragmentary memories of a nightmare.
The final episode of his journey is the most absurd, and the most creepy: Culla falls into a river, breaks his leg, and comes out from the water to meet the three people who have been following him. These three men are carrying his son, the child Culla abandoned. The child is horribly wounded, with a torn eye. The men accuse Culla of fathering the child, and of abandoning him. Then one of the trio slays the baby.
The ending of the novel is swathed in the surrealistic light of madness: after surviving his creeping adventures, Culla makes friends with a blind man. He watches the blind man walk towards a swamp: certain death. The novel ends with Culla thinking: "Someone should tell a blind man before setting him out that way."
The fake glory of the colonization of the West is recounted here as a nightmare, as a foggy meandering between violence and fear and abjection.

WRATH

From the nightmare of McCarthy to the historical reality of John Steinbeck — I was reminded of the most important American novel of the 1930s while reading an article from the far-right libertarian financial blog *Zero Hedge*, an interesting reference for white supremacy.
As a reader of this repugnant but useful rag, my attention was captivated one day by an article titled "The Old America Is Dead: Three Scenarios For The Way Forward." Written by Wayne Allenswroth, the article was about John Steinbeck's novel *The Grapes of Wrath* and the 1939 film adaption by John Ford.
The novel stages a community of farmers in Oklahoma in the days of the Great Depression. Due to debt, and due to the financial context that the farmers are unable to understand, one day they receive a visit from the landowner's men, who bring the message that they are evicted:

> Some of the owner men were kind because they hated what they had to do, and some of them

were angry because they hated to be cruel ... And all of them were caught in something larger than themselves. Some of them hated the mathematics that drove them, and some were afraid, and some worshiped that mathematics because it provided a refuge from thought and from feeling. If a bank or a finance company owned the land, the owner man said, the Bank — or the Company — needs — wants — insists — must have — as though the Bank or the Company were a monster, with thought and feeling, which had ensnared them ... The bank — the monster has to have profits all the time. It can't wait. It'll die.[2]

Steinbeck describes here, in a quite vivid way, the impotence that workers, and functionaries, experience when facing the monster of financial capitalism. But the interesting thing is that the pro-Trump *Zero Hedge* resurrects Steinbeck now, as the scenario of the Depression returns through the conditions triggered by the pandemic. Steinbeck continues:

> At last the owner men came to the point. The tenant system won't work anymore. One man on a tractor can take the place of twelve or fourteen families. Pay him a wage and take all the crop. We have to do it. We don't like to do it. But the monster's sick.[3]

The tenants sit on the ground while the landowner's lawyer finally tells them:

> You'll have to get off the land. The plows'll go through the dooryard.
> And now the squatting men stood up angrily. Grampa took up the land, and he had to kill the Indians and drive them away. And Pa was born here, and he killed weeds and snakes. Then a bad year came and he had to borrow a little money. An' we was born here. And Pa had to borrow money. The bank owned the land then, but we stayed and we got a little bit of what we raised.[4]

But the owner's men are inflexible:

> We're sorry. It's not us. It's the monster. The bank isn't like a man ...
> The tenants cried, Grampa killed Indians, Pa killed snakes for the land. Maybe we can kill banks — they are worse than Indians and snakes ...
> And now the owner men grew angry. You'll have to go ...
> We'll get our guns, like Grampa when the Indians came. What then?
> Well — first the sheriff, and then the troops. You'll be stealing if you try to stay, you'll be murderers if you kill to stay. The monster isn't men, but it can make men do what it wants.[5]

These pages illuminate the sentiment and the mythology that lie beneath Trump, and make up his strength. The white people who earned this land by killing Indians are under threat because of liberal globalism. Trump is their weapon against the globalist threat. The people of the Second Amendment are facing their last opportunity to save their social dominance: this opportunity is Trump. Just read what Allenswroth writes at *Zero Hedge*:

> Our people, our culture, our history, everything we hold dear, is under relentless attack by the Main Stream Media, politicians, "activists," and kritarchs in the courts, aided and abetted by enemies within, often our own kith and kin, who have internalized the blood-libel Leftist narrative of an irredeemably "racist" America that must be razed to the ground ...
> Our enemy, in this case is the globalist Blob and its militant would-be Che Guevaras and LARPing Leninists, the MSM, the bureaucracy, the courts, the big corporations, and the education establishment. Yet, for the most part, until recently, the Blob has not confronted the Historic American Nation head-on. The Blob has been patient, killing us by the death of a thousand cuts, taking ground steadily through subversion, using propaganda and misinformation, censorship via Tech Totalitarians, and the slow encroachment of what the late Sam Francis called "anarcho-tyranny," with mass immigration ("the Great Replacement") as its weapon of mass destruction. The Blob is amorphous, a slippery, slimy thing that probes and gropes its way into whatever social-economic-political cracks it can exploit, eventually engulfing its prey like quicksand. Then Donald Trump was elected president. The Blob was shocked. Orange Man Bad seemed to threaten its plans to finish off the Historic American Nation. And so, ever since November 8, 2016, the MSM have kept the country in hysterics with one manufactured crisis after another. Fake news via a social media, a hybrid warfare tactic, kicked into high gear: Russiagate, Ukrainegate, the Chinese Virus panic and ensuing lockdown and economic crash, and now the myth of St. George Floyd and blacks being "hunted" by whites that catalyzed the mobs that have looted and burned American cities. Using the Chinese Virus and Floyd riots as cover, the Blob and its militant wing — Antifa and Black Lives Matter — ratcheted up anarcho-tyranny to new heights.[6]

This narrative is rooted in racialized memory and supported by an army of white people who own weapons and who Trump has unified with the definition "people of the Second Amendment."
At the end the article, Allenswroth turns to an open invitation to prepare for civil war:

> If we bank solely on electoral politics, we will lose, especially as the demographic ring closes. The winners will show no quarter. Political life as we knew it in America is over. Again, the America we grew up in and loved is dead. Elections are a holding action at best. It seems highly unlikely that Trump (or anyone else, for that matter) can, for instance, deport and encourage to self-deport tens of millions of illegal aliens, even assuming a desire to do so.[7]

Trump cannot do the job alone, is the claim. "We" must take our weapons and do the job: deport tens of millions of illegal aliens, right? We did a century ago, when we deported indigenous people, when we slaughtered them. And now, goes the racist white position, we have to do it again.
Madness? Yes, but what the political pundits cannot grasp is this: madness, and only madness, is now ruling a world that is totally out of control.
Allenswroth wonders, *What if Trump loses the election in November?*
And this is his answer:

> Trump loses, and the Blob and its allies triumph. But because this is a country now and not a nation, with no shared sense of common identity and agreed-upon history, culture, beliefs, or language, only a full-blown police state can hold it together. Even that might not ensure order in a chaotic post-America, and the diminishing number of whites will surely not enjoy the protection of the state. At some point, white Americans might well be living like white South Africans, ever in fear for their lives. If order breaks down, vigilante groups, even criminal gangs, will step into the void, as vigilantes have done in Mexico and Hispanic gangs have done to protect their neighborhoods during the Floyd riots. The good news: white men have followed suit when mobs threatened their homes and history.[8]

THIS COUNTRY IS FRIGHTENING

From the years of the Great Depression I jump to the 1960s, when progressive consciousness spread out from black revolts and from universities.
In *American Pastoral*, Philip Roth stages the tragedy of a man who has grown up in with a somnambulant trust in the American Dream. Suddenly, he is obliged to face the reality of a mental breakdown that traverses his family, his village, his country, and the world as a whole. He is called the Swede, but he is a young Jewish man from New Jersey. He's tall, handsome, a good baseball player. We are in the '50s and life looks joyful and glorious for him. He marries Miss New Jersey, and they have a child, Meredith, aka Merry. Merry is affected by a pronounced stutter. There's no way to heal this flaw, this small stain on the picture of perfect American joy at the beginning of the '60s.
Then Kennedy is killed, and one day while Merry is watching TV she's shocked by the image of a Vietnamese priest, dressed in saffron, who lights himself on fire and stays still until the moment he falls, a human inferno. For Merry, this is the beginning of a monstrous mutation. She recoils from this image, she cries, she babbles. Then more Vietnamese priests kill themselves, and the girl's brain is forever scrambled.
The new American reality tears a whole in the fenced-off garden of the Swede's American Dream. The black uprisings erupt: Watts is on fire, Newark is on fire. The Swede protects the factory that his father bequeathed to him. But everything is changing all around. Most importantly, Merry has gone crazy: she does not come back home at night, spending her nights with communists and anarchists instead.
Then comes the tragedy, the irredeemable tragedy. Merry becomes a murderer, a terrorist: she sets off a bomb that kills an innocent passerby. Merry is on the run, Merry will never come back, her mother has a nervous breakdown. Then Merry meets up secretly with her father, but she is as thin as a rake, she's dirty, she's ruined. Merry has been raped.
The world of the Swede has broken down, but he must resist, the factory must go on, his wife is out of her mind, she's fucking the heinous neighbor, an intellectual. The Swede calls his brother, his cynical brother, and tells him that nothing is left of his world. His brother replies:

> "You think you know what this country is? You have no idea what this country is ... This country is frightening. Of course she was raped. What kind of company do you think she was keeping? Of course out there she was going to get raped ... She enters that world, that loopy world out there, with what's going on out there — what do you expect?"[9]

Earlier in the same chapter Roth writes:

> Yes, at the age of forty-six, in 1973, almost three-quarters of the way through the century that with no regard for the niceties of burial had strewn the corpses of mutilated children and their mutilated parents everywhere, the Swede found out that we are all in the power of something demented. It's just a matter of time, honky. We all are![10]

It's just a matter of time, says Roth. We are all under the power of something demented.
Now the time has come, I guess.
No one would have ever fathomed that America — the greatest country in the world with "the greatest economy ever" — could be on the cusp of another civil war. Now, after more than one hundred and seventy thousand dead in the unspeakable massacre that the American health system has committed, after the killing of George Floyd and the explosion of protests with continuous escalations in police violence, after Trump's warning about the coming electoral fraud by the Democrats, after the call-to-arms he issued to the people of the Second Amendment, after the lines of people buying weapons in the early days of the pandemic, after the armed mobs protesting against the lockdown, I think that civil war is the most likely prospect for this country that is the terminal malady of humankind.

SENILITY

> The madness of an autumn prairie cold front coming through. You could feel it: something terrible was going to happen. The sun low in the sky, a minor light, a cooling star. Gust after gust of disorder. Trees restless, temperatures falling, the whole northern religion of things coming to an end.[11]

This is the opening of *The Corrections*, Jonathan Franzen's 2001 novel that marks the passage to the new century — a century of swift disintegration, beginning with the disintegration of the human brain:

> Alfred lacked the neurological wherewithal. Alfred's cries of rage on discovering evidence of guerrilla actions — a Nordstrom bag surprised in broad daylight on the basement stairs, nearly precipitating a tumble — were the cries of a government that could no longer govern.[12]

Alfred Lambert is an old father of three, and husband to Enid. The Lambert family is the protagonist of the novel.

Indeed, *The Corrections* is an account of the decomposition of the American brain, through the story of a couple of old people: Enid, a woman on the brink of depression who discovers the magic of psycho-pharmaceuticals, and Alfred, who is wandering on the border of Alzheimer's disease.

The world is getting less and less comprehensible, objects are sliding out of hands, actions get confused, overlap, lose their meaning and their functional relationships.

Not only because of neuro-chemical degradation, but also because of the transformation of the mental environment, reality has grown incomprehensible for the old brain:

> Black man performing oral sex on white man, camera shooting over left hip sixty degrees behind full profile, crescent of high values curving over buttock, knuckles of black fingers duskily visible in their probing on the dark side of this moon. She downloaded the image and viewed it at high resolution. She was sixty-five years old and she'd never seen a scene like this. She'd fashioned images all her life and she'd never appreciated their mystery. All this commerce of bits and bytes, these ones and zeros streaming through servers at some midwestern university. So much evident trafficking in so much evident nothing. A population glued to screens and magazines.[13]

Astonishment, sorrow, and absurdity are spreading everywhere.

> And there was a very important question that he still wanted answered. His children were coming, Gary and Denise and maybe even Chip, his intellectual son. It was possible that Chip, if he came, could answer the very important question. And the question was. The question was.[14]

I use the word "senility" to refer to a condition of extreme dissociation of cerebral flow and the surrounding universe; it happens when the brain loses nervous system integration that is needed to consistently elaborate both semiotic and natural impulses. Senility, thus, is an individual condition that is encapsulated in a confused mental state of the old mind. But the expanding presence of old people spreads this condition well beyond the limit of a marginal pathology. Many signs in the present American situation point to a political diagnosis: the American brain is irreversibly rotten. But before political senility it is psychological senility. And before being psychological it is a neurological dysfunction.

The contemporary widespread perception of an apocalyptic vertigo is not only generated as a reckoning with the long history of racial violence, industrial pollution, and economic hyper-exploitation. It is also the result of widespread neurological degradation, and of the inability of the American mind to come to terms with senility and impotence.

In the movie *Nebraska*, directed by Alexander Payne, a police officer discovers Woody Grant walking on the highway. Woody is then picked up by his son David, who learns that Woody wants to go to Lincoln, Nebraska, to collect a million-dollar sweepstakes prize he believes he has won. When David sees the sweepstakes letter, he knows immediately that it is a mail scam designed to get gullible people to purchase magazine subscriptions. David brings his father home, where his mother Kate becomes increasingly annoyed by Woody's insistence on collecting the money.

It is a heartbreaking story, the story of people (most white Americans) who have grown up with fake mythologies and have been nourished with horrible food (in both the physical and spiritual sense), and are now sleepwalking towards the swamp, but still trust in their superiority.

UN-AMERICAN QUICHOTTE

In the surrealistic baroque of the novel *Quichotte*, Salman Rushdie recounts the story of an Indian-born writer living in America who works for an opioid pharmaceutical enterprise (the producers of Oxycontin, by the way) and falls in love with an Indian-born TV star. He travels from California to New York City with his fictional son Sancho Panza, and is confronted by countless acts of racist rejection and aggression from the true white Americans who do not love the brown pair.

> "I want us to speak to each other in that language, especially in public, to defy the bastards who hate us for possessing another tongue."[15]

This is the best definition of Americans: those bastards who hate us for possessing another tongue (and also, it must be said, for speaking better English than they do). Ignorance is the bedrock of American supremacy. They know nothing about the world, about the numerous and infinitely different countries of the world, they do not speak any language except an impoverished form of English, they do not know, and they protect their ignorance as the origin of their strength. And they have some reason to do this, because ignorance has been the force of those who don't want to be distracted by beauty, by unpredictability, by complexity, so that they can focus only on winning the miserable game of competition, profit, accumulation.

This has been the force of the American people during the last two centuries. But now?

Don't forget that there is another side of American power, which is the contrary of ignorance: knowledge.

American universities and other cultural enterprises are the places where knowledge is stored, processed, transformed, created. By whom? By people who come from India, Japan, Italy, China, and many other countries. Silicon Valley would be nothing without the Syrian Steve Jobs, without the Tamil Indian Sundar Pichai, and countless engineers and designers who come from all over the world. The movie industry would be nothing without Italians and Jews. And so on and so on.

The ambiguous greatness of America has been the result of the marriage between Anglo-Saxon brutality (and ignorance) and cosmopolitan curiosity.

Now, for the first time in history, the integration of these two cultural components is breaking down. The anti-global reaction wants to expel, to forbid, to reject, to build walls, erase multiplicity, and reduce complexity.

The core of the process of disintegration is to be found here: in the social blame surrounding intelligence, irony, consciousness, and imagination.

TOO MUCH AND NOT ENOUGH

Then I read the e-book (not all of it, for God's sake) that Mary Trump has devoted to the psychoanalysis of her uncle. *Too Much and Never Enough: How My Family Created the World's Most Dangerous Man* is a useful book, written with some understanding of the psychoanalytic background of the current catastrophic situation. The author is not only a professional psychologist, but also the niece of this horrible man, who is also a poor unfortunate whose life has been miserable, as is often the case with people who are obliged to defend a self-image that is profoundly fake.

Trump's father, Fred, was a highly functional sociopath, according to Mary Trump. After describing the philosophy that the father transmitted to his son, Mary comments:

> "Fred's fundamental beliefs about how the world worked — in life, there can be only one winner and everybody else is a loser (an idea that essentially precluded the ability to share) and kindness is weakness — were clear."[16]

Then Mary recounts some family anecdotes. After having a bowl of mashed potatoes thrown on his head, Donald Trump feels humiliated:

> Everybody laughed, and they couldn't stop laughing. And they were laughing at Donald. It was the first time Donald had been humiliated by someone he even then believed to be beneath him. He hadn't understood that humiliation was a weapon that could be wielded by only one person in a fight. That Freddy, of all people, could draw him into a world where humiliation could happen to him made it so much worse. From then on, he would never allow himself to feel that feeing again. From then on, he would wield the weapon, never be at the sharp end of it.[17]

In Mary's opinion, Donald has a double problem: he had too much, and not enough. Too much ego, a resentful ego, nourished by a father incapable of providing affection. And not enough love, because his mother was sick, absent, and psychologically dependent on the sociopath.

This looks like a good introduction to the psychogenesis of the president of the United States of America. But also, I guess, it's a good introduction to the psychogenesis of American white males, and of America itself: the psychogenesis of the American abyss.

Journal #111 - September 2020

1 Roger Cohen, "The Masked Versus the Unmasked," New York Times, May 15, 2020
2 John Steinbeck, The Grapes of Wrath (Viking, 1939), 32–33.
3 Steinbeck, Grapes of Wrath, 34.
4 Steinbeck, Grapes of Wrath, 34.
5 Steinbeck, Grapes of Wrath, 35.
6 Wayne Allenswroth, "Old America is Dead: Three Scenarios for the Way Forward," Zero Hedge, June 29, 2020.
7 Allenswroth, "Old America is Dead."
8 Allenswroth, "Old America is Dead."
9 Phillip Roth, American Pastoral (Houghton Mifflin, 1997), 276.
10 Roth, American Pastoral, 256.
11 Jonathan Franzen, The Corrections (Picador, 2002), 3.
12 Franzen, The Corrections, 6–7.
13 Franzen, The Corrections, 303.
14 Franzen, The Corrections, 159.
15 Salman Rushdie, Quichotte (Random House, 2020), 151.
16 Mary L. Trump, Too Much and Never Enough: How My Family Created the World's Most Dangerous Man (Simon & Schuster, 2020), 43.
17 Mary L. Trump, Too Much and Never Enough, 46.

THE VERTIGO OF THE CORPORATE SOUL

by
Pujan Karambeigi

It was 1966, and Theodor W. Adorno was in the middle of feverishly writing what would become his last and posthumously published book, *Aesthetic Theory* (1970), when he found himself in a radio discussion with one of his many archenemies, Arnold Gehlen: "It is precisely because the surface of modern life is so tremendously dense, i.e., because the social fabric has become so concentrated, that the essence of this society can hardly be penetrated anymore," he tried to legitimize his retreat from empirical sociology. In fact, it was the "density" of the ideological surface that was preventing the sociological method from operating properly, rendering art to be the last remaining domain still affording the depth of a "sociological experience."

More than a mere side-note, Adorno's comment was certainly intended as a rebuke not just of Gehlen but, most importantly, of his old friend and former colleague Siegfried Kracauer and his 1927 essay *The Mass Ornament*. More specifically, he was arguing against Kracauer's proposition for a sociological method that had guided much of the Frankfurt School's research output in the 1930s and 1940s, including his own. "The surface-level expressions, however, by virtue of their unconscious nature, provide unmediated access to the fundamental substance of the state of things," Kracauer argued famously. Being something of an unconscious of capitalist production, it is the surface, or more precisely, the ornamental level, that would afford the most succinct view into the state of things. Ornaments are here defined by two symbolic characteristics: First, they never appear by themselves but in "regularity," in a series or a pattern. Second, as much as it "consists of lines and circles [...] and also incorporates the elementary components of physics, such as waves and spirals," ornamentation doesn't coalesce into figuration. For Kracauer, these seemingly superfluous lines, circles, waves, and spirals were crucial as they functioned as "the aesthetic reflex of the rationality to which the prevailing economic system aspires." In short, an analysis of the ornament would afford grasping the ways in which capitalism was both producing and legitimizing the production of its surplus.

Sure, four decades had passed between Kracauer's and Adorno's remarks, and much had changed on the level of production to justify a renewed discussion around the relation between surface and depth, ideology and reality. However, for those less convinced of Adorno's retreat into the formal analyses of art, 1966 also offered a second and lesser-known trajectory within the Frankfurt School that remained closer to its sociological beginnings while attempting to update its tools. I am speaking here of *Monopoly Capital* by Paul Sweezy and Paul A. Baran. Very much part of the productivist line of the New Left that was forming in the 1960s, and somewhat opposed to the culturalist tradition organizing synchronously around the Birmingham School of Cultural Studies, they were eager to look at how the capitalist base was running. At the center of their analysis lies the falling rate of profit, putting immense pressure on corporations to engineer new ways of maintaining their surplus. For Sweezy and Baran, this pressure results in the emergence of a new social unit within the capitalist order: "the giant corporation."

In their eyes, this new scale of the corporate enterprise renders a series of distinctions to earlier corporate forms necessary: "Control rests in the hand of management" and not anymore in the hands of tycoons or entrepreneurial individuals that the Right and the Left still understood to be the center of capitalism. Moreover, these giant corporations are defined by "corespective behavior," by which they mean their systematic avoidance of price wars, competition, and any type of conflict. On the level of production, this results in a constant state of overcapacity since the mechanisms of competition were annulled. A crucial effect of this is that, rather than investing their surplus into improving methods of production, the giant corporation's surplus flows into "expenses of representation." This fulfills two functions simultaneously: For one, a corporation builds monuments to itself to stage and legitimize its success. Second, and most importantly, these expenses function as "emanations of the corporate soul," as ways to create and solidify their internal identity.

It is only in a footnote that Sweezy and Baran give an example for the way in which the pressures of the falling profit rate are transfigured into a representational expense: The recently finished Chase Manhattan Bank Plaza (1961/1964). (fig 1) In fact, as Sweezy and Baran were analyzing the emergence of giant corporations over the course of the 1960s, they had probably come across the 1955 merger between Chase National Bank and the Bank of the Manhattan Company: By combining the former's focus on the international handling of corporate credit with the latter's focus on private customers, Chase Manhattan had become the second largest bank in the United States, now handling the entire sphere of circulating liquidity. To advertise this newly formed corporation, employees, customers, and newspapers received a cartoon depicting the merging as a wedding, emphasizing that the state had sanctioned the eternal tie of two individuals.

Only a few months after this publicity campaign, Chase announced it would build a new headquarters, a few blocks below what would soon become the Silver Towers (1966). This was not really a matter of not being able to house the 7,500 employees in one single structure, since the Bank of the Manhattan Company owned the iconic French Gothic tower 40 Wall Street, which afforded more than enough space. Rather, Chase aimed for a new form of architecture, one that would distinguish itself from the "cathedrals of commerce" from the 1920s and 1930s. To do so, they hired Skidmore, Owings & Merrill (SOM), one of the earliest architectural representatives translating the international style into the United States, to devise a new sixty-floor skyscraper in Lower Manhattan.

VERTIGO

Visiting parts of the SOM and Gordon Bunshaft archives to get a better idea of what might have led Sweezy and Baran to highlight Chase Plaza, I came across one particularly strange photograph. (fig 2.1) Most striking is its angle: Whose position is this supposed to be? Why the slight tilt which ends up distorting the purity of a bird's eye view? Is the image supposed to capture the view of someone falling down from 40 Wall Street, the former headquarters of the Bank of the Manhattan Company? In a way, it seems like it is neither somebody's nor nobody's gaze. It is almost as if it is solely created to evoke the kind of experience one gets from looking down a dam, the way in which the immense verticality — the abyss opening up in front of you — pulls you downward. Certainly, there is a kind of kinship between verticality and hallucination, one we already know from films like Hitchcock's *Vertigo* (1958). But there is a difference: Whereas in *Vertigo*, the experience is a product of a kind of psychological trauma, the photo renders the experience to be a pure symptom of the architectural reality we are invited to contemplate, the mere surface effect of a structure we can only guess at.

To be sure, the photo is not depicting the real building but an analog model of what would later become Chase Plaza. The slightly tilted top-down view dramatizes the grand marble plaza with its Isamu Noguchi sculpture *Sunken Garden* (1964) that was still under construction when the photo was first published in SOM's in-house publication *Architecture of Skidmore, Owings & Merrill* (1962). In fact, it occludes that there were going to be seven basalt rocks from the Uji River in Japan, not just five, as the photo seems to indicate. Moreover, one clearly doesn't feel what the many commentators highlighted when the plaza first opened to much public applause. It "invites quiet contemplation in an area devoted to commerce," the anonymous *New York Times* editor wrote in 1964. Implied here might have been the sound of water so crucial to Noguchi's sculpture, with the pipes being able to create different effects such as spray or bubbling. Or, the contemplative feeling was sparked by the water lilies and their reference to Monet's high modernism. In any case, far from any experience of vertigo, the commentators on the ground emphasized the way in which the space afforded a rest from the pressures of corporate life.

So, if it's not the "ground experience" that the photo is capturing, whose experience is it? Since what it captures seems to be antagonizing what the public feels, it could be assumed that it depicts what the bank's executive feels: At the mercy of the stock market's uncertainty, threatened by global competition and the difficulties of expanding surplus while the rate of profit is shrinking ever more rapidly, every day at the bank would be like facing an abyss.

But looking at the images depicting how the newly forming banking elite was supposed to behave in the modernist temple, it remains rather questionable whether facing an abyss was really what they saw when looking up from the realities of numbers piling up on their desks. A good example here is another photograph I found in Gordon Bunshaft's archive: What we see are five empty chairs, a marble table, and four ashtrays designed by Ward Bennett — just one of the many custom-made accessories made for Chase Plaza. Behind the table, there is an army of bouquets organized in a grid, and on the very right is an Abstract Expressionist painting. But the center of the composition is clearly taken up by what appears to be a modernized French Gothic façade, with a seemingly endless horizon stretching in the background. The photograph is taken in the executive dining area on the sixtieth floor. The setting is thus explicitly devoid of tables for secretaries, typewriters recording memos, and ringing telephones. Moreover, the floorplan tells us that the observer is facing 40 Wall Street, the former headquarters of the Bank of the Manhattan Company, which the freshly merged Chase Manhattan sold in 1956 to acquire the real estate for its new headquarters. In that case, is the landscape supposed to dramatize a view onto the past of the corporation? Or is this about the southern-facing horizon behind the architectural colossus, anticipating the bank's expansion into the Latin American and African economies?

Two additional photographs put these questions into action by staging subjects now taking on the perspective of the camera. The first one shows two men — transfigured into anonymous black silhouettes by way of the lighting — in what could either be a conversation or a discussion. (fig 2.2) In the second one, four men in dark suits are observed gazing out, seemingly taking in the view silently. In fact, the photographs are staging what Bunshaft, the SOM partner in charge of Chase Plaza's design, wanted the executives to see, feel, and do once entering the sixtieth floor. As it is recounted in *The Chase*, Bunshaft had "early plans to place a spectacular piece of sculpture just off the 60th floor elevator landing." However, after the construction of the floor had been finished, "the designers discovered that the necessary piece of sculpture had already been provided, [...] the spire of 40 Wall Street." In short, the photographs' transfiguration of the urban reality into a seemingly passive and timeless space was far from arbitrary. Rather, they staged the way in which Rockefeller and SOM imagined the relation between the bankers and their community: In safe distance from the conflicts taking place on the ground, the world was turned into a painting waiting to be contemplated.

VERTICAL INTEGRATION

If the vertiginous photo neither depicts the view of the public nor that of the executives, there is a third option: It is a picture from the building's perspective. SOM's own captioning of the photo in its 1962 publication offers a glimpse of that: "View of model from above demonstrates the dynamic rise of the office tower from its plaza. The exterior columns emphasize the height of the building." In fact, the primary function of the building is to manage, obfuscate, and channel height. This simultaneous organization and repression of height are rendered feasible by providing its users with an aesthetic experience. Not just present in the view on the sixtieth floor but, most prominently, in the systematic employment of art within the corporate space.

As much as this was itself a trend that had already started in the early 1950s, Chase Plaza pioneered an intricate system of art as a subjective training program for its employees — with different modalities depending on the position taken up in the corporate hierarchy.

That there was an astonishing amount of art inside the office spaces was a fact few commentators at the time forgot to mention. Touring through the building shortly after its opening, an anonymous *New Yorker* journalist commented that it was "like miniature art galleries." What was less reported on was the way art was distributed among the different office spaces, and the ways in which the selection of artworks was organized. Three interrelated scales are crucial here: (1) the hallways and open floor office spaces, (2) the executive offices, and (3) Chase's art collection. As we will see, understanding this interrelation will offer us a glimpse into the ways Chase Plaza was both symbolizing and channeling an internal coherence to its users while inscribing them into a vertical order.

Let's begin with the largest scale: Chase's art collection. In 1959, two years after construction had begun, McCloy and Rockefeller managed to convince Chase's board to form a committee for an art collection to decorate the new headquarters equipped with a rather handsome sum of $500,000. Severinghaus noted later how this sum was calculated: "We marked all the places where small, medium, and large paintings and sculpture might be needed. We then assigned an arbitrary price for each class of item, ranging from $100 to $10,000." For the committee, which was presided by McCloy who was joined by Rockefeller, they invited Bunshaft in addition to prominent museums professionals: MoMA's former director Alfred H. Barr Jr., Guggenheim's director James Johnson Sweeney, Metropolitan Museum of Art curator Robert B. Hale, the Boston Fine Art Museum's Perry Rathbone, and Barr's assistant Dorothy C. Miller. (fig 3.1)

The selection process was roughly the following: Once a month, the committee would meet, with each member bringing works they were proposing to be bought, at times "as many as 150 items," as Miller recounts two decades later. These objects were then displayed in a room together, with each member presenting the works they selected, as well as indicating price points. This was followed by a discussion and a secret vote from 0 to 3, with 3 being a definite yes and 0 a definite no. Every item with eleven or more votes was bought, approximating the selection process to the board meetings on Chase Plaza's seventeenth floor. Except for major pieces, small and medium works were not bought with specific places in mind.

"Our only object was quality," Miller explained later. However, that there was a second objective becomes clear when reading the briefing notes: "March 21, 1960: Mr. McCloy was still concerned that there was a continuing tendency toward abstract and a brief discussion centered around the long history of the bank. ("We were founded in 1799 and therefore the past should be represented.") It was generally conceded that the art program should reflect our own times and we should have courage to look ahead." In fact, the selection process can be understood as an attempt to negotiate between two poles, namely a representation of the corporate history on the one hand, and aesthetic quality on the other. Similarly, the committee's function was to approximate two professions and their respective fields of expertise, bridging the gaps between bankers and connoisseurs.

To a degree, this negotiation process taking place within the committee was then generalized in different configurations for Chase's entire staff. The executive offices offer a clear picture: Being able to either hang art from their own collection or, as it was encouraged, from the pre-selected collection that had been set up in the warehouse on the thirtieth floor, there were two guiding principles that were assessed differently depending on one's position within the executive hierarchy. The first step here was expert interviews with each executive, "some several times," to then make suggestions accordingly. These suggestions were supposed to synthesize the individual personality and the professional expertise, a delicate balancing act that was far from arbitrary. One way this could play out can be seen in the office of the Vice President of Chase's African accounts. As the writers in *The Chase* note, "appropriately, an African weaving hangs behind his desk." In other words, professional and aesthetic identity were merging into one, just like when Chase National Bank and the Bank of the Manhattan Company merged in 1955.

Moving further up the ladder, however, executives were encouraged to rebalance these poles. David Rockefeller's own office is a case in point. In a much-reproduced image, the viewer sees a Kenzo Okada painting and a sculpture by an anonymous Oceanic sculptor. (fig 3.2) The other less well-known photos offer a glimpse at works by Milton Avery, Charles Burchfield, Jose Guerrero, Josef Albers, Jean Dubuffet, and Mark Rothko, in addition to a little Cézanne lithograph in the washroom. As The Chase concludes: "Rockefeller's office was furnished as an extension of his personality." But again, this only gets at half the truth, since the combination of modernist painting and what was at the time circulating as "primitive art" was certainly not an expression of Rockefeller's individual personality. Comparing the pictures from Rockefeller's office with photographs of Bunshaft's Travertine House or his Manhattan apartment, the strong correlation is impossible to miss. In fact, much more than expressing individuality, the employment of art was supposed to showcase a specific technique. In neither relying on stylistic unity nor on geographical identity, Rockefeller's selection exhibits something that had already been a central ambition to the collection committee: The ability to synthesize differences across time and space. In other words, managerial and aesthetic expertise are approximated here due to their shared ambition for synthesis.

Outside of the executive floor, aesthetic expertise operated differently. The contrast here seems to have been not so much gradual as binary, with a clear sense of distinction between executive and non-executive labor. As *The Chase* highlighted, over its 1,200,000 square feet of office space and 7,500 employees, it had only 150 private offices. The rest were open floor offices. This is not to say that art took place only on the executive floor. Rather, for the 7,350 remaining employees, art seems to have been less a medium to showcase the ability to synthesize difference than about breaking with the rigid rationality modern architecture is usually associated with: "Compared with most modern office buildings of the first rank, Chase has colors more muted, more intricate, and, on the whole, warmer." SOM partner Severinghaus even went so far as to claim Chase Plaza formulated a break with modernism altogether:

Modern architecture, based on Bauhaus-inspired functionalism, had essentially eliminated the use of traditional ornament and sculpture as an integral part of a structure. However, Skidmore, Owings & Merrill believed that the simplicity of modern structures called for a sympathetic approach to the use of sculpture, paintings, and furnishings to complement the prevailing architectural simplicity to create a harmonious environment for both public and private areas.

That is, far from the anti-ornamental temple Chase Plaza is usually understood to embody, art was supposed to bring warmth and motivation to what, by the late 1950s, appeared as modernism's lifeless structures. There is a second side to this ambition, however: not just making the workplace more human but also educating the employees' senses. In contrast to the executive floor, this education was conceived in a strictly top-down manner. As Miller recounts enthusiastically: "At some companies, if a secretary doesn't like a picture, it is immediately removed. At Chase, they let the person grow up with the picture. That process of education was usually successful." Miller hints here at two things at once: First, conflict was absolved through hierarchy. As already hinted at in the sixtieth floor panorama, this disappearance of conflict was by far not confined to the non-executive labor but extended well into the relation to the "banker's community" as well as the internal dynamics within the executive branch. Again, this becomes most clear when looking at the selection process of art. A Newsweek report with one of the executives depicts the handling of conflicts in the following way:

What happens, the reporter asked, if one of the vice presidents wants elks' heads on his walls? "Nobody in the bank hunts," was the answer. What if a man paints, or if his wife paints? "Nobody in the bank does." What if a man's taste in art differs from Chase Manhattan's? "Well, a bad Maxfield Parrish chromo would be heavily discouraged on policy grounds."

The report was quickly denied by Chase, but it depicts a "workplace culture" in which art was a medium to interweave the unwritten and written rules to create immense pressures to conform.

The second point Miller hints at in her enthusiasm is that aesthetic sensitivity was vertically organized. The further up one goes, the closer one was to it, making clear why the transfiguration of the cityscape into a contemplative painting was reserved for the sixtieth floor. That is, Chase Plaza is less about collapsing the inside with the outside than about manufacturing a rigid distinction on the bottom while at the top, just for a brief moment, one might be awarded an ability to project the inside outward.

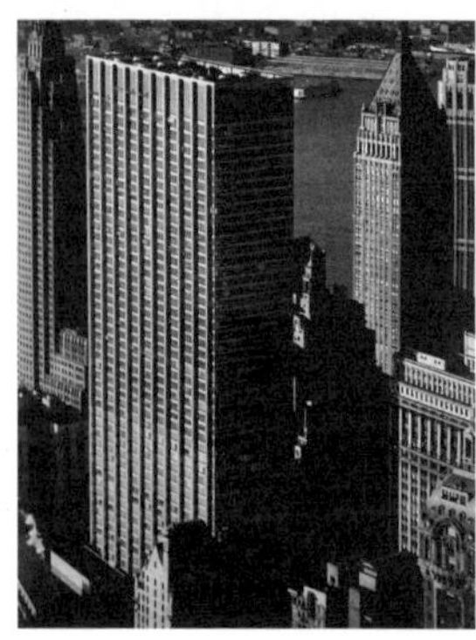

Fig. 1
Photograph taken of Chase Manhattan Bank Plaza by Erich Locker, in: *Gordon Bunshaft architectural drawings and papers*, 1909-1990, Box 4, Folder 4.2, Avery Drawings & Archives.

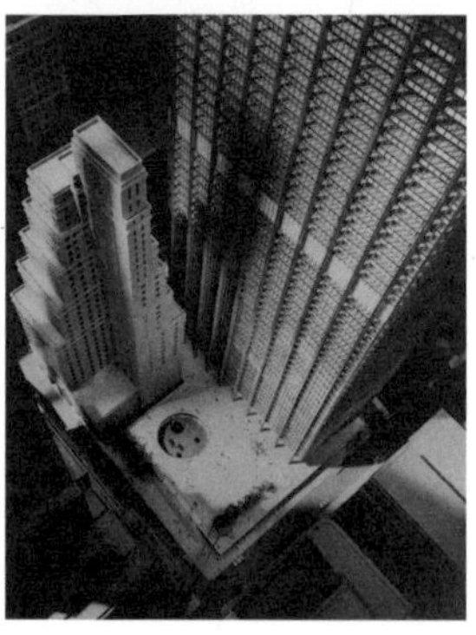

Fig. 2.1
Photograph taken of Chase Manhattan Bank Plaza, in: *Skidmore, Owings, & Merrill Photographs Collection, Bunshaft architectural drawings and papers*, Box 3, Folder 1, Avery Drawings & Archives.

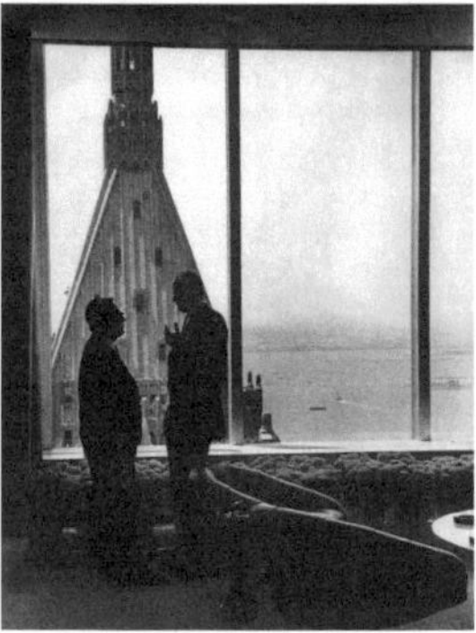

Fig. 2.2
George Zimbel, photograph, reprinted in: Tanner, "THE CHASE," p. 85.

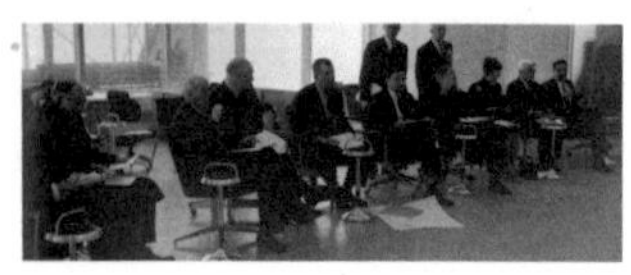

Fig. 3.1
First meeting of the committee in 1960, beginning second from left: Alfred Barr, John McCloy, James Johnson Sweeney, Gordon Bunshaft, David Rockefeller, Robert B. Hale, Dorothy C. Miller, John J. Scully, J. Walter Severinghaus, reprinted in: *Chase Manhattan Bank, Art at Work: The Chase Manhattan Collection*, New York: E.P. Dutton (1984), p. 17.

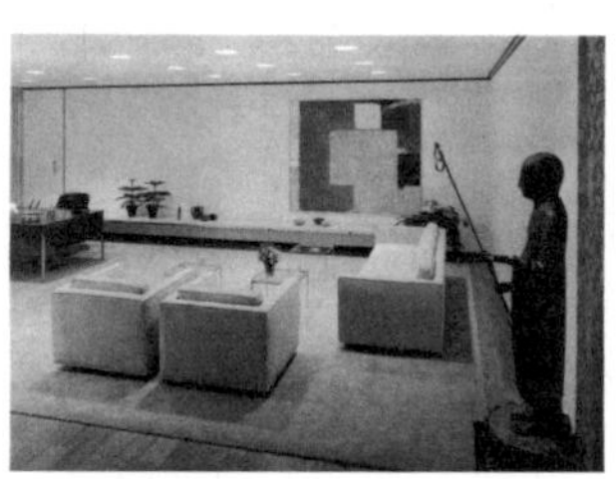

Fig. 3.2
David Rockefeller's office as President of Chase Manhattan, reprinted in: Tanner, "THE CHASE," p. 77.

FALLING

by
Anna Lena Seiser

"A cross section of today's social structure would have to show the following: At the top, the feuding tycoons of the various capitalist power constellations. Below them, the lesser magnates, the large landowners and the entire staff of important coworkers. Below that, and in various layers, the large numbers of professionals, smaller employees, political stooges, the military and the professors, the engineers and heads of office down to the typists. And even further down what is left of the independent, small existences, craftsmen, grocers, farmers e tutti quanti, then the proletarian, from the most highly paid, skilled workers down to the unskilled and the permanently unemployed, the poor, the aged and the sick. It is only below these that we encounter the actual foundation of misery on which this structure rises, for up to now we have been talking only of the highly developed capitalist countries whose entire existence is based on the horrible exploitation apparatus at work in the partly or wholly colonial territories, i.e., in the far larger part of the world. Extended regions in the Balkans are torture chambers, the mass misery in India, China, Africa boggles the mind. Below the spaces where the coolies of the earth perish by the millions, the indescribable, unimaginable suffering of the animals, the animal hell in human society, would have to be depicted, the sweat, blood, despair of the animals.

[...] The basement of that house is a slaughterhouse, its roof a cathedral, but from the windows of the upper floors, it affords a really beautiful view of the starry heavens."

Max Horkheimer, "The Skyscraper"[1]

IN CONTROLLED DESCEND / COMMODIFIED WINGS

A human falls out of the sky. Four minutes and twenty seconds in free fall, from the stratosphere to the earth's surface. Around the world, eleven million people — a number rarely reached before — watch in front of televisions and computer monitors. They hear his breathing and follow in real time the data measurements on the speed of the fall, the remaining oxygen supply, and the duration of the fall, which are superimposed in a second layer on the image of a small white dot moving against an infinitely black background at a speed that the eye can hardly assess. The body's gravitational pull alone serves as an indicator of where up and down are to be located in the image. "He is falling in controlled descent," says the commentator after three minutes and fifty-five seconds of fall. It is precisely this contradiction that accounts for the spectacle's tremendous public interest and thus its advertising appeal: a human being hurtling through the sky in free fall is ascribed the highest possible degree of control, the whole event is staged as an experiment and, at the same time, a controllable scenario.

It is October 14, 2012, and Felix Baumgartner dives into the history books, deliberately, trained, and introduced with carefully prepared sentimental remarks. The jump from the stratosphere was made headfirst, with arms outstretched. A human against the laws of nature, elevated in the most modern machinery and surrounded by a human control unit of top-class scientists. Not only from the uppermost floors, one can watch him from all floors of Horkheimer's skyscraper. In almost every respect, this falling event differs from any other form of falling: The fall is announced, receives a coordinate in the time-space structure that can be planned. It can be consciously viewed, and though exciting, viewing this particular fall is done without fear or shame. Excitedly, with benevolence and astonishment, one observes how this human body shoots at over 1300 km/h through the atmosphere. Because this human falls for records, he falls as a model; he falls cherished, within the framework of the system. And he lands softly. On his feet, so to speak. With his head held high, he ascends to a higher floor immediately afterward.

Falling triggers something elemental in us.

Both the person who falls — whether physically or symbolically — and the contemplation of a fall touches something in us, although or perhaps precisely because it is a fundamental constant of our existence. Between shame and misfortune, loss of control, social decline and death, falling opens up a whole history of decline. The viewer's reaction and the post-fall behavior, or the physical or social consequences that go along with it, decisively determine the quality of the event.

Felix Baumgartner's "fall" is an absolute exception that contradicts every logic of falling. A media event that deliberately stages a successful "after the fall" that stylizes an encounter with contingency not as a sudden event but as a conscious challenge to be actively and productively faced. The global corporation Red Bull, which organized and paid for the stratospheric jump an undertaking based on a NASA experiment from the 1960s — and shaped it according to its claim "Red Bull gives you wings," underscores the role models of our time. Man as an indestructible existence that defies the laws of nature, potent, successful, willing to take risks, never tired, and always capable of peak performance and (superhuman) records.

THE COMMON CASE / FALLING AND FAILING / FALLING AS DIFFERENCE

Who among us has not fallen? If you haven't yet, you will — "in the end, we are all dead."

Brian Massumi / John Maynard Keynes, *"Everywhere You Want to Be: Introduction to Fear"*[2]

What happens during the classic fall?

Falling is neither a conscious movement nor a state. In most cases, one falls unintentionally and unexpectedly. Every fall is an event (Old High German *irougen* =

to happen, ouge = eye), with which, in the etymological sense, something is "put before our eyes." [3] There is an element of surprise in falling. It happens mostly spontaneously, it is an accident. Perhaps one could even say falling is something passive. It happens. It happens to you. ("It can happen to anyone!") In Crowds and Power, Elias Canetti describes the moment of falling as a change of position to "lying down" as particularly powerful because it is unexpected: "Such people have the misfortune to remind those who can stand of a wounded animal. They are marked. They have taken a long step downhill towards death." [4] Certainly, one can only fall if one is not already on the ground, that is, if one is at a certain height. Therefore, there is a topological and qualitative difference between the state before the fall and the state afterward. Falling means a shift, a transition into another state of being. A person who falls loses more than just briefly the ground under his feet.

The sight of large numbers of prostrate and lifeless bodies has a terrible effect on anyone who experiences it: he comes to feel as though he himself had struck them all down and his sense of power increases rapidly and uncontrollably. [...] ... there is always, even amongst civilized people, a faint feeling of contempt for anyone to whom this happens. They procure him the help he needs, but in doing so expel him from the society of the erect. For a time, he is not considered fully adult. [5]

According to Canetti, the lying person in themselves, but the involuntarily lying person even in a heightened form, symbolizes a "passivity." [6] A fall thus initiates a power gradient, at the lower end of which the person lying on the ground, ergo, the fallen person, finds himself "not considered fully adult."

The "upright," those who move on two legs, these are humans. Canetti straightforwardly associates an existence close to the ground directly with the animal, one that is defenseless, injured, or even dead. The person lying on the ground does not receive pity but contempt for having "come so far." Who collapses or falls indicates that he / she has lost control (over his / her own body). Even if only briefly, but still in a way that made it, publicly, unconcealed, before the eyes of all.

It becomes clear that falling is something that should not happen. Falling is a disturbance, an accident, something that should be remedied (lifted) and compensated for as soon as possible.

In time of peace anyone who falls down in a crowded place and is unable to rise has a different effect on the many who see him. In their own time and fashion, and to differing degrees, they all identify themselves with him. One, though perhaps with a bad conscience, will pass him by; another will take the trouble to help him. If he manages to get to his feet fairly quickly all the onlookers will feel pleased that this man, who is themselves, is on his feet again. If he fails he is handed over to the care of the appropriate institution [...]. [7]

At the moment of falling, an awareness of our potential vulnerability and even the inevitable transience and destruction of our bodies crashes over us. Canetti calls it a "misfortune" that establishes itself and is "a long step downhill towards death." [8] That is never solely true of the actual "fallen" person; it is precisely the observers of the event who are equally ashamed and unpleasantly reminded that the same thing could easily happen to them.

UP AND DOWN / FALLING AS PERMANENT CONDITION / GRAVITY

When you walk, each step is the body's movement against falling — each movement is felt in our potential for freedom as we move with the earth's gravitational pull. When we navigate our way through the world, different pulls, constraints, and freedoms move us forward and propel us into life. [9]

Brian Massumi, *Navigating Movements*

There is much to suggest that the fall in the sense of an accident can equally be understood as a fundamental constant of human existence. While in the biblical story of creation, the fall is described as a moral decline, in evolutionary theory, the elevation from the ground to an upright walk marks the central moment of Homo Sapiens' genesis.

Philosopher Vilém Flusser, in turn, describes humanity's moment of initiation as an accident, a continual lapse and unfinished process, the effects of which have left the planet unbalanced to this day. In his short, polemic essay Vom Hebel (From the Lever, 1992), Flusser describes human history as a history of mechanics, the archetype of which he sees the lever "as a machine for outrage from baseness, that is, as a machine for becoming human." [10] In a deliberately sharp-tongued and lumbering abbreviation, Flusser traces the development of man back to a "series of failed leaps" by great apes between the treetops. [11] For Flusser, falling, in the sense of failure, is as much genuinely human as the repeated and mostly technically supported straightening up after the fall. "People keep getting up, building ever more perfect levers, cranes, and other elevating machines, and the higher they climb, the harder they fall to the ground." [12] Canadian philosopher Brian Massumi expands the view from mechanics to the constant play and balancing act of our bodies with the physical forces that affect us. Even walking, Massumi says, can be described as a controlled form of falling: "There are always constraints. When we walk, we're dealing with the constraint of gravity. There's also the constraint of balance, and a need for equilibrium. But, at the same time, to walk you need to throw off the equilibrium, you have to let yourself go into a fall, then you cut it off and regain the balance. You move forward by playing with the constraints, not avoiding them. There's an openness of movement, even though there's no escaping constraint." [13]

A decisive criterion of the fall is undoubtedly the landing, the ground, the base that opens to us in the fall. But what if there is no ground and also no reason (in the sense of logic) that awaits us?

GROUNDLESSNESS / AMBIENT FEAR / THE SAFETY BELT / CONTINGENCY

The commodity is a time-buckle, and the time-buckle is a safety belt. The consumer "good" reassures us that we are, and, traditionally, will continue to be, unfallen from our groundless peak. Buying is prevention. It insures against death.

Brian Massumi, *"Everywhere You Want to Be: Introduction to Fear"*

Flusser and Massumi agree that our existence is bottomless, without roots, that is, "without a rational basis."[14] The realization of our uprooted, absurd existence puts us in disarray. It gives us "the dizzying feeling of floating over an abyss in which the concepts of 'true' and 'false' no longer apply."[15]

According to Massumi, it is not only falling but also free-falling that establishes our generic identity as human beings in late-stage capitalism.[16] All the more heroic is the one who survives a deep fall and then (again) continues to master life successfully. Representation of this success and of not having fallen finds its expression in consumption. By purchasing certain products, we generate our subjectivity, mark our distinction, our status of "upright," which in the best case will ensure an afterlife even after our demise by passing on the associated goods to the next generation.[17] Success is marked by possessions, which are supposed to protect us from shame and transience.[18] But no matter how much we invest, our bodies continue to be attracted to gravity.

Restlessness and the need to anchor oneself, to look for the "safety belt" in consumption before a free fall into the bottomless pit, finds its reason beyond that in a social shift, a kind of "ambient fear": "Terrorists, feminists, flower children, black power militants, people who don't buckle up, guilty smokers, eaters, polluters, closet exercise resisters ... Everywhere, imminent disaster. [...] These faceless, unseen and unseeable enemies, operate on an inhuman scale. The enemy is not simply indefinite (masked, or at a hidden location). In the infinity of its here-and-to-come, it is elsewhere, by nature. It is humanly ungraspable."[19] Instead of explicit images of the enemy, causal cause-and-effect schemes, or the one great catastrophe, danger now lurks everywhere and at all times, "[i]n a word, the enemy is the virtual."[20]

Fear is an insight into the untenability, the absurdity, the contingency, and the danger of falling off the grid physically and/or socially or of being excluded. It is an insight into the impossibility of absolute control, which opens up to us when we fall. Danger lurks outside as well as inside, and our place in the system is always up for debate. With the fall, as big or small as it is, we encounter an invisible border space, which Giorgio Agamben calls the "dislocating localization" and from which every form of life and every legal norm can be virtually grasped at any time.[21]

For Flusser, man can only establish a continuously renewed relationship to the world and his meaning in it through his actions. In doing so, he reflects: "It is of no use to want to be outraged by baseness and to build a lever, if one has not first found a fulcrum on which the lever is to be set. Such a fulcrum, however, cannot itself be within the competence of mechanics. ..."[22] Today, for Brian Massumi, such a fulcrum can only be found in constant play with the forces and ideologies acting upon us. Resistant actions can offer anchorage only if they are experimental and distributed over different areas of life and learn to detach themselves from any simple causal logic.

AT THE EVENT HORIZON / FALLING APART / FALLING AND DISAPPEARING / THE ASTRO-END

"I know the whole world is watching now. I wish you could see what I can see. Sometimes you have to be up really high to understand how small you are... I'm going home now."

Felix Baumgartner, before his jump from the stratosphere

Let us imagine a lever that could transport us not only into the stratosphere but also to unimagined heights, light years away from the earth to the edge of an event horizon. That would bring us to that frontier surface of space-time at the edge of a black hole, from which events in principle withdraw from visibility for human beings. Although everything that could happen here would be neither usable nor analyzable, in this zone beyond observability lies the dream of many a physicist. So, let's imagine falling over this border of visibility and letting ourselves fall together with light, space, and time in absolute surrender to the forces of gravity into the ultimate bottomless pit, into the abyss of the universe.

Astrophysicist and science journalist Neil deGrasse Tyson calculated the scenario and described it this way: "As you fall in, the gravity at your feet becomes rapidly greater than the gravity at your head, so your feet start falling faster than your head does. That's a bad situation to be in. [...] Initially, it feels like a stretch, but what happens is that stretch continues beyond comfort levels. You reach a point where — And they're called the tidal forces, tides on your body basically. The tidal forces become so great that they exceed the intermolecular forces that bind your flesh. The point comes where you snap into two pieces, likely to happen at the base of your spine. Now you are two pieces. I know you didn't ask about this, but it turns out you will survive that snap because below your waist, while there are important organs, there are no vital organs below your waist. Your torso will stay alive for a little while until you bleed to death, but this all happens much faster than it would take to bleed to death. These two pieces then feel tidal forces, and then they snap into two pieces. Then they snap again into eight, and then sixteen, and then you're bifurcating your way down. Eventually, it's your head and multiple other parts. That will continue until you are a stream of atoms descending toward the abyss, and it turns out that's not the worst of it. The worst — it turns out, the fabric of space and time funnels down towards a black hole, so the space that you occupy up here is larger than a space you occupy down here. In fact, while you're getting stretched, you're getting squeezed, extruded through the fabric of space like toothpaste through a tube."[23]

The Astro-End.

1 Horkheimer, Max: "The Skyscraper," in: Dawn & Decline: Notes 1926-1931 and 1950-1969, New York, 1978, p. 66.
2 Massumi, Brian: "Everywhere You Want to Be: Introduction to Fear," in: The Politics of Everyday Fear, University of Minnesota Press, 1993, online: http://allanmccollum.net/amcimages/Brian_Massumi/Everywhere_You_Want_to_Be_Introduction_to_Fear.html
3 Cf., Kluge, Friedrich: Etymologisches Wörterbuch der deutschen Sprache. 24th edition, de Gruyter: Berlin, New York 2002, p. 253.
4 Cf. Canetti, Elias: Crowds and Power. Continuum: New York, 1981, p. 392.
5 Ibid.
6 Cf. Canetti, p. 394. Kneeling, on the other hand, is a form of active powerlessness.
7 Canetti, p. 393.
8 Ibid.
9 Massumi, Brian: Navigating Movements: An Interview with Brian Massumi and Mary Zournazi, 2003, online: https://archive.org/stream/InterviewWithBrianMassumi/int-massumi_djvu.txt
10 Flusser, Vilém: "Vom Hebel," DIE ZEIT, No. 12, March 15, 1991, p. 71. From the ZEIT ONLINE archives: http://www.zeit.de/1991/12/vom-hebel
11 Cf., Ibid.: Due to long periods of cold, according to Flusser, the trees in the steppe of East Africa became fewer and grew at a greater distance from each other. As a result, the apes fell more often when jumping between the trees.
12 Flusser, Vom Hebel, op. cit. "From this," Flusser continues, "it can be concluded, on the one hand, that all revolutions are technical revolutions, because it is always a matter of building new machines after a fall. And on the other hand, it can be concluded that something is fundamentally wrong with technical progress, with progress in general, with history, with man in general. After all, we are still lying lowly kicking on the ground, and we haven't progressed since the East African steppe, the Neander Valley, and Archimedes. That's because of the lever."
13 Massumi, Navigating Movements, op. cit.
14 Flusser, Vilém: Bodenlos. Eine philosophische Autobiographie, Bollmann Verlag, 1992, p. 9.
15 Ibid.
16 Cf. Massumi, Everywhere You Want to Be, p. 26 f.
17 Cf., Ibid., p. 4: "[I]dentity is an act of purchase predicated on a condition of groundlessness. The commodity stands (in) for our existence. The ground(lessness) it stands on is the accident in its most general expression—the accident-form, exemplified as downfall, the unqualified or generic founding event."
18 Cf., Ibid., p. 9: "When we buy, we are buying off fear and falling. Filling the gap with presence-effects. When we consume, we are consuming our own possibility. In possessing, we are possessed, by marketable forces beyond our control. In complicity with capital, a body becomes its own worst enemy."
19 Cf. Massumi, Everywhere You Want to Be, p. 7 f.
20 Ibid., p. 8. "The content of the disaster is unimportant. Its particulars are annulled by its plurality of possible agents and times: here and to come. What registers is its magnitude. In its most compelling and characteristic incarnations, the now unspecified enemy is infinite. Infinitely small or infinitely large: viral or environmental." (Ibid.)
21 Cf., Agamben, Giorgio: Homo Sacer. Sovereign Power and Bare Life. Stanford University Press: Stanford 2002, p. 175.
22 Flusser, Vom Hebel, op. cit.
23 Radiolab, "Falling," aired September 17, 2020, transcript of the program online: https://www.wnycstudios.org/podcasts/radiolab/episodes/91726-falling